OTHERWISE ENGAGED

Donald Spoto was born near New York City in 1941 and received his PhD from Fordham University in 1970. He is the author of 24 books, including internationally bestselling biographies of Alfred Hitchcock, Tennessee Williams, Marlene Dietrich, Marilyn Monroe and Ingrid Bergman. His acclaimed biography of Audrey Hepburn, *Enchantment*, is available in paperback from Arrow. He is married to the Danish academic administrator Ole Flemming Larsen. They live in a quiet village an hour's drive from Copenhagen.

Also available by Donald Spoto

Joan: The Mysterious Life of the Heretic who Became a Saint
Enchantment: The Life of Audrey Hepburn
In Silence: Why We Pray
Reluctant Saint: The Life of Francis Assisi
Jacqueline Bouvier Kennedy Onassis: A Life
The Hidden Jesus: A New Life
Diana – The Last Year
Notorious: The Life of Ingrid Bergman
Rebel: The Life and Legend of James Dean
Dynasty: The House of Windsor from Victoria to Diana
A Passion for Life: The Biography of Elizabeth Taylor
Marilyn Monroe: The Biography
Blue Angel: The Life of Marlene Dietrich
Laurence Olivier: A Life
Madcap: The Life of Preston Sturges
Lenya: A Life
Falling in Love Again: Marlene Dietrich – A Photo-Essay
The Kindness of Strangers: The Life of Tennessee Williams
The Dark Side of Genius: The Life of Alfred Hitchcock
Stanley Kramer: Film Maker
Camerado: Hollywood and the American Man
The Art of Alfred Hitchcock

OTHERWISE ENGAGED
The Life of
ALAN BATES

DONALD SPOTO

arrow books

Published by Arrow 2008

2 4 6 8 10 9 7 5 3 1

Copyright © Donald Spoto 2007

Donald Spoto has asserted his right under the Copyright, Designs
and Patents Act 1988 to be identified as the author of this work

This book is sold subject to the condition that it shall not,
by way of trade or otherwise, be lent, resold, hired out,
or otherwise circulated without the publisher's prior
consent in any form of binding or cover other than that
in which it is published and without a similar condition,
including this condition, being imposed on the
subsequent purchaser

First published in Great Britain in 2007 by
Hutchinson
Random House, 20 Vauxhall Bridge Road,
London SW1V 2SA

www.rbooks.co.uk

Addresses for companies within The Random House Group Limited can be found at:
www.randomhouse.co.uk/offices.htm

The Random House Group Limited Reg. No. 954009

A CIP catalogue record for this book
is available from the British Library

ISBN 9780099490968

The Random House Group Limited supports The Forest Stewardship
Council (FSC), the leading international forest certification organisation.
All our titles that are printed on Greenpeace approved FSC certified paper
carry the FSC logo. Our paper procurement policy can be found at
www.rbooks.co.uk/environment

Typeset by Palimpsest Book Production Limited, Grangemouth, Stirlingshire

Printed in the UK by CPI Bookmarque, Croydon, CR0 4TD

for Paul Sidey
with gratitude for three decades of friendship

'Soave sia il vento . . .'

'The truth of people's lives
is what you've set out to do, and it's usually a phenomenal story.
Let's have that person!'

Alan Bates, December 1997

Contents

Acknowledgements

During the autumn of 2004, I received a telephone call from Michael Linnit, whom I had met almost twenty years ago through our mutual friends, Laurence and Mary Evans. With Rosalind Chatto, Michael directs the highly respected London theatrical agency, Chatto & Linnit Ltd. He asked if I would be interested in undertaking the authorised biography of Alan Bates, whom he and Ros represented for many years. Michael further informed me that I would have the full and enthusiastic support of Alan's family. Immediately, I responded affirmatively, as my high regard for this great actor went back many years. Throughout my research and the writing of *Otherwise Engaged*, I had the constant help of Michael and Ros, and I begin these acknowledgements with a deep expression of gratitude to them for their confidence in me and my work, for the many introductions they provided, and for their wise counsel and guidance.

Soon after that, I had my first meetings with Alan's son, Benedick Bates, and with Alan's brother, Martin Bates. I owe Martin and Ben far more than I can say for their extraordinary kindness to me; their undiluted trust; their generous, full and honest sharing of memories during interviews, telephone calls and letters; and their ready transfer to me of the complete cache of Alan's personal and professional papers, letters, documents and ephemera – box after box, bag after bag, file after file, which they turned over without editing or censorship. From the beginning, Martin and Ben were my major allies and chief supporters; they also became my good friends. In Alan's family, too, his brother John and his niece and nephew, Lauren and Karl, shared especially warm, touching and amusing memories.

In the offices of Chatto & Linnit, their longtime associate, Lucy Robinson, at once came aboard as my de facto research assistant. How fortunate I was in having her daily assistance; her extraordinary knowledge of theatre history in general and of Alan's career in particular; her quick access to important facts and sources; her good humour despite my many requests, phone interruptions and electronic communications – and in her case, too, the offer of abiding friendship.

In the New York offices of International Creative Management, I was fortunate to be welcomed by another much respected agent, Boaty Boatwright. She also knew Alan well over many years and facilitated my work in Manhattan and my introductions to his colleagues and friends in the United States. Boaty's assistant, Kevin McEleny, has my thanks, too, for his kindness and help.

In the course of my research, many people who were significant in Alan's life and career granted me important interviews. Their memories, impressions, insights and contributions provided a unique kind of rich understanding, and I am very grateful to them all for their generous assistance and their confidence:

Niema Ash, Alan Bennett, Jaffray Cuyler, Lauretta Feldman, Rosemary Geddes, Nickolas Grace, Elizabeth Grant, Simon Gray, Georgina Hale, Sir Peter Hall, Yardena Harari, Gerard Hastings, Glenda Jackson, Gemma Jones, Felicity Kendal, Arthur Laurents, Michael Lindsay-Hogg, Marie Malavieille, Hayley Mills, Conrad Monk, Joanna Pettet, Angharad Rees, David Storey, Paul Taylor, Ian White, Gareth Wigan, Peter Wyngarde.

Tony Gooch, a knowledgeable and generous film collector, enabled me to view several especially obscure Alan Bates films. For various other kinds of help I warmly acknowledge Mart Crowley, Mary Evans, Davie Evans, Lewis Falb, Charles Marowitz and Gerald Pinciss.

My brother-in-law, John Møller – not for the first time and doubtless not the last – devoted liberal time and his remarkable artistic talents to preparing for publication the many photographs for this book. Indeed, many people helped me in so many ways during the preparation of *Otherwise Engaged* that I am fearful of having omitted a name; if I have, I ask forgiveness – and a prompt letter of correction.

* * *

Karl and Mona Malden always have a special claim on my deepest thanks for their abiding devotion to me and my work; my life would be much the poorer without their faithfulness and loyalty.

My London agent, Elizabeth Sheinkman, in the offices of Curtis Brown Ltd, is a treasure. I do not know how she does all that she does, but I am glad and grateful for her many gifts – among them her intelligence, perception, humour, warmth and promptness.

Every day I am sustained in ways past counting by Ole Flemming Larsen, with whom I share my life. With his customary endless patience and astute insights, he watched something like sixty-five Alan Bates movies and television dramas with me, always providing valuable comments and raising important questions for my consideration. Especially in the last stages of the manuscript, he was my strongest support. Ole's commitment to me, and his nurturing of my work, defy my comprehension, not to say articulation, and his sheer goodness almost takes my breath away. My life is very blessed indeed.

I first met Paul Sidey almost thirty years ago. Our friendship has endured without interruption, it has continued through a number of publishing collaborations, and we are at work on future projects. I place his name on the dedication page of this book with gratitude and honour.

Paul is, quite simply, the ideal editor – earnest and swift to respond, invariably encouraging and sympathetic, good-humoured and loyal. Widely respected for his unerring literary sensibility, he has been a precious friend to me over these many years. I am grateful to him; to his wife, Marianne Velmans; and to his entire family, for all they mean to me. It remains only for me to state, with utmost certainty, that Alan would have admired and loved Paul Sidey, too.

D.S.
Christmas 2006

List of Illustrations

I

'Hug and Kiss Me, Please'

Almost precisely equidistant from the North and Irish Seas and from Scotland and the Channel, the county of Derbyshire features some of the most varied topography in England. The mountains of the High Peak overlook rich pastureland in one direction and austere moors in another, while at some points inhospitable cliffs disturb the tranquillity of a chocolate-box panorama. For centuries, Derbyshire has offered travellers constant surprises: views and vistas shift and change, even along a mile or two of one's journey.

At the end of the nineteenth century, the county census listed 325,000 citizens. Most men worked in coal mines, on farms or in foundries, while women were domestics, cotton spinners or dressmakers. Set apart by vast tracts of land from the modest cottages of ordinary folk stood Derbyshire's great historic houses, dominating the scenery and reminding everyone of the enduring wealth of the aristocracy: Chatsworth House, residence of the Duke and Duchess of Devonshire, with its splendid grounds planned by Capability Brown; and Kedleston Hall, Haddon and Sutton Scarsdale. During the twilight of the Victorian era, the pace and tone of life in Derbyshire had little of the rush and clatter of London, 130 miles to the south. But change was imminent, and soon a new company, Rolls-Royce Ltd, chose Derbyshire as the site of its large first factory.

In 1895, twenty-four-year-old Arthur Bates was working as a tram supervisor in Derby, the county's primary city. The job paid a decent wage, but he derived greater satisfaction from his off-hour diversions – practising the cello, for which he had real talent, and refining his skills as a gifted oil painter and watercolourist. An imposing, attractive young man, Arthur conducted an amateur orchestra at a local Methodist church, and there he met Alice Scattergood, a dressmaker and part-time landlady. They were married after a proper courtship and had two children, Harold and Edith. Everyone was delighted when Harold replicated his father's aptitude for the cello and attended London's Royal College of Music, where he won the prestigious Scholefield Prize for performance on a stringed instrument. Edith studied voice and became an admired singer.

Mr and Mrs Bates predicted a significant career for Harold as a cellist, but this was not to be. He never took to the pace of London, nor was he keen on travelling with orchestras in the provinces. Instead, he returned to Derby, where he restricted his performances to local concerts, gave private music lessons during evenings and weekends, and, for his living, took a job as an insurance salesman. Harold did join the Derby Light Orchestra under the celebrated conductor John Pritchard, and orchestras in Birmingham and several Midland towns occasionally invited him to play with them as a soloist; otherwise he was, as Pritchard said, a flower in the wilderness.

In 1932, while he was an assistant supervisor for the Refuge Assurance Company, Harold met a lively young Derby woman named Florence Wheatcroft, who always preferred to be known by her middle name, Mary; she not only shared his love of music, she was an accomplished pianist.

Born in 1904, Mary was the daughter of Edward James Wheatcroft, a devout Baptist and sometime lay preacher who incurred the disapproval of his abstinent church brethren by holding the position of chief accountant at Worthington's Brewery in Derby. Edward's wife, the former Mary Ann 'Polly' Hands, was a dutiful soul, but she developed a mode of remarkably eccentric and even outrageous behaviour. Her husband and children were accustomed to her habit of hiding behind doors and yodelling loudly for the benefit of family and visitors. She also blithely purloined the clothing of guests and occasional lodgers, and, thus freshly attired, made a grand descent on the family staircase.

Edward and Polly had three children: William, a talented draughtsman and illustrator; Eddy, an amateur actor and musician who sometimes appeared in local repertory theatre productions; and Florence Mary. The girl was much adored by her parents and brothers, and she loved being the centre of attention – a trait, her own children recalled, that never faded with time. As a teenager, she was an avid reader and theatregoer, and at school she learned elocution, deportment, good manners and the home-making arts.

But by her early twenties, Mary was alone in the world: her parents had died, her beloved brother William had been killed in the World War, and Eddy was working in France. Forced to sell the family home and its contents, she was for a time quite desolate. Nevertheless, Mary had admirable resilience, and her wit, strength, humour and prettiness guaranteed a healthy social life; she also impressed others with her lively intelligence, her romantic temperament and her love of a good time. But Mary went in for none of her mother's antics. She was, on the contrary, a model of proper decorum and impeccable manners – qualities which, along with her love of music, endeared her to Harold Bates. Like him, Mary had studied theory and practice, and she received an honours certificate in piano in 1925.

Harold and Mary were married in a local Baptist church on 13 April 1933. Their home was at 3 Derwent Avenue, Allestree, then being developed as a suburban village within Derby's city limits. Notable for its scenic open parklands, Allestree's features included a lake, cool forests, verdant roadside fields thick with wild flowers and a profusion of silver birches. At a nursing home in this picturesque village, on 17 February 1934, Mary bore the first of their sons, christened Alan Arthur. Soon afterwards the family moved to 105 Western Road, Mickleover. Later, Harold and Mary had two more boys: Martin Edward was born on 28 March 1939 and John Roy Adrian on 20 August 1945.

Harold Bates was a handsome, deeply emotional man and a devoted father. 'You always knew where you stood with him,' said Alan. 'Behind a certain outward bluster and authority, there was a glint in his eye, and you knew there was humour.' Occasionally, Harold could be irritable and short-tempered, perhaps because he felt some remorse for not pursuing the career in music for which he had received first-rate training and had shown such promise. 'I think', Martin said years later, 'that he sometimes wished he had gone for greater recognition.'

'Your father is a home bird and wants to stay in Derby,' Mary often lamented to her sons, making no secret of her yearning for travel and excitement. 'But what is he going to achieve in Derby?' She thought it a pity that her husband rejected invitations for them to give dual cello-piano recitals in England and abroad. Later, the great John Barbirolli offered Harold the opportunity of a position as cellist with the Hallé Orchestra, but he politely declined, citing his job as an insurance salesman – which, he said, offered steadier employment than that of a seasonal travelling musician. 'I think he could have been something, but he didn't push hard enough,' according to Alan.

'Dad was always worried about money,' Martin added, 'and he was not ambitious or adventurous, nor would he promote himself. He must have had an inner assurance about his music, but he had a general lack of security and confidence – there was a kind of timidity about him. There he was, a brilliant cellist who had once studied in London and then played in regional engagements, and he settled into a humdrum career as an insurance salesman. But he stuck it out for the sake of his family.'

As for Mary, she was a proud, genteel woman who insisted that her sons speak and act politely, demonstrate good manners and proper diction, and always consider the feelings of others. These were, of course, fine qualities so far as they went, but there can be disadvantages in placing too much stress on gracious altruism: a certain self-effacement, along with passivity and a habit of indecision. These did not combine to make for weakness in Alan, Martin or John, but as boys, they evidently had to work hard to assert themselves, to establish their independence and individuality. Still, if there was a predominant characteristic in the Bates family, it may have been that of goodwill – the cultivation of genuine interest in others, an astuteness of judgement and compassion for the problems of others.

Mary was determined to enjoy life and she encouraged the same attitude in her sons, spurring on all their interests, especially in aesthetic and cultural subjects. She loved anything to do with music and theatre; she played tennis into her sixties and the piano right up to her death at ninety-four. An incorrigible flirt, she often giggled like a schoolgirl. 'She said she didn't know when she was born, which of course wasn't true,' recalled Alan's son, Benedick. 'It was a source of some family amusement that she never revealed her age and she always tried to ignore her birthday. But she was a woman of high ideals, and she saw to it that her family was exposed to a highly cultivated life. She could be very grand, but she was also the rock of the family.'

Perhaps because of the loss of her family and the concomitant period of loneliness in her youth, it was as if Mary (in Martin's words) 'threw a fortress around her family once she was happily married. She gradually became more possessive and defensive of her sons as the years went by, and this could be damaging – for example, many of our girlfriends and even our wives had a difficult time. She was of course intensely loyal to her husband and family, and there was always a very special relationship with Alan. But her early training had emphasised all the social graces necessary for her to take her place as the charming and dutiful wife of a professionally successful gentleman.' In this aspiration she was disappointed.

Hence, while Harold was frustrated artistically, Mary felt hindered socially. Forced to remain at home and to abandon her desire for more frequent travel, she became, as if by default, possessive and extravagantly doting. 'Sometimes we felt suffocated,' Martin recalled, 'and our girlfriends felt shut out if, in her eyes, they did not match up to her expectations.' Fearful of losing others as she had lost her own family, Mary often risked alienating those she most loved.

Year-round, Allestree was very much a paradise for active children, and so it was remembered by Alan and his boyhood chums. They built tree houses, played football and fixed up a makeshift raft, which promptly sank in the lake. 'We sent Alan out to test it,' recalled Peter Barry, a boyhood friend, 'and he was soon a foot under water.'

Most of these after-school activities earned the disapproval of Mary, who much preferred that Alan and Martin learn to play piano. But this notion met with boyish resistance, and off they went to lark about with their mates. 'She shuddered at the way Alan lived his life,' according to another childhood chum, John Ash. 'To us, it was just boyish pranks, but she thought we were leading him astray. She also pulled us up about our grammar – she seemed determined to bring Alan up as a gentleman.' In fact, Mary corrected Alan's speech even more than she enjoined music lessons. As she had learned at a school for young gentlewomen, proper diction signalled good breeding, which (it was implied) was almost a religious virtue.

Shy and affectionate, and with a winning smile even as a boy, Alan nevertheless had a naughty side to his nature. He and a few friends were involved in minor shoplifting, purloining and then exchanging among themselves some of their parents' possessions (a wristwatch or two); they smoked on the sly; and they dared pranks that were sometimes dangerous. No matter that Mary had to school and scold him, she never wavered in the special bond she felt for her eldest son.

In 1942, the family moved from Western Road back to Derwent Avenue. England was enduring the deprivations of World War II, and the Bates family shared the general austerities: food, paper and fuel, among other necessities, were severely limited. 'I remember the strictness, the rations,' Alan recalled years later, 'but music was played a great deal' – and that brought a certain serenity despite the grim daily news.

In 1942, Mary's predilection for good diction and fine oral communication inspired her to enrol eight-year-old Alan in the Herbert Strutt School, a respected academy with an admirable tradition of speech and drama education. Located in the nearby town of Belper, the building resembled a Tudor manor house where classes were small, and the students were encouraged to pursue artistic as well as athletic pastimes. Mary also took a special interest in Alan's music education – a subject taught by the petite but formidable Miss Rudd, who terrified the children into submission.

According to another teacher, Miss Harris, Alan was 'very quiet, almost retiring'. Such apparent diffidence faded when, as so often, his refined diction made him the obvious choice to read lessons or to recite a poem before the entire school at assemblies. 'At first, I had a huge resistance to speaking in public at grammar school. I would panic and withdraw from it. Then I suddenly reversed – I just jumped and couldn't wait to do it.' Later, he tried to analyse this shift in feeling, 'but I've never been able to.'

During that first year at Strutt, Alan developed a lifelong habit of sending letters and notes to his family. At Christmas 1942, for example, he took up his pen and wrote separate holiday greetings for his mother and father, who lived no further from him than the next room.

Dear daddy

I hope you like your card and all the other presents that you have. I just forget what egsact day I did the card but I know it was a few days before. Do you like it? My writing I mean. I gave Mummy a note like this one to. When you have read the letter hug me and kiss me please? I am so sorry I cant think of anything els to tell you but in the next letter I write to you I will do. Good-by.

Love from Alan and Martin to daddy.

Dear Mummy

I hope you had a very nice Christmas and I wish you a happy new year. My writing is very small but still I cant help that I am writing very quickly. I did not fill my pen so I have to keep dipping it in the ink pot but now I have finished talking about ink pots. Do you like my writing if you do tell me so hug me and kiss me please. I mean when you have read the letter. I know it is very nigh to say good-by.

Love from Alan

Except for public speaking and letter writing, he had little interest in school. 'I wasn't academic at all – not before my late twenties did I ever really like the idea of actually studying.' He managed mostly pass grades, although not in mathematics, which seemed especially useless to his boyish judgement.

'It was not an unhappy childhood,' Alan reflected later,

> but I reacted very strongly against my middle-class environment. I had to get away from it . . . There is something about the atmosphere of suburbia that I find stifling and inhibiting . . . [and] I felt frustrated . . . Everyone lived with the lid on . . . and there was a tremendous sense of there not being much to do. A night designated for going into town for fish and chips and hoping the fairground was open – that was about it.

There was, however, significant diversion. His mother, who fancied anything dramatic, exotic or sentimental, routinely took Alan to amateur theatricals and to movies appropriate for a boy of his age. By the time of his eleventh birthday, in 1945, he was addicted to the cinema. That summer, three films were on in Derby – a George Formby comedy; one of the *Tarzan* series; and *Thunderhead, Son of Flicka*. 'I want to see them all!' he wrote in a note to his mother and, that season, he began to keep a diary of the films he saw, rating them and the actors with one to five stars. His list of favourite titles over the next three years indicates not the typical childhood fare but adult dramas remarkably sophisticated for a boy between eleven and fourteen: *Great Expectations, Odd Man Out, Uncle Silas, Blanche Fury, London Belongs to Me, Good Time Girl, Desire Me* and Laurence

Olivier's *Hamlet*, which he saw no fewer than three times when he was fourteen.

Recalling his visits with his mother to plays at the Derby Little Theatre, Alan said that he 'became infatuated – I *had* to go every week.' More to the point, he soon announced, 'I can do what we've seen on that stage tonight!' As he later added, 'I'd found what I wanted to do, and what I thought I could do. It just hit me, and then it became an absolute obsession. I didn't care about anything else.' He was especially impressed when he saw his Uncle Eddy Wheatcroft perform in an amateur production of *The Seagull*.

Martin remembered going to Alan's 'secret acting place – a clearing in the nearby woods, where he enacted simple scenes, using me as his "foil" while he practised entrances, exits and quick exchanges on things like attack, alarm and escape. If I made fun or expressed impatience, he became quite cross.'

When Alan told Harold and Mary that he wanted to be an actor, 'they took it to be a childhood whim and humoured me, thinking it would pass as I grew older'. Still, they permitted him to appear in the non-speaking part of Mercutio's page, in six performances of *Romeo and Juliet* at the Railway Institute in February 1948, an offering of the British Empire Shakespeare Society in Derby, which had been operating almost every year since 1909. This role, not mentioned in character lists of Shakespeare's plays, was a walk-on, along with the masquers, the citizens of Verona and other supernumeraries; in the text, the page is singularised only when Mercutio is dying: 'Where is my page? Go, villain, fetch a surgeon.' Exit the page.

Participation, even with no lines to speak, must have been exhilarating for a stage-struck fourteen-year-old, and Mary saw an advantage to her son's youthful enthusiasm. If, as he said, Alan was committed to the idea of acting, then he ought to enrol in voice and diction lessons – a social advantage, she reasoned, no matter his professional future. Harold at once arranged for Alan to study with a respected and charismatic teacher named Claude W. Gibson. After listening to the boy read, Gibson recognised an inchoate talent and, potentially, an impressive voice; he also observed the boy's natural charm and engaging appearance.

That autumn, Alan joined a group of students travelling to Stratford for a performance of Shakespeare's *King John*, a production that featured, among other players, Paul Scofield, Claire Bloom, Clifford

Williams, Paul Hardwick, Esmond Knight, Robert Helpmann and Anthony Quayle. From that evening, Alan told his parents, his future was fixed and firm – and he asked to have more tutorials with Claude Gibson. 'He really knew how to draw something out of you,' Alan recalled. 'He got me to really articulate and taught me to breathe properly.'

But Harold and Mary had growing reservations about Alan's theatrical aspirations and so approached one of his teachers at the Strutt School. 'His mother and father came to a parents' evening,' recalled Miss Harris. 'They were worried because they thought there was no money in a theatre career,' although they evidently saw no contradiction in having encouraged a musical one. Together, the teacher and the parents devised a plan, which they presented to Alan: 'They filled me with all the warnings, saying, "If you haven't succeeded by the time you're twenty-six, then think about something else."'

Still, Mary could not bear to disappoint her eldest son. She knew George Revill, a producer at the Derby Shakespeare Society, and in February 1949 Alan appeared with the company again – this time in a speaking role as Prince Arthur, in six performances of *King John*, which he had read and studied carefully since his visit to Stratford. The highlight of his performance was the long fourth-act dialogue between Arthur and the henchman sent to blind him. The scene presents a challenge even to a seasoned actor, for the frightened boy must dissuade his would-be torturer by a combination of sincere affection and frank terror:

> If heaven be pleased that you must use me ill,
> Why then you must. Will you put out mine eyes?
> These eyes that never did nor never shall
> So much as frown on you?

'I was smashing,' Alan recalled proudly, 'even though I forgot to take off my wristwatch while I was playing a thirteenth-century prince.'

Douglas Marsden, who co-produced the play with Revill, had the task of preparing younger cast members, 'but Alan was obviously gifted and needed little coaching,' he recalled. A local newspaper critic agreed: 'Arthur, the boy prince was played by A. Bates, whose manner, particularly in the famous scene with Hubert, the gaoler who is to put out his eyes, was natural and very moving.' Impressed with Alan's preparation and intensity, the producers then cast him, in February 1950, as Edward, Prince of Wales, in *Richard III*, and to similarly good effect. Moreover, that spring he won an honour certificate in a local verse-speaking competition. With that, Alan, who openly complained to friends and family that he was supremely bored at the Strutt School, boldly wrote to the Royal Academy of Dramatic Art in London, asking for information and the requirements for acceptance. 'I was attracted to the glamour and the famous people,' he admitted later.

The allure of fame and the appeal of beautiful actors were much trumpeted by a young actor and soon to be director named John Dexter, who was nine years older than Alan; he was then working in and around Derby, and he was not at all shy about being homosexual. 'Alan formed a friendship with John Dexter that my father was not happy about,' recalled Martin, 'and he gave Alan a lecture.' Harold's objection could not have concerned matters theatrical but rather the nature of the relationship between twenty-four-year-old Dexter and fifteen-year-old Alan – or perhaps what Harold judged it to be. But Harold's instructions had to be softened, for Dexter's father was a good friend who also performed in the Derby Orchestra.

Meanwhile, Alan continued to study with Gibson, who lived in a rambling, book-strewn Victorian house in Derby. Because the elocution lessons were conducted under the formal aegis of the government, Gibson was required to report on his students' progress, grading them on enunciation, sight-reading and voice control. To pass with distinction, students had to attain at least 130 out of a possible 150 points; Alan earned 140.

Appropriately, he had prepared Hamlet's injunction to actors:

> Speak the speech, I pray you, as I pronounced it to you, trip-pingly on the tongue: but if you mouth it, as many of your players do, I had as lief the town-crier spoke my lines. Nor do not saw the air too much with your hand, thus, but use all gently; for in the very torrent, tempest, and – as I may say – whirlwind of passion, you must acquire and beget a temperance, that may give it smoothness.

By the end of that year, Gibson reported that Alan had recited verse 'with considerable lyric understanding' and rated his speech from *Julius Caesar* as 'remarkable for its insight and dramatic intensity'.

When the teacher learned of his student's desire to attend the Royal Academy of Dramatic Art at the age of seventeen, he wrote a cautionary letter to Mary:

Alan told me about the suggestion [perhaps made by Marsden or Revill] that he should take the RADA audition at the end of December. It is necessary to realise that RADA is no ordinary dramatic school for bright boys and girls, but the leading dramatic school in England, in which places are sought from literally all over the English-speaking world: there were many Americans there when Joy [his daughter] was there. All ages under 30 were represented, but anyone younger than 18, unless there is unusual brilliance, promise and a mature outlook and appearance, is not welcome.

If Alan were successful too early in gaining admittance – and the competition is extremely keen for the relatively few places – he might well regret it later. To find oneself younger than the average may not be a pleasant experience. I feel one would enjoy life at RADA far more at 19–20 than at 17–18. RADA is looked on as the university of the stage, and I feel sure that the preference is for an older type already very well equipped. Whereas in the old days a certain standard of attainment was required for admittance, it is now a question of competition and many find themselves unable to get to RADA.

Time, I feel, is all on Alan's side, and men, in any case, can always afford to wait. For his own sake, I should advise him not to hurry. My own opinion is that however much Alan dislikes school, he should [continue with his studies] – his knowledge would become wide, pass or fail, and his mental outlook would be broader. And he would have advanced to a much higher standard in his dramatic work. At present, although most promising in his work, he has not and will not have for some time independent command of his medium. This is not intended or expected at this intermediate stage of his training.

Then, too, staying longer at school would mean less difficulty over a grant. I do not think the County authorities would be very generous with a grant if in one of their schools a boy wished to leave with a School Certificate only, especially if the grant were to subsidise a boy in attempting a career of little value to the education authorities.

I fear Alan won't like this advice. Forgive me for giving you and
Mr Bates so much to read . . .

Yours very sincerely,

C. W. Gibson

Not long after Mary and Harold received this letter, Alan had yet
another triumph at school – as Jack, in a school production of Wilde's
The Importance of Being Earnest. 'Alan Bates was not only an extremely
able player himself,' wrote a Belper critic, 'but one also who, by his
own acting, encouraged and stimulated the rest of the cast to give a
performance to match his own.' This was the first mention of a
generous trait regularly praised by colleagues throughout his lifetime:
Alan regarded himself as a member of an ensemble – he was never
a performer fixated merely on burnishing his own star.

Gibson's caveats notwithstanding, Alan begged to be allowed to
pursue his application to RADA; finally his parents consented and,
after a time, even Gibson agreed to write on his behalf. But Alan had
perhaps not fully considered the matter of tuition, which was several
thousand pounds per annum. Financial support for arts students was
extremely difficult to obtain during post-war austerities, and such a
sum was beyond his father's capacity.

Two acquaintances came to the rescue – John Dexter's influential
father and an officer for the Derbyshire County Council's Education
Department. They championed Alan's petition and the awards
committee provided a generous grant. The course of study at RADA
normally extended for two years, but the money was initially offered
only for the first. After that, Alan would be eighteen, and it would
be time to fulfil his obligation of military service; support for subsequent studies would be taken up by the committee in due course.

Alan took his final tutorials with Claude Gibson during the spring
of 1951: 'He shows great possibilities and is already very good,' noted
Gibson. 'I enjoyed the unadorned sincerity [of a fragment from Keats's
"Hyperion"] and his very good grasp of character and situation [in
an excerpt from Shakespeare].' By mid-June, seventeen-year-old Alan
Bates was living in London.

That summer, much of the capital was still in ruins after the destruc-
tion of World War Two, and physical and spiritual rehabilitation was
badly needed. The Festival of Britain, held from May to September,

recalled the centenary of the Victorian Great Exhibition and was devised as a tonic for a weary nation: it tried to give the English people a sense of recovery as they set about rebuilding towns and cities following the war. Art and design exhibitions were held all over Britain, and Battersea Park, south of the Thames, was transformed into the Festival Gardens; many of its blocks of flats were hastily refurbished, and leafy paths, fountains and sculpture were installed to suggest the spirit of new residential neighbourhoods.

When the class met for the first day at RADA, Alan was assigned a locker next to another new student. 'We seem to be the youngest here,' he said as they deposited books, supplies and ballet slippers into their compartments. 'Shall we be friends?'

The classmate he addressed was Ian White, a talented and genial young man who became a lifelong friend. 'Alan was of true-bred Derby stock,' Ian recalled,

> with his dark hair and blue-green eyes, the slightly florid face, the strong constitution. Alan had a strong sense of presence, of his talent and of himself generally, which came from his solid, secure and protected background – from the strength provided by his family, whose darling he was. He had lived in a confined cultural space and within a limited geography, with a very powerful mother who was a cut above her husband. But his father had enormous charm and humour, and these qualities Alan inherited in full measure.

John Dexter, by this time also living in London, had found a flat in a boarding house in Hampstead. Alan took a room there too, only to discover that his house mates included a group of rather wild dancers whose antics made him uneasy. Coincidentally, Ian was in a similar predicament at a London YMCA, so they decided to look for a flat to share. As Ian recalled, they were both fairly innocent, serious boys in those days, and they did not want to pursue bohemian or louche lives. 'Alan became like a brother,' Ian recalled. 'We discovered London and life together, we found out who we were, and we formed a firm friendship that endured for over half a century.' They found a flat at 127 St George's Drive, Pimlico, where the proprietor was a serious character who left excruciatingly prolix notes all over the place: 'Kindly switch off the lights before you depart the room . . . Please leave the bathroom in the condition in which you would like to find it . . .'

In 1951, the principal, or director, of RADA was Sir Kenneth Barnes, then seventy-three; he had run the school since 1909, five years after its founding by the actor-manager Herbert Beerbohm Tree. The original council of the academy had included James M. Barrie, W. S. Gilbert and George Bernard Shaw, who, at his death in 1950, left a third of his royalties to RADA.

By the time Alan arrived, the long list of notable alumni included John Gielgud, Vivien Leigh, Charles Laughton, Cedric Hardwicke and Athene Seyler. The work was serious, but the place was shabby, a maze of cold rooms, with poor lighting and ancient plumbing. After the wartime bombing, the walls needed patching, the banisters required repair and the electricity wanted replacement. RADA was also emerging from a period of imprudent decisions. As the school's historian wrote, 'When Barnes packed in as many as 250 students, to maximise income, many [of them] had little real ambition.' That began to change in the early 1950s, as the United States underwrote grants to RADA for veterans who were or wanted to be actors, and as young American men and women were encouraged to study abroad.

Alan retained mixed impressions of the place:

> It was concerned with technique – how to speak, how to move, how to dance. I was there in the last years of a wonderful character called Sir Kenneth Barnes, who was running the place and was really at the end of his powers. The teachers were varying degrees of good and not so good, and there was a highly competitive feeling – which was quite good training, although not really what drama schools are meant to be about. For the wrong reasons, perhaps, it got you quite used to the rat race – trying to get into the public show, trying to get jobs.

His first task on arriving at RADA was to lose his regional Midlands accent: 'It's nice to be able to use it when necessary – but not to be forever saddled with it,' he said later. The change in his speech and manner was a source of some bemusement to his family when he returned for a visit to Allestree that autumn. Martin remembered feeling 'in awe and even a bit baffled. Alan brought some friends home, and I recall thinking, "What have we got here?" There were all sorts of colourful characters, with their extravagant, theatrical way of speaking' – and, no doubt, with the unintentionally droll affectation of young drama students who often take themselves so very, very seriously. 'I assumed', Martin added, 'that he was having a thrilling life – indeed, he was! – with girlfriends, good mates, quite daring exploits, popularity, knowing exactly what he wanted, a growing ambition, and the love and support of parents and tutors.'

That season, Alan learned that the Herbert Strutt School was holding a speech competition, in which former students could compete; at the Founder's Day prize ceremony, he won the Lady Inglefield Cup for achievement.

Back in London, Alan easily made more new friends at RADA, where everyone quickly learned that he was certainly among the wittiest students. 'He drew people naturally,' according to Ian, 'because he was amusing, a good listener, and never pompous. He was just terribly, wonderfully likeable, and he had a gift for reaching out to people. Of course, sometimes others took advantage of his kindness, but he shrugged that off.'

Teachers were often the objects of Alan's hilarious impersonations, and students the subjects of his incorrigible love of gossip. As for himself, there were no quirks or mannerisms to satirise and no fodder for tittle-tattle; and, it seemed, there were no romantic dalliances – this despite the fact that he had grown to be strikingly handsome and slim at five foot ten, with a warm and sometimes seductive smile, and blue-green eyes that seemed hazel in some lights and were so described on several official forms.

Keith Baxter, soon to begin a successful career in England and America, was also a classmate. Occasionally, Bates, White, Baxter and a few others were able to obtain passes to West End productions, where they learned as much about acting as they did from their teachers: they saw, for example, Noël Coward's *Relative Values*, starring Gladys Cooper; N. C. Hunter's *Waters of the Moon*, with the trio of Edith Evans, Sybil Thorndike and Wendy Hiller; and the hit musical *South Pacific*, imported from America with its jaunty star, Mary Martin.

On his eighteenth birthday, 17 February 1952, Alan began rehearsals for a RADA production of Goldsmith's 1773 comedy, *She Stoops to Conquer*. Cast in the pivotal role of Young Marlow, he smoothly conveyed the desperately shy young man as both awkward swain and lecherous rogue, depending on the social status of the young lady of the moment. According to all reports, he was word-perfect from the first run-through, and his vocal pitch was beyond criticism – properly alternating between a petulant whine and a seductive stage whisper. Friends lamented that there was no recording of the performance.

At the conclusion of his first year at RADA, Alan was summoned for a medical examination and was found immediately eligible for National Service – which he duly began in November at the Royal Air Force station at Syerston, a wartime bomber base that had become a post-war training camp. There, according to his service record, Alan operated telephone switchboards, maintained traffic records and installed simple field phone systems. To family and friends he made clear the intensity of his dislike for this time of his life, but it had to be done. His rank on discharge was that of Senior Aircraftsman.

There were frequent and even extended leaves accorded to those at Syerston in peacetime. But in Alan's case, his first trips away from camp were neither enjoyable nor auspicious, for Harold Bates had suffered a psychological collapse that led to profound clinical depression. 'He could no longer work, and he had to stay at home,' Martin recalled. 'Mother knew what to do, and she got him through this time.' After a long and difficult recovery, Harold was able to return to work, in the humble position of a clerk with a local building firm. Alan could do little other than visit his family during this difficult time, but he did so regularly and devotedly. Fortunately, Syerston was but a short journey from Derby.

2

Someone Else's Property

L ike most of his friends at Syerston in peacetime, Alan had a regular but not very demanding schedule in National Service: his office duties occupied him from eight in the morning to four in the afternoon, but then he had considerable leisure time and, with permission routinely granted, he could leave the base in the evenings. But the more freedom he was offered, the more Alan hated his required duty with the RAF: he was bored and, he soon judged, he was wasting valuable time. The experience was not, after all, providing him with creative nourishment for his future.

To no one's surprise, he took advantage of this freedom to appear in plays at a cooperative theatre centre ten miles away, in Nottingham. This was an amateur enterprise run quite professionally, according to Conrad Monk, who was enrolled in an elocution class with Alan at the centre and became a lifelong friend.

'One of the first things I noticed was that he hated pomposity,' Conrad said years later. 'He could not endure people with airs and attitudes. And even at that early stage, long before he became famous, he was the golden boy wherever he went. He was one of those people everyone wanted to do things for. He never seemed to have to make any effort – it all came to him. I don't mean that he was lazy or demanding, but with his humour, good looks and charm, everyone was drawn to him and wanted to help him.'

No list of classes or performances during their time at Nottingham has survived. But at least one other project appears on the record during the period of RAF service. As a guest with the Derby College of Art's theatre class, Alan appeared as Orpheus in two performances of *Point of Departure*, an English adaptation of Jean Anouilh's play *Eurydice*, staged by none other than John Dexter. One local newspaper critic praised the 'melodious language, so well delivered' – but no actor was named.

Alan's work at Syerston, his visits to his family and his classes at Nottingham provided the only reprieve from an otherwise bland two-year period. Finally, on 18 November 1954, he was officially discharged. His superiors assessed his conduct as 'exemplary', his technical ability, leadership aptitude and cooperation merely 'good'. As for his personal appearance, it was judged neither 'very smart' nor 'untidy', but 'smart'. He behaved himself, in other words, but he did not otherwise make much of an impression on officers of the Royal Air Force. No one thought it likely that he would pursue a military career.

Before the end of 1954, Alan returned to London and RADA, where he was glad to find his friend Ian White, who had come back from service in Singapore. There were about seventy-five students completing the two-year course, and the advisory council that year included Laurence Olivier, Sybil Thorndike and Edith Evans.

'It was a terrifically good year with a great clutch of people,' Alan said, recalling the names of other notable students: 'Richard Briers, John Vernon, Brian Bedford, John Stride, Albert Finney, Peter Bowles, Peter O'Toole, Roy Kinnear, Keith Baxter, Rosemary Leach, James Booth – it was really quite astonishing. We were always competing with each other, perhaps without knowing it.' Peter Bowles remembered that 'Finney, O'Toole and Bates were all swaggering around. They threw down the gauntlet. They said, "There – that's my Macbeth – beat that!"'

At first, Alan and Ian shared a flat with Brian Bedford in Hampstead, but Alan wanted to live near the Thames, so they found a large flat, 20 Primrose Mansions, Prince of Wales Drive, Battersea. 'It became a famous theatrical apartment,' according to Ian. 'Roy Kinnear joined us, and then virtually everyone from RADA seemed to move in for either a short- or long-term residency.' The place became, as Martin Bates recalled, 'a kind of typical bohemian student hostel'.

'It was a friendly, sprawling, airy, big flat,' according to Keith Baxter, 'with four bedrooms and a kitchen. We each paid one pound a week.' The low rent enabled Alan to buy a used record player for his growing collection that ranged from the classics to opera, jazz to popular music

– cheap entertainment that often welcomed a crowd of visitors. There was no late-night transport in London at the time – hence if other students or their friends were nearby, they tapped on the door and sought temporary lodging at Primrose Mansions, no matter the hour. 'It was a kind of crash pad: we just made space for whoever was floating around,' Baxter added. 'Some were straight, some were gay, some didn't know quite what they were, and some helped out in the rush hour according to the flow of the traffic.'

The students heard one another's lines, they shared their concerns about their future, and the men worried about being recalled to National Service during the Suez crisis – but most of all they talked about acting, and there were virtually endless parties. 'What a crew!' said Alan. 'Did we have fun!' Company from RADA included the likes of Peter O'Toole, Tom Courtenay, Frank Finlay, David Warner and Claudine Morgan, who had a serious infatuation for Alan. But he preferred to be her friend, not her lover.

RADA teachers popped in occasionally too, among them the scholar and theatre historian Muriel St Clare Byrne, who had once collaborated on a play with Dorothy L. Sayers. Then about sixty, Byrne had fallen hopelessly in love with a young, strikingly beautiful female student named Dalia Punianski, who was unresponsive to Byrne's charms. 'Dalia!' Byrne called out one boozy evening. 'Ask Alan what underpants he wears! I wear men's underpants, and I think all girls should – they give a girl a lift!' Her social idiosyncrasies notwithstanding, Byrne was a gifted and caring instructor who recognised Alan's talent and offered him constant encouragement.

He very much needed that. Cast in the title role of Shakespeare's *Richard II* for his final RADA performance, Alan was woefully disappointing to himself and his teachers. 'I was sorry you missed the show,' he wrote to his father, 'but on the other hand, glad, because I know that I was not as good as I should have been.' He was not quite so frank to others, however. In a letter to a friend of his parents, Alan wrote, 'I was able to play the one part I wanted more than any other, Richard II. Things just turned out splendidly – and I'm glad to report that the staff of the school were all favourably impressed.'

But as he admitted years later, 'I blew it – I absolutely blew it. Everyone else did well except me. I felt terrible that night [10 February 1955]. I was so shattered that I just walked around London for hours, saying to myself, "This will never happen to me again." It was a very early experience of absolute frustration – a feeling of having thrown everything away. I didn't go to anyone for help or advice, I was just determined that in the time I had left, I would get on with it. But I was determined that it would never happen to me again.'

That determination was evident to everyone, and there was an early pay-off. That autumn, he shared a coveted prize for Shakespearean recitation, named for the great actor Sir Johnston Forbes-Robertson (1853–1937), considered, in his time, the finest Hamlet in England and America. The award was presented to Alan, and to another student for a separate recitation, in the presence of Queen Elizabeth the Queen Mother, who was visiting the Academy and decided to remain for the brief ceremony. On hearing of this royal encounter, Alan's mother nearly fainted from excitement.

Despite the setback occasioned by his Richard II, the final reports from Alan's teachers at RADA were overwhelmingly positive: Clifford Turner, a Shakespearean scholar and voice teacher, judged Alan 'a very excellent student [who] needs to make quite sure that uncertainty over breathing does not cause uncertainty of voice'. His student took the caution to heart. The actress Winifred Oughton, who taught at RADA, reported that Alan was 'a sensitive, imaginative young actor whose talent develops all the time. He works very hard and takes just as much trouble to perfect a small part as a long one. His acting – and indeed his whole personality and appearance – are coming on so well that I have great hopes for his future in the theatre.' She noted, however, that there were 'moments of inaudibility, particularly in emotional, poetic passages'.

As for Sir Kenneth Barnes, he observed in his 'Principal's Remarks' that Alan had 'real talent, which took some time to develop. His performances established his ability to act Shakespeare with the romantic and unaffected emotion needed for expressing the beauty of the words. We look forward with interest to his future on the stage.'

But that summer there was another disappointment. On the basis of his studies at RADA, Alan had hoped to receive a concurrent diploma in drama from London University, with which RADA was linked. But this he failed to achieve. Muriel Byrne, never easy to please, sent Alan a handwritten letter:

I feel your career at the Academy has been a triumphant success; and though naturally I should have liked you to have that extra reward and encouragement, I do not, as you probably know, set all that store by exams. Your foot is now firmly planted on the actor's road, and I am sure a fine career lies ahead of you. But I think you only really 'found' yourself with Richard, and your development then took place at such an amazing rate that I don't see how you could have come on at the same pace for the other part of your work. So I hope you won't be too disappointed at missing the University diploma: for your own private information, you just didn't do enough on any of your papers – they were too slight. But the intellectual quality is there in you, just the same as the emotional powers that you are now discovering; and I am sure that you have gained by doing the L.U.D. work. I look forward to real solid success for you, and send you every possible good wish for the future.

At the same time, Alan received a note from Mary Pilgrim, another teacher. John Fernald, the new principal of RADA, had agreed to assume a small role in *It's Never Too Late*, a movie about a housewife who becomes a successful screenwriter. The picture required another actor to appear in a one-minute excerpt from *King Lear*, and Fernald wanted a RADA student. Alan saw a casting notice on the school's news board, was coached by Miss Pilgrim, turned up at the production office and was hired on the spot. He smeared on heavy ageing make-up, dispatched the uncredited task in a few hours (on 9 August) and pocketed twenty pounds. This was his first time before movie cameras, and he liked everything about it except the brevity of his appearance. *It's Never Too Late* then vanished from all but the most esoteric film vaults.

Later that month, Alan wrote to Frank Dunlop, the artistic director of the Midland Theatre Company, a professional repertory troupe that staged classic and modern plays in Coventry, Dudley, Loughborough and other Midland towns. Dunlop often came to RADA in search of new talent, and he invited Alan to join the company that autumn. The salary was almost nothing, and the acting assignments would be varied, but the opportunity to graduate from amateur to professional status was irresistible.

Before he headed north, Alan fulfilled an earlier commitment, to appear as Romeo with the non-professional Stockwells Players. Five performances were given in gardens in Berkshire and Oxfordshire, and the Bates family attended the première in late July. 'A summer visit with Harold, Martin and John to see Alan playing Romeo,' wrote Mary in an album she was compiling. 'A quite unforgettable weekend and evening of happiness with my family.' Later, Alan offered his own review: 'I was terrific.' At the zenith of his youthful good looks, that is as it may have been. Something important was taking shape in Alan's life and personality: his appealing carriage as a young actor, his ability to charm audiences and colleagues, his expert diction – all this fulfilled his parents' own frustrated artistic and social ambitions.

Of Alan's private life at the time nothing can be definitely determined. Even bohemians like the residents of Primrose Mansions did not speak openly of their romantic liaisons in the 1950s, except to very close friends. One might be keeping company or 'stepping out' with someone (and therefore assumptions might be whispered), but in polite circles, little was said publicly, and discretion was always a high art. Then and later, Alan was very much of his times: he kept his counsel, and he had a positive horror of offending his mother's Victorian sensibilities. The regular flow of her letters and cards to him over the years made frequent references to her pride in her sons' manners as those of *gentlemen*, and the injunction to maintain that status was not lost on them. Hence the bachelor Alan never identified anyone who was the object of his affections, especially during the formative RADA-Midland years, nor has anyone of that era claimed to have been his lover.

Protracted virginity has perhaps never been found in vulgar profusion among worldly young men. It may not be prurient, therefore, to assume that a healthy, handsome and amiable twenty-one-year-old actor, living and working amid a freewheeling crowd of bold young hopefuls, must have had some initiation into a carnal life. More to the point, he would have been thought remarkably strange had he kept a monastic discipline in this regard. In any case, there was considerable gossip at the time. If others believed the rumours, Alan would have been considered a typical and popular young man; and if they did not, some would regard him all the more fervently as fresh quarry.

The chit-chat among fellow students and apprentices mostly concerned Alan's friendships with male colleagues – and the concomitant observation that apparently no young woman attracted him to anything more than social flirtation. At that time, the spirit of the Marquess of Queensberry still prowled the land, and Englishmen lived in terror of being accused of the sin of Oscar Wilde. Laws against homosexual conduct were harsh and ruthlessly applied; many careers were summarily ruined if 'sexual deviance' or 'perversion' were proven or even strongly suspected; and the decriminalisation of same-sex relations among consenting adults was still more than a decade away. There had been a great deal of winking and nodding, of course, and some people in the performing arts (Noël Coward, Ivor Novello, John Gielgud and Robert Helpmann among very many others) were essentially granted special status that left them immune to public opprobrium. But most gay men and women who resolutely refused to marry, like adulterers or unmarried heterosexual lovers, had to lead extraordinarily discreet private lives or risk ostracism.

The result was a kind of furtive subculture, ringed with fear and a great deal of self-denial, especially by young people not yet established in significant careers. By 1955, for example, there had been some whispers about a John Dexter–Alan Bates affair, but neither man ever spoke of it, and no third party claimed to have held the lamp.

In Coventry the Midland Theatre Company performed on a small stage in a cavernous, barn-like auditorium that was part of a technical college. Although a touring group, they offered high-quality productions of Shakespeare and Shaw, as well as new plays by British writers and lectures by guest speakers.

To his credit, Dunlop was unafraid of controversial themes: the topic of Philip King's *Serious Charge* was a boy's claim to have been molested by a clergyman. There was much local muttering over this production, especially compared with the rest of the 1955–56 season, which presented more routine fare – *You and Your Wife*, for example, a thin, unmemorable comedy featuring the professional debut of Alan Bates in a small role. He was apparently more impressive as a twin in Shakespeare's *The Comedy of Errors*; and he was credibly passionate as the young lover, Horace, in Molière's comic masterpiece *The School for Wives*. This latter role is usually as enjoyable for a young actor as it is for the audience, mostly because the appealing Horace has scenes both of deft humour and touching romance.

'It was a very, very strong and well-thought-of company,' Alan said later, adding that he was more fortunate to have gone to the Midland than, for example, to the more famous company at Stratford, 'where they would keep you for a very long time before they let you begin to emerge'. With Dunlop, on the other hand, Alan appeared in no fewer than six plays in as many months, including a Christmas pantomime for children based on *Treasure Island*. His last assignment was a momentary turn as a comically nervous waiter in Thornton Wilder's *The Matchmaker*.

He would have continued with Dunlop through the spring of 1956, but an interesting opportunity brought Alan back to London early that year. Sheila Ballantine, an actress working with him in Coventry, had heard about a new repertory group called the English Stage Company, and she urged him to audition. 'I didn't really know what I was getting into,' he said later. 'I'd not heard of this new theatre, which was to be a writers' theatre. I went in quite innocently.'

The English Stage Company had been founded in 1955 by a governing council consisting of playwright Ronald Duncan, producer Oscar Lewenstein, composer Benjamin Britten and the Earl of Harewood (the queen's cousin and an enthusiastic patron of the arts). As artistic administrator they chose George Devine, an actor and director who had come from the Oxford University Dramatic Society and was working at the venerable Old Vic in both capacities. Passionate about theatre and zealous for it to be a more important force in British life, Devine invited as his associate an imaginative young director named Tony Richardson, who had just staged *Othello* for television.

Their first task was to find a professional home. The old Kingsway Theatre, Covent Garden, was available but required major rehabilitation. Their next choice was more feasible: the intimate Royal Court Theatre, on the east side of Sloane Square in Chelsea. Its distance from the West End soon became the symbol of an independent new theatrical identity and fresh artistic goals.

The aim of the English Stage Company was to offer a serious programme of plays – not necessarily to be ultra-modern or overtly activist, nor to be associated with a political agenda, but to be a popular company mounting plays rejected by the less adventurous commercial theatre, as well as experimental efforts by young playwrights and the best contemporary plays from abroad. The ESC also wanted to appeal to a younger audience, less interested in stars and glamour than the typical patrons of the West End; hence the company hoped to draw plays, playwrights and actors from the working classes and those sympathetic to them.

This was a risky programme, for in and around Shaftesbury Avenue, London theatres and careers survived by offering standard thrillers like Agatha Christie's *The Mousetrap*; lighthearted musicals like Sandy Wilson's *The Boyfriend*; American imports (there were fourteen in 1955); and an endless array of breezily artificial drawing-room comedies. The West End, in other words, was very much aimed at those who preferred undemanding and polite fare, of which very little related to contemporary English life. Characters were often dinner-jacketed sophisticates with champagne glasses and cigarette holders, gathered in elegant town homes or on vast country estates. The rarefied blank verse of plays by T. S. Eliot and Christopher Fry were discussed in reverential tones, and it was difficult to find ordinary, recognisable characters confronting the real social and personal problems of the 1950s. American playwrights like Arthur Miller, Tennessee Williams and William Inge had tackled unconventional social issues on Broadway, but English producers seemed hesitant to offer anything controversial.

Devine and Richardson, on the other hand, agreed that their primary concern was to find plays that were new, worthwhile and challenging – and above all to respect the text; hence, there was to be a close collaboration between director and writer, as well as an unwavering commitment to the possibilities of evolving theatrical art. Devine's vision was, therefore, to produce works that explored issues of the time. He looked for uncompromising new English writers and he longed for the ESC to be a repertory company that would stimulate fresh thinking.

Devine had placed an advertisement in *The Stage*, inviting writers to submit new plays. Hundreds of manuscripts jammed his post box, and so began the process of reading and winnowing. But even as they turned pages, Devine and Richardson had to get the ESC up and running, and the Royal Court duly occupied, so they announced open auditions for their first two offerings, to open in repertory that April.

Alan Bates was among the applicants, and he came to Sloane Square on an icy day in February 1956. Devine and Richardson asked him to read lines from Angus Wilson's play *The Mulberry Bush*, which had been revised since its Bristol Old Vic première and was to be the ESC's first offering. Alan won an inconsequential role in that play and, a few days later, he received an equally small part in the British première of Arthur Miller's *The Crucible*. The two plays, both under Devine's direction, opened in repertory on 2 and 9 April; the critics, unimpressed, lamented the absence of a new British work for the first night and did not much like the Miller play; their coolness even extended to the esteemed actresses Gwen Ffrangçon Davies and Rachel Kempson.

As the press offered little support and ticket sales dwindled, Alan began to wonder if he had erred in leaving Coventry. But he had one more commitment to the ESC that season: a substantial role in a new work, scheduled for May. Despite all the expressed hopes, there was considerable anxiety among the members of the new company over that play, too.

The writer Anne Piper recalled the desperate measures then taken within the company. She lived at 7 Lower Mall, near Hammersmith Bridge, and George Devine resided with his family in a flat at number 9. Devine's wife, stage designer Sophia Harris, made an odd request of Piper: would she and her family please buy tickets for *The Mulberry Bush* and rise up from their seats during the performance, shouting, 'This is rubbish!' and 'How disgusting!' before storming out into Sloane Square. The idea was that this would be reported in the press, and the public would come to the Royal Court in great numbers to see the cause of such a fracas.

Dutiful good neighbours, the Pipers purchased tickets for a mid-May performance of *The Mulberry Bush* and privately rehearsed their little scheme – but by then the melodramatic ruse was unnecessary. On the eighth of that month, the ESC presented their third offering – at last, a new play by a young English playwright – and the subsequent journalistic controversy, as well as the surprising appeal the play made to young theatregoers, surpassed anything that might otherwise have been devised as a marketing tool.

Among more than 700 plays submitted to Devine and Richardson, this one manuscript had impressed them more than all others, although they had doubts about its box-office potential. The play was *Look Back in Anger*, by twenty-seven-year-old John Osborne, and West End producers had universally rejected it. Among the cast of five, Alan had the supporting role of the Welshman, Cliff Lewis – which he very nearly lost. 'I stage-managed all the auditions for the company,' recalled Osborne. 'One of the actors selected was Alan Bates, and he was among those asked to give readings for Cliff. I favoured Nigel

Davenport, but Tony [Richardson] dismissed him' – and insisted on Alan.

The audition for *Look Back in Anger* was in early April, just as *The Mulberry Bush* was about to open; its cast and that of *The Crucible* worked at night, and those about to appear in *Look Back in Anger* prepared each day. 'In rehearsal,' Alan said later, 'I don't believe any of us realised how important [the play] was going to become. All it meant to me at the time was the chance to work in London.' While the cast met under Richardson's direction (who recalled that 'rehearsals were tense and a bit glum'), Devine – pragmatist as much as idealist – decided that the Osborne play would have only a short run, to be followed by two verse dramas by Ronald Duncan. During the rehearsal period, Alan asked Welsh-born Keith Baxter to teach him the correct accent for the role of Cliff.

Meanwhile, George Fearon, press officer for the ESC, informed Osborne that he doubted he could interest the press in *Look Back in Anger*. 'I suppose', Fearon told Osborne gloomily, 'you're really an angry young man?' With that casual query, a new phrase entered the lexicon of contemporary English.

Look Back in Anger concerns Jimmy Porter (played by the estimable Kenneth Haigh), a pitiless but articulate critic of English class distinctions, who humiliates his wife Alison (Mary Ure), hates just about everyone and finds contemporary life repellent. His foil is his patient friend and lodger, Cliff Lewis (Alan), a sympathetic chap with whom the audience can readily associate.

From its opening night, audiences found nothing that was comforting or amusing in the play's dialogue or setting, an attic apartment in the Midlands. 'Let's pretend that we're human beings and that we're actually alive,' says Jimmy maliciously at the outset and from that point he rails, with undiluted cynicism, against society and all the people in his small world: 'Nobody thinks, nobody cares – no beliefs, no convictions and no enthusiasms' redeem modern life and he loathes living in the new 'American age'. Against his temper and ill-concealed inclination to violence, Jimmy is forced to see that his friend Cliff, though poorly educated, is warm and affectionate, far more humane and therefore likely to get on better in the world.

For the most part the London critics recognised Osborne's talent but were cool to the play. Kenneth Tynan, writing in the *Observer*, became its pre-eminent champion: 'I doubt if I could love anyone who did not wish to see *Look Back in Anger*. It is the best young play of its decade.' Notwithstanding Tynan's standard for loving, his review provoked a critical dialogue but no rioting in the streets.

Finally – and perhaps to the amazement of Devine, Osborne, Richardson and everyone else – the conservative censor C. D. Heriot, reading the play on behalf of the Lord Chamberlain, asked for a few minor changes but praised the work as an 'impressive new play that breaks new psychological ground. The play's interest, in fact, lies in its careful observation of the anteroom of hell' – a judgement worthy of a seasoned critic. As for the actors, critics reviewed them collectively. Some could not accept that the characters spoke for a new generation; others agreed with Tynan that the actors gave 'fresh and unforced' performances corresponding to real life. Philip Hope-Wallace, in the *Guardian*, liked the way Alan – as 'a cosy young puppy' – brought Cliff to life.

As a brouhaha bubbled in the press and on the radio over *Look Back in Anger*, there was hope for more box-office activity. But during May and June, the ESC was still not drawing audiences in significant numbers. In August, Devine and company decided to cancel the Wilson and Miller plays, and to present the Osborne alone. Still, ticket sales were disappointing. Things began to shift favourably only after the influential and savvy Lord Harewood introduced a twenty-five-minute extract of it on the British Broadcasting Company's television network in October.

Condemned by many as the vulgar archrival to theatre, television saved the play and, as Tony Richardson said, 'made us the theatre of the moment, the place where it was happening, take it or leave it, love it or hate it'. *Look Back in Anger* ran for 151 performances at the Royal Court and transferred to the West End for three more weeks. A touring company staged the work in a number of other English cities, and soon it was sufficiently respectable to be named the best new play of the year by the *Evening Standard*.

Seen or read without prejudice, the Osborne drama is, for all its astonishingly cruel dialogue and its painful confrontations, very much in the tradition of the well-made play about a troubled marriage and not much at all about politics. It was the quotidian setting, the realistically dreary scenery and the blunt-force language of the play that set off fireworks among critics in 1956, making the ESC and John Osborne conversational topics over which people took sides – much as they had in New York in 1947, following the première of *A Streetcar Named Desire* by Tennessee Williams.

After *Look Back in Anger*, common life itself became an acceptable dramatic setting for the English theatre. Onstage, country houses, French windows and uniformed servants suddenly seemed drearily outmoded, and ironing boards, household squalor, frank talk of sex and sometimes overtly political content were purposefully introduced. A new wave of young British playwrights – among them Harold Pinter, Arnold Wesker, Edward Bond, Simon Gray and David Storey – were free to explore fresh forms and to express impolite, rude, radical and even violent emotions in their work.

The changes went beyond the theatre. In 1956, rock'n'roll was not widely heard in England; the following year, a pair of teenagers named John Lennon and Paul McCartney were trying new chords on their guitars and playing for friends and neighbours in Liverpool. Censorship itself, taken with utmost gravity in 1956, was gradually but insistently ignored, finally falling to the spirit of the times in 1968, when the last of the Lord Chamberlain's critiques was issued. Sexual stereotypes and acceptable prejudices began slowly to crumble, as significant changes in popular culture were soon evident and widespread.

Alan's performance as Cliff Lewis was appealing but appropriately restrained: he conveyed a touching sensitivity, a kind of tense tranquillity and persuasive composure opposite the feral ranting of Kenneth Haigh's Jimmy. Most of all, there was a subtle emotional economy that was never merely cool. According to some theatregoers, his stillness commanded attention even while characters around him were hysterical. His portrait was eloquent for hiding something of Cliff, who seemed to go along with all the games around him even while he kept an emotional distance.

'It was the first time I was seen in a recognised play, and people took notice,' he recalled. 'It was a real stroke of luck in terms of finding my feet and getting on and being acknowledged. I sometimes look back and think, "Oh, was I there, doing that then?" I don't think you ever do realise that you are in the middle of something unique and special. Obviously, John Osborne was a fine writer and we were conscious of that – and we also heard people talking about the play after it opened. But I think that Kenneth Haigh and

Mary Ure might have felt as I did: we were too involved in the play to see its immediate significance.'

Alan was working a fierce schedule. While rehearsing *Look Back in Anger*, he was also appearing in the plays by Wilson and Miller, and from June to August he alternated the serious role of Cliff with a farcical character in Nigel Dennis's satire *Cards of Identity*. That play had a disastrous reception, recalled John Osborne, who was also in the cast, as he was in the Duncan verse plays. 'Booing is a strange sound in the theatre,' Osborne wrote, 'and I had never heard it in such pure form [as during the performances of *Cards of Identity*].' Two months later it vanished from the repertory.

Devine's production of Wycherley's seventeenth-century comedy, *The Country Wife*, fared better when it opened that December. With film star Laurence Harvey in the leading role and Alan in a minor one, the production was pleasant for everyone involved and, when it was taken to the West End in February 1957, Alan went with it for another 172 performances. Then, when *Look Back in Anger* returned to the Royal Court in March 1957 for another thirteen weeks, he was again busy every night. 'I just felt lucky to have some work,' he said. 'It was nice to have the aura of an angry young man without having even thought of it! It wasn't until the play moved to New York that I realised this was big.'

Before the end of the year, scouts from American and British movie studios, who were always on the lookout for attractive young actors, were tapping on his dressing-room door, eager to discuss long-term deals. When Alan learned that they had no specific film projects or roles on offer – merely a weekly salary – he politely bade them good-night. Representatives from the Rank Organisation, England's most powerful and diverse combine, also came forward waving a lucrative contract. 'Even though it offered security, I felt it meant being owned by somebody,' he said, preferring to take his chances amid the un-certain, shifting fortunes of a self-directed career. 'I didn't want to be someone else's property and be told what to do.'

Years later, that was precisely how he described the subsequent long period of his private life. That autumn of 1956, there came an offer of another sort of security and it, too, came with risks. But this time Alan accepted the proposal – which concerned a relationship, not a film contract. One evening, the actor Peter Wyngarde came backstage at the Royal Court to praise Alan's performance. An alliance was evidently struck almost at once for, within weeks, Alan and Peter were living together.

Peter had hopscotched the world as a child and grew to be strong of features and robust of purpose, angularly handsome and invariably self-confident. By 1956 he had appeared onstage with Peggy Ashcroft in *The Good Woman of Setzuan* and had established a firm footing on British television; he had also recently completed a role in a feature film (*Alexander the Great*, with Richard Burton, Fredric March and Claire Bloom). With his imposing sophistication and social poise, Peter cut an impressive figure, and he found Alan an attractive and engaging partner with whom he could share aspirations.

So began a decade during which the couple shared their lives and homes. Peter was only six months older than Alan, but he had travelled widely and was more urbane and experienced in the tangled byways of the actor's life and the thickets of professional politics. Alan, on the other hand, was vulnerable, even pliant. Unsure of any future success and in many ways untutored, he was captivated by Peter's decisive and dynamic personality – qualities of which he was unsure in himself.

Before long, he decided to introduce Peter to his family. 'The most forceful among the lively and extrovert characters Alan brought home', said Martin, 'was Peter Wyngarde. I remember Peter saying to me, "Alan has the sort of face that falls in love with the cinema screen"' – not, it should be noted, 'the sort of face the cinema screen falls in love with', but the reverse, although it was equally true that the camera certainly favoured his good looks.

At the same time, Alan lived within an envelope of numbing fear that the precise nature of his life with Peter at 1 Earls Terrace, Kensington (and later at a country home) would become known – which, of course, it did, at least within certain theatrical and journalistic circles. While preparing a long article about Alan for *Time* in 1972, freelance correspondent Jerene Jones interviewed no fewer than two dozen friends and fellow actors. In a long summary of her research, she wrote from London to the magazine's New York office: 'Bates went through a homosexual period, [and] lived for a time with actor Peter Wyngarde.'

This was not mere gossip, as many knew. 'He doesn't want his private side public,' Jones added. 'He doesn't need to spill the beans.'

Hence, from this time forward, Alan rigorously avoided interviews and questions about his private life. He knew he needed publicity, and sometimes he had to sit for questions and answers. But he always tried to steer the interviewer away from personal enquiries: he wanted to retain a wide distance from the press, and he was not the only actor or celebrity to realise that, if he intended a career in public, this was virtually impossible.

3

Extreme States

Alan continued to gather admirers in London during the successful second run of *Look Back in Anger*, from 11 March to 15 June 1957. As the ESC returned briefly to a repertory season, he also assumed minor roles in two plays: Jean Giraudoux's *The Apollo of Bellac*, directed by Tony Richardson; and a single Sunday reading of *Yes, and After*, a new play by twenty-year-old Michael Hastings. At the same time, Devine and Richardson concluded negotiations for the ESC to bring the Osborne play to the Sixth International Youth Festival in Moscow.

The cast arrived in Russia that July to find the main streets of the capital festooned with multicoloured flags representing many nations and, instead of the hammer and sickle, the festival symbol was Picasso's doves of peace. Musicians from America played jazz, which had been banned as decadent by Stalin; there were exhibitions of European abstract art, which violated the canons of socialist realism; films from all over the world were screened without censorship; and masses of foreign visitors mingled with Soviet citizens socially, at modern dance recitals and at readings by young dissident poets. 'I can't believe I'm in Moscow!' Alan wrote on a postcard to his family. He found it 'grand and friendly', and praised its stimulating theatre life.

In such an atmosphere, *Look Back in Anger* was received without shock or outrage; indeed, its Russian première was warmly welcomed – perhaps as much for its implicit criticism of British imperialism (especially after the 1956 Suez crisis) as for its indictment of the class system.

By late summer, the cast was back in London, preparing to depart for the New York première. Peter, who was employed in a successful television series, suggested that he and Alan look for a country cottage to use as a weekend retreat from London. Peter would search for the right place while Alan was in America – an absence neither of them expected to be longer than a few months.

Rehearsals in New York proceeded smoothly, and before their opening night the cast had a few weeks to see other plays in the evenings – among them Eugene O'Neill's *Long Day's Journey into Night*, which Alan found much the best drama he had ever seen.

Look Back in Anger opened on Tuesday, 1 October at the Lyceum Theater on West Forty-fifth Street, a grand old house but, with almost one thousand seats, too cavernous for an intimate, single-set drama. As Richardson recalled, there was not much response from the audience at the première and only polite applause when the final curtain rang down at about eleven thirty; more ominously, no one came backstage to offer the traditional first-night congratulations. The show's American producer, David Merrick, escorted Osborne, Richardson and the cast to Sardi's, the nearby restaurant patronised by theatre people. Merrick ordered one drink for each of them, then a long and gloomy silence prevailed as they awaited word of the first reviews. 'We all felt', Richardson said, 'as though we were carrying some unnameable, unspeakable social disease. As the hours crawled along, Merrick looked more and more anxious and edgy.'

The apprehension finally lifted at about two in the morning, when early copies of the *New York Times* were brought to the restaurant, whose kitchen overlooked the newspaper's loading docks. 'Five British actors give Osborne's savage morality drama the blessings of a brilliant performance,' wrote the senior drama critic, Brooks Atkinson, who cited Alan for 'a vigorous performance in a more fluid style' than the rest of the cast. As favourable reviews accumulated over the coming days and weeks, *Look Back in Anger* settled in for a year-long run and eventually moved to the John Golden Theater. In 1958, while performances were still being offered, the New York Drama Critics' Circle named it the best foreign play of 1957–1958.

But success was not immediate, even with fine notices. Within a week, Richardson and Osborne went to a performance. 'Kenneth Haigh was not only not performing,' according to Richardson; he was also 'totally inaudible and cutting some of the most brilliant monologues in John's play'. The director gathered his cast and criticised Haigh, who gestured towards Alan and Mary Ure, the leading lady.

'Why do you always pick on me? [Haigh asked]. Why don't you blame *them*?' But *they* were giving impeccable performances, Richardson replied: why was Haigh cutting his speeches? The actor's answer was astonishing; he could not feel the lines deeply that night. 'Do you want me to give the audience *lies*?' Richardson was adamant: 'Yes – I want 'To be or not to be,' whether the Hamlet feels it or not!'

Once that matter was resolved, Richardson and his cast had another brief obstacle to negotiate. Merrick, an ingenious promoter, sometimes went over the top. A few weeks into the run, he hired a young lady who pretended to be outraged by the attitude towards women expressed by the character of Jimmy Porter. She rushed from her seat, jumped on to the stage and hit Kenneth Haigh hard in the face – all for the benefit of the press and rather in the spirit of Sophia Devine.

The show became a hit and its cast became Manhattan celebrities, but they certainly did not become wealthy. As in London, salaries for all but a few stage actors compared unfavourably with the compensation paid to movie stars; more to the point, the cast of *Look Back* was a company of unknowns who could not command substantial pay cheques. Alan received about one hundred dollars a week, and after taxes and commissions to agents, he could afford only a modest apartment on nearby Sixth Avenue that was located (in the words of John Osborne) in 'little more than a red-light apartment block on a sleazy street'.

At that time, all Broadway shows had the same performance schedule – Monday through Saturday evenings, and matinées on Wednesday and Saturday; hence it was impossible for Alan to see other plays once his had opened. For his ventures outside Manhattan, he was limited to the hours from late Saturday night to Monday afternoon. On many weekends, he travelled north to scenic mountains and east to the beaches; he was also invited by some wealthy New Yorkers to their summer homes on Fire Island, east of Manhattan, where he was, for a time, part of a privileged but rather louche society of Broadway denizens. 'He was sexually very precocious,' according to Paul Taylor, later a companion in Alan's life. 'He had been very passionate during his time in the RAF – as he was later in New York.' Neither boasting nor contrite, Alan discussed his highjinks with a few close friends.

But life that year was not primarily a party. Eager to expand his capacities to include singing, dancing and guitar-playing, he took notes while listening to the singer Martha Davis at the Blue Angel night-club. He also attended an Actors Benefit performance of *West Side*

Story, a musical whose vitality and freshness had an enormous impact on him. 'I think I'm a baritone,' he wrote to his family after he began sessions with a voice coach, 'but naturally I want to be a tenor.' Music, after all, was virtually in his genes and at least once he auditioned, unsuccessfully, for a musical.

His ticket to *West Side Story* benefited him far longer than an evening of superb theatre. The author of that show was the award-winning playwright, director and screenwriter Arthur Laurents; very quickly, Alan formed an enduring friendship with him and his life-partner, Tom Hatcher, whose many talents included the construction and renovation of homes and the design of a magnificent private park on Long Island. From this time they were among Alan's closest confidants. 'We always had a good time with him,' Laurents recalled years later. 'He came to our house in Greenwich Village and out to Quogue on Long Island to stay with us there. He was a cautious man, and he was nervous, for example, that Tony Richardson, who had affairs with men, would tell all about himself in his book. Alan thought that was a mistake.'

As his brother Martin recalled, Alan was buoyed by his success and delighted in meeting intelligent and creative people like Laurents, as well as working actors in New York – among them Fredric March, Richard Burton, Julie Harris and Henry Fonda. Paul Newman and his wife, Joanne Woodward, invited Alan to their Connecticut home for Christmas dinner, and he had drinks one evening with Laurence Olivier ('very charming and very, very funny,' Alan wrote to his family). Young, ambitious and not long away from his roots in a quiet provincial Midlands town, he reported that he was 'intoxicated' living in New York and 'fascinated' by things he saw every day, including the city's astonishing array of ethnic neighbourhoods.

'I'm looking well,' he wrote to his mother, answering her enquiry. 'In fact, I've never looked better – my skin is clear, I'm much thinner – I think a bit taller [!], dandruff under control! The comforts of New York agree with me.' Mary was showering him with letters, cards and baked goodies that year, and of a holiday fruitcake he commented, 'The cast shared it, but I ate an awful lot of it!' His mother knew his sweet tooth and kept his caloric cravings satisfied during his time in New York.

Nor was Alan slow to reciprocate. When he was away from England he always remembered to post presents to his family at Christmas and on their birthdays, however modest they had to be on his limited income at that time. Later, as his fortunes increased, everyone at home received boxes of quality clothing; he sent cash gifts to his brothers; and he bought his father a new car. In the years following, he took his parents and brother John to Venice, brought Mary and Harold to New York and Canada, and treated Martin and his wife to a Mediterranean holiday. 'He was generous in the extreme,' John remembered, 'uniquely understanding, highly entertaining and amusing – always exceptional company.' John never forgot Alan's look of feigned shock at a restaurant table as he said to his guests, 'This bill is enormous! What the hell have you all been eating?'

The New York production of *Look Back in Anger* ran for fifty-one weeks and 407 performances before its closing on 20 September 1958. By that time, as Alan admitted, 'I got stale. Long runs are very bad for an actor – you just stagnate, and that's death in this business. I lived with *Look Back in Anger* for over two bloody years, and it almost ruined me. Well, actually it made me, so I can't really complain about *that*.' Then and later he was, as John Bates rightly said, 'a valiant ambassador for Britain and British theatre'.

Alan did not remain with the show through its entire run, nor did he accept the offer to play Cliff in a film version. He was, as he wrote to his family several times, 'fed up with the play [and] I have really lost the inspiration for the part!' Besides, he was homesick for England: 'I don't think I could be happy here,' he wrote to his family. 'I'm looking forward to coming home, but I've now got a desire for travel worldwide!' Instead of staying with the Osborne play or working on the film, he preferred to take on a role in the British première of *Long Day's Journey into Night*, to be directed by José Quintero, who had staged it in New York. Alan left his colleagues on Broadway in late June 1958.

He returned to London for a long and arduous rehearsal period prior to a week of performances at the Royal Lyceum Theatre, Edinburgh, from 8 to 13 September, where it was part of the annual festival. On the fifteenth, there was one performance at the King's Theatre, Glasgow, then the production moved to London's Globe Theatre (later the Gielgud) on 24 September, where it ran until the year's end. The Bates family came en masse to London, where they saw the play and gazed proudly at Alan's name in lights outside the theatre.

Before the Scottish première, Alan and Peter drove from London to the village of Kilndown, near Lamberhurst, Kent, where they found an eighteenth-century cottage with a wide view over the meadows;

one of their neighbours was the great actress Dame Edith Evans. The cottage became mostly a private refuge, although occasionally they invited a friend or two in whom they could put their trust.

A lengthy, sad and difficult play, *Long Day's Journey into Night* usually runs over four hours and exhausts both players and spectators. Depicting one very painful day in the life of an early-twentieth-century New England family (surrogates for O'Neill's own), it has challenging roles for actors cast as an alcoholic father (in this production Anthony Quayle), a morphine-addicted mother (Gwen Ffrangçon Davies) and two doomed sons (Alan and Ian Bannen).

Once again cast in a complex, tricky supporting role, Alan played the younger and more poetically inclined son who, returning home after travels as a sailor, learns that he has tuberculosis and must again be dependent on his father for support. His performance, as critics observed, was moulded from small bits of business (some of which he learned under the warm tutelage of Ffrangçon Davies) – the carefully timed, anxious flutter of his hands, for example, and the shrewd but never exaggerated bursts of a consumptive cough. There was a sense of bedraggled melancholy about him, and he delivered the conclusion of his longest monologue with an almost unbearable poignancy: 'It was a great mistake, my being born a man; I would have been much more successful as a sea gull or a fish. As it is, I will always be a stranger who never feels at home, who does not really want and is not really wanted, who can never belong, who must always be a little in love with death.'

Alan's performances were the most exacting of his career thus far, and the play's bleakness often left him weary and dispirited. Peter, too, was working a full schedule in television plays, so their fore-shortened weekends in Kilndown were much anticipated. About this time, they purchased two shiny sports cars, a new Sunbeam Alpine coupé for Peter and a 1934 Lagonda four-seater, which Alan later gave to his brother John. Neighbours and friends were duly impressed, as was Alan's family. They were once invited to tea with Dame Edith, who, referring to *Long Day's Journey*, confided to his mother, 'Alan's awfully good in that play.' Edith's judgement was confirmed by British Actors Equity, which awarded Alan the Clarence Derwent Award for the best supporting performance of 1958.

But honours do not always translate into work and at the start of the new year 1959 there was nothing on Alan's horizon in which he could be 'awfully good'. And his agent, Philip Pearman, had no calls for him in theatre or film. But Peter had some useful contacts in television, among them the producer Sydney Newman. A Canadian impresario, Newman had only just arrived in Britain, where he was invited to be head of the drama division of the Associated British Corporation (ABC), the franchise holder for the BBC's rival, ITV. Thus began Alan's successful work in British television, both at ITV and eventually with the BBC.

In 1954, the BBC's monopoly had been legally terminated, and commercial broadcasting quickly became a formidable rival with the launch of Independent Television (ITV) the following year. A wave of new programming required a cascade of new scripts, fresh ideas, and young and attractive faces, but the constant demand for product resulted in uneven quality. Some of the programming was entertaining and a few scripts were provocative, but many were hastily sutured from a feeble premise. Such was the situation when Sydney Newman arrived in Britain.

By 1958 ITV had become enormously successful with long-running variety entertainments (*Sunday Night at the London Palladium*), quiz shows (*Double Your Money*) and the American import *I Love Lucy*. But the company wanted something fresh as well as prestigious, to counter the BBC and to widen their audience.

'At that time I found this country to be somewhat class-ridden,' Newman said years later with characteristic understatement. 'The only legitimate theatre was of the "anyone for tennis" variety, which on the whole gave a condescending view of working-class people. Television dramas were usually adaptations of stage plays and invariably about the upper classes. I said, "Damn the upper classes: they don't even *own* televisions!"' His approach, he continued, was to cater to people who were buying soap – ordinary people to whom advertisers aimed their commercials. Had he chosen to work in theatre, these sentiments might have made him a colleague (or rival) of George Devine.

Newman was on the mark. Television fare that year was, for the most part, comfortably cosy, consisting of dramatic series like *Dixon of Dock Green*, more variety shows such as *The Good Old Days* and quiz shows spun off from their American originals, like *What's My Line?* In 1958 a great deal of British television programming was either directly bought from the United States – *Dragnet, Alfred*

Hitchcock Presents and *Wagon Train*, for example – or creatively sten-cilled from it.

There had been occasional heavily edited television productions of classic English and Continental plays by Maugham, Wilde, Coward, Strindberg, Maupassant, Ibsen and Gide, but to Newman these were productions 'for the upper classes'. He had seen a West End revival of *Look Back in Anger* very soon after he arrived in April 1958, and he at once recognised that television, too, must reflect a changing society with new works created especially for home viewers.

Newman took over an anthology series called *Armchair Theatre*, with which he changed forever the style and content of British tele-vision drama. He commissioned original works by young writers like Harold Pinter, whose drama *A Night Out* was seen by six and a half million viewers in one evening – almost certainly more people than ever saw his plays in theatres. And Newman signed talented young directors like Philip Saville and Ted Kotcheff; for a time it seemed that only Newman himself was over the age of thirty.

Television plays at the time were for the most part transmitted live. This greatly restricted even the most imaginative writers and directors, much as early sound films, with their enormous and noisy cameras, had also limited camera movement. For television the action was static, the viewpoint much like a spectator in a theatre. ITV came up with a revo-lutionary approach in its presentation of Terry Southern's adaptation and Ted Kotcheff's direction of Eugene O'Neill's *The Emperor Jones* (broad-cast on 20 March 1958), which featured tracking and point-of-view shots with moving cameras. But there were expensive requirements – large sets and multiple cameras, for example, which made productions both awkward and difficult. And then something happened that changed the medium forever. Millions of viewers watched in horror as the young actor Gareth Jones collapsed and died during the live transmission of *Armchair Theatre's Underground* in November 1958. The change from live to filmed programmes occurred almost immediately.

As if by convention, the great British stage actors declined offers to appear on television. But Laurence Olivier broke the tradition that season, when he filmed Ibsen's *John Gabriel Borkman* for television. And, in 1959 alone, a virtual *Who's Who* of the English stage followed his lead: John Gielgud, Gladys Cooper, Michael Redgrave, Margaret Leighton, Joan Greenwood, Donald Pleasance and Robert Helpmann among others.

To his credit, Peter Wyngarde was attentive to these developments and he was convinced that an interview with Sydney Newman could work only to Alan's advantage; besides, a number of other young actors were lining up for television work – Tom Courtenay, Diana Rigg, Maggie Smith, and Peter himself. On his side the producer needed no persuasion when he met Alan: he knew of his performance in the original cast of *Look Back in Anger,* and he had seen him in *Long Day's Journey into Night.* He had just the project for Alan's television debut: a leading role in a drama called *The Thug,* by Jane Arden, to be directed by Philip Saville.

Things happen quickly in television production, and that era was no exception. After two days of rehearsal, Saville directed his cast in one day of filming and *The Thug* was then broadcast on Sunday, 15 February 1959. Alan played the title role, a delinquent who meets a sad, lame girl. 'The production,' according to *The Times*'s reviewer, 'was exciting whenever Mr Alan Bates was on the screen. His broodingly lonely and savage performance gave the part a profundity never suggested by the lines alone.'

At once, Alan was offered a number of teleplays and, with Peter's encouragement, he accepted them all. Twelve days after *The Thug,* viewers saw Alan in Arthur Miller's long one-act play *A Memory of Two Mondays,* based on Miller's experience as a warehouse worker during the Depression and directed by Silvio Narizzano (like Kotcheff, one of Newman's fellow Canadians). With a flawless American accent, an admirable sensitivity and the restraint necessary for the camera's close-up, Alan portrayed Kenny, a young Irish immigrant who knows that poverty is crushing his poetic gifts: 'They're gone,' he says about his lyrics. 'There's too much to do in the country for that kind of stuff.'

Granada Television, ITV's weekday contractor for viewers in the north of England, then featured Alan as another hooligan: in *The Jukebox,* broadcast on 17 April, he played a gang leader who shows little interest in girls until he meets the beleaguered daughter of an Italian immigrant. On 9 June he was seen as a boxer in *The Square Ring,* with Sean Connery, who had already launched his career in movies. That week, Alan was featured in several national magazines, where he was described as a dynamic newcomer with an avalanche of fan mail. On 18 August he was a medical student in an adaptation of Merton Hodge's play *The Wind and the Rain,* directed by Peter Wood.

Alan's next project was *Three on a Gas Ring*, which told the story of an unmarried and unrepentant pregnant girl who decides to raise a baby on her own rather than marry the father (Alan), whom she does not love. But the finished programme was judged too controversial and was never broadcast. In January 1960 Alan appeared – as a bright but unscrupulous man-next-door – in a teleplay called *Incident*. His co-star was Stephen Dartnell, whom he had known at RADA, who played a renegade soldier whose emotional breakdown triggers a crisis that affects all his neighbours.

Alan was television's unofficial man of the year – or 'the number one pin-up boy of British television,' panted *Picturegoer*, which detailed his every appearance with jubilant devotion. 'He is among the brightest and handsomest actors on TV.'

John Osborne and Tony Richardson held the same opinion. Since *Look Back in Anger*, playwright and director had collaborated again. *The Entertainer* was written at the request of Laurence Olivier and for him; in the role of Archie Rice, he had one of the great achievements of his career, as a fading provincial music-hall performer. After its success at the Royal Court in 1957, Osborne and Richardson had formed a movie production company, and in the summer of 1959 they were ready to film *The Entertainer*, as they had *Look Back in Anger*. In the role of Frank, one of Archie's sons, Osborne and Richardson wanted Alan, who at once accepted; Mick, Archie's other son, was played by Albert Finney. Both would be making their feature-film debuts; both were on screen very briefly, supporting Olivier and other players.

Before working at Shepperton Studios in Surrey, the cast and crew spent several weeks that summer of 1959 on location in and around the appropriately weathered and worn atmosphere of Morecambe, Lancashire, on the Irish Sea coast. Working with Olivier was often a daunting prospect for young players, but whatever awe Alan may have felt he concealed. 'I think he was seeking out something new with *The Entertainer*,' he said of Olivier. 'He had sought out the new dramatists and had made a very conscious effort to place himself at the forefront of all that.' The veteran and the novice had only a few moments together in the picture, but Alan acquitted himself smoothly.

Lean and graceful, Alan played Frank Rice utterly without affectation – a patient son, but not one to sacrifice his own life to his father's sad follies. This was not a major role, but amid the story's prevalent squalor and the cinematographer's properly flat lighting, Alan shone: some consider that in this film, at the age of twenty-five, he was at his most alluring.

His most important scene in the picture occurs during a breakfast conversation, in which Frank states, in the form of a question, Osborne's ultimate challenge. Exploiting his own original Midlands accent, Alan-as-Frank quietly asks his sister, 'Can you think of any good reason for staying in this cosy little corner of Europe? Who are you? You're nobody, you have no money and you're young. And when you end up, it's pretty certain that you'll still be nobody, you'll still have no money – and the only difference is you'll be old.' Spoken without rancour or sarcasm – but as a simple fact of feeling and of encouragement to others – the words highlighted his character's function in the story, despite the brevity of his appearance. Quietly effective, he made it matter very much that he was there.

In early 1960, playwright Harold Pinter and director Donald McWhinnie were casting Pinter's new work, *The Caretaker*, a three-character play about two eccentric and destitute brothers in a derelict house, who allow a querulous, disreputable vagrant to live, for a time, in their attic. Donald Pleasance and Peter Woodthorpe had already been chosen as the tramp, called Davies, and the mentally unstable brother, Aston; the role of the mercurial, brutal Mick was not yet assigned. Then, on 22 January, Pinter saw *Incident* on television. 'I watched Alan leaning against a wall, smoking a cigarette,' he recalled years later, 'and at once I called the director and said, "We've found our Mick."'

The script was immediately sent to Alan's agent at MCA Artists, Philip Pearman, who duly forwarded it along with a concurrent offer from the BBC for Alan to appear as Hotspur in a television production of Shakespeare's *Henry IV, Part I*. Alan read the two plays and met with Pearman, who said, 'Well, there isn't much to say about all this, is there? Obviously you are going to play Hotspur.'

'I'm rather drawn to this play,' Alan said, pointing to the Pinter script.

'Over my dead body,' replied Pearman. 'The Arts Theatre? For six pounds a week? In a play which I find completely incomprehensible? I'm ringing the BBC now to accept Hotspur on your behalf!'

'Wait!' Alan rejoined as his agent picked up the phone. 'I know the play is not easy to understand at first sight, but I also know that it's a marvellous piece of writing – and I want to do it.'

As Alan recalled years later, 'Philip put the phone down and looked at me with an expression that seemed to suggest I would shortly be dropped from the MCA client list. Ten per cent of six pounds per week is not exactly what agents go into the business for.' And so, against his agent's counsel, Alan took on the role of Mick in *The Caretaker*, the play that confirmed Pinter's permanent place as a great modern dramatist and that remains perhaps his most famous work. 'I didn't immediately understand the play,' Alan said, 'but I just knew emotionally that it was wonderful.' Rehearsals were under way in early March.

'It is a study of people in extreme states,' he said about *The Caretaker* years later; it is also an uncompromising and poetic exploration of the need for illusion and the desire to dominate. 'However mystifying or alarming it may initially be,' Alan continued, 'it haunts and resonates in a hugely dramatic way.' And this it achieved in a setting of insistent disarray – a junk-filled attic in a decaying house, a garret cramped and claustrophobic, without a single item to please the eye or a character to evoke enduring sympathy.

The play's language is realistic and ordinary, but allusive; the words are quotidian and common, but equivocal; and the characters' actions are recognisable, but ambiguous in their intent and effect. When a few critics in 1960 objected to the lack of clear and definite behaviour in the action of his plays, Pinter countered, 'I don't find my own behaviour definite and clear. To pretend to find your behaviour clear is to engage in a conspiracy with other people who would like to find their own behaviour clear. Most of the time, we're elusive, evasive, obstructive.'

As they prepared for the première, the trio of actors found the rhythms in the play's pauses – in the interruptions that are never arbitrary, in the tense overlappings and repetitions that reflect the tangle of ordinary life and discourse. And while they found little in the way of plot, they discovered a wealth of inference about human possibility. Not all life is like this, the play seems to say – but some of life is like this, and life itself is in danger of becoming like this: an anti-world, fragmented, disconnected, isolated, cruel, empty of meaning and purpose.

The Caretaker opened on 27 April 1960 at the Arts Theatre, a cramped and airless auditorium seating 340 in Great Newport Street, which is little more than an alley connecting Charing Cross Road to Upper St Martin's Lane. The cast, director and author took more than a dozen curtain calls, and Philip Pearman came backstage to congratulate his client. 'Never listen to me again,' he said. 'The play is brilliant.' Next day the critics ransacked their vocabularies for superlatives: *The Caretaker* was generally regarded as the finest drama in London – 'a national masterpiece', as the critic, director and playwright Charles Marowitz said at the time. In due course it won the *Evening Standard* Award as best play of the year.

'I went with fear and dread,' wrote Noël Coward in his diary. '*The Caretaker*, on the face of it, is everything I hate most in the theatre – squalor, repetition, lack of action, etc. – but somehow it seizes hold of you. It was magnificently acted by Peter Woodthorpe and Alan Bates and effectively by Donald Pleasance. Nothing happens except that it does. The writing is at moments quite brilliant and quite unlike anyone else's . . . I loathed [Pinter's] *The Dumb Waiter* and *The Room*, but after seeing this, I'd like to see them again because I think I'm on to Pinter's wavelength.' Soon, he made public his private esteem. Writing in the *Sunday Times*, Coward – the defender of orthodox theatrical conventions – astonished readers:

> Mr Pinter is neither pretentious, pseudo-intellectual nor self-consciously propagandist. True, the play has no apparent plot, much of it is repetitious and obscure, and it is certainly placed in the lowest possible social stratum; but it is written with an original and unmistakable sense of theatre and is impeccably acted and directed. Above all, its basic premise is victory rather than defeat.

The cast was highly praised, with Alan (as one critic wrote), 'playing the most straightforward character straightforwardly [and] managing at the end to compress the brothers' secret into a single nod and half-smile'. His Mick, a mysterious and unpredictable character with large claims about his business and larger dreams about his future, alternated between courtesy and violence.

'Mick is a fantasist,' Alan said. 'He's got a fantasy of the life he wants to lead, and a place in which he wants to do it. His brother is disturbed, and Mick is instinctively, hugely protective of his brother – which means loyalty, in this case. And because he's a protector, he's jealous of the tramp. I understood all of that instinctively. I didn't need to have anything more specific than that.'

Onstage in this play, Alan was nothing like the gentle, long-suffering Cliff of *Look Back in Anger*, nor the wasted dreamer, Edmund, in *Long Day's Journey into Night*. Here, he was a man whose best instincts have been firmly suppressed – a sneering, leather-jacketed, over-age delinquent, perhaps partly redeemed by his evident refusal to abandon his psychologically derailed brother. Alan's Mick was limned with oily charm and pitiless intensity – an entirely new character in his anthology, one frankly risking his audience's disaffection. With an intensity previously untapped, Alan became the character, saying that he understood these 'three rather isolated people and their need to belong, and to find some kind of purpose. I find them all very moving characters. I understand them. I know who they are.'

Four weeks after its première, the play transferred to the Duchess Theatre, Covent Garden. Somewhat more comfortable and more capacious than the Arts Theatre, the new venue was sold out almost every night for the next year, and Alan's salary rose slightly from six pounds weekly. During that time, actors from all over the world came to the Duchess: Joanne Woodward visited in October and sent Alan a laudatory telegram, saying that she was bringing Paul Newman over from Paris (where he was filming) to see *The Caretaker*. The play finally closed on 27 May 1961, after 425 performances.

During the run, Alan performed in two more television dramas. The first, broadcast on 7 June 1960, was the Harold Brighouse comedy *The Upstart*, in which he was a fatuous idealist who makes a bid for a seat in parliament. His character revels in 'the glorious sensation of holding a crowd in the hollow of your hand', so his friends deflate his vanity. (Peter Woodthorpe, his 'brother' at the Duchess, was also in the cast.) The second show was televised on 17 August: *Treviso Dam* concerned a man's death in a notorious construction accident. Alan's co-stars were the great Italian actor-director Vittorio de Sica, in his 111th role; and Judi Dench, who had not yet appeared in a feature film.*

---

* According to the British Film Institute's online data base, Alan appeared on 3 October 1960 in the 'BBC Television *World Theatre* Production' of *The Seagull*. But neither the BFI nor the BBC provides any details about such a broadcast; nothing was mentioned in the press, then or later; and there is no information about it in Alan's files. He did, of course, assume the role of Trigorin in *The Seagull* in 1976.

In answer to a question about performing a role eight times a week, Alan was forthright:

> I think eight performances a week are killers, really. Singers don't do that, violinists don't do that, pianists don't do that, dancers don't do that – only we do it. I don't know why. I don't know why we think we can. I know we always have, for probably hundreds of years, but it's odd, isn't it? It's madness, really! You should do an evening, but not a matinée on the same day.

He was convinced, for example, that the preparation for a performance started hours earlier with a conservation of energy and an effort to keep himself free – 'very loose, so that something can happen' – even if it was unlikely to be what happened the night before, or what he thought might happen or should happen. Something had to remain, as he said, alive and flexible. He tried always to recollect what he had decided to do in a scene – and then develop a mechanism for keeping it fresh and alive, which was a process he began that year.

> You can't really get to the same depth of feeling every night, and I think you have to trust the fact that once you have found something, even if you don't feel it the next time, you have *been* there, and you will be convincing to an audience. Representing someone else is convincing yourself that you are in someone else's shoes.

Hence, Alan did not approve of the tradition in which actors have a conception of a role from day one and never alter that idea:

> I do believe in going [deeply] into a part. I like to let the part creep up on me, just take it on slowly, with thought. Maybe that's my version of [The] Method. I rather like parts where you can crawl around them for a bit. Sometimes you don't feel the change in yourself, but it's happening, because you're doing it slowly. Well, there are really no rules.

That year Alan began to make some analogous slow changes in his personal life at Earls Terrace and in Kent. He continued to look to Peter for advice on just about everything and he gave himself to their life together. But at about this time he started to feel that the dynamics of their relationship were those of the dominant Peter and the dominated Alan. To be sure, Peter toughened him for the business side of acting; Peter advised him on what to read; Peter introduced him to influential producers and writers; and Peter encouraged him at the right times.

But Alan felt that Peter's strength and his zealous instructions had an element of precisely the kind of dominance Alan recognised and found so frightening in *The Caretaker*; he also told friends that he feared becoming overwhelmed – and that he resented his own passivity, his willing subordination. 'I understand them,' he said of the characters in Pinter's play. 'I know who they are.' Later, Alan described the years with Peter as 'the dark period of my life'; it was also a time when some of Alan's friends and colleagues referred to Peter – perhaps harshly, perhaps not – as 'The Major'.

On the other hand, at least some of the shadows in this dark period were cast by Alan's own carefully created public image, which was necessarily at odds with his private life. Hence he felt enormous inner tension at this time and a growing uncertainty about his future. There were bright times in his life with Peter, who seems not to have felt the same terror of censure; but years later, Alan would not discuss the compensations of their relationship. In 1960, theirs was becoming an unpredictable and tortuous voyage, but they still hoped that any potential storms could be weathered.

Between 1957 and 1960 Alan had appeared in three major plays; within eighteen months, he was seen in no less than nine television productions. Always eager to work, he became anxiously restive on holidays or between projects. Martin retained vivid memories of his brother's impatience for the next job, the next task: 'He often moved furniture around, redecorating or having alterations made to his homes. I lost count of the number of times he loaded his car with furniture, paintings, linen and ornaments and shunted different mixes of them' from one residence to another. Alan knew he was fortunate to have so many offers so often, and in the years to come they only increased. 'I'm very lucky, you know,' he said more than once. 'There are a lot of good actors out there.' Aware of the competition even as he was confident of his talents, he often enjoined on others his own unofficial axiom: 'You've got to be driven – *driven!*'

4

On the Run

On 20 February 1961, Harold Pinter stepped for two months into the role of Mick in *The Caretaker* at the Duchess Theatre. Acting for neither the first nor last time, the actor-playwright was (thus *The Times*) 'wholly convincing, [and] his presence, timing and diction fulfil all the demands made' – demands imposed, of course, by Pinter himself.

Although Alan greatly disliked performing eight times a week and had already logged more than 300 performances in this play, the reason for his temporary absence was suitably professional. That winter he had been offered an important role in a film script he much admired – *Whistle Down the Wind*, based on a novel by Mary Hayley Bell. It was to be filmed quickly on location in Lancashire, in the bleak midwinter, and many of the scenes were set outside or in an icy barn. But as always, if the story gripped him, Alan accepted the physical challenges and seasonal discomforts. In addition, he liked working with novice craftsmen: the actor-writer Bryan Forbes would be directing his first film, from a screenplay by Keith Waterhouse and Willis Hall.

The star of the picture, however, was a seasoned professional – fourteen-year-old Hayley Mills (daughter of Mary Hayley Bell and the actor John Mills), acting in her fifth movie. After a week of rehearsals, filming began in Burnley and at the Worsaw End Farm, Downham. 'How very lucky I was to have him in the first film I directed,' recalled Bryan Forbes. 'He had an instinct for truth and honesty, even during those long winter weeks in that drafty, cold barn in the country!'

The story and screenplay have a disarming and deceptive simplicity, beneath which are issues of faith and credulity that must have appealed to Alan's sharp sensibility as a script reader. In *Whistle Down the Wind*, a girl named Kathy (Hayley Mills) goes to the family barn one day to feed her kittens and is shocked to find a bearded stranger (Alan) in hiding. Wide-eyed with fright, she asks, 'Who are you?' The man realises that he has been discovered and mutters 'Jesus Christ!' before collapsing, exhausted, in an animal's stall. The child takes his reply as an answer to her question and so the dilemma is set in swift motion. 'He's in our barn!' the girl tells her younger sister and brother. 'He's come back! He's asleep in the hay!'

The conflict derives from the unwanted but inevitable publicity that accumulates around the fugitive, as schoolchildren come in great numbers to see (as they think) Jesus Christ himself, while the sound-track rings with the musical phrases of 'We Three Kings'. Kathy urges her friends, 'Don't tell the grown-ups, or they'll take him away – like the last time,' but that is just what happens. The secret gets out and the police – eager to question the man about a murder – arrest him as he spreads out his arms, cruciform. (During a scene in the village we see a 'Wanted' placard with the stranger's name: 'Arthur Alan Blakey, from Derby', which is close enough to Alan Arthur Bates, from Derby, to reward the attentive moviegoer.)

The title of the book and film originates in Shakespeare's *Othello* and refers to releasing a hawk after its quarry: 'I'd whistle her off and let her down the wind, to prey at fortune.' But by 1900 the phrase 'whistle down the wind' also came to mean simply letting go of some-thing – thus the double reference, both to Kathy's final plea to have the man freed and of her own 'letting go' of him.

Curiously, most reviewers and many spectators wrongly took Blakey for a killer, which is not unambiguously established in *Whistle Down the Wind*. He is obviously on the run, but we cannot be certain of the reason; he *may* have committed a crime, but there is nothing to warrant a wholesale presumption of guilt. This is a significant aspect of Mary Hayley Bell's complex story, which (however unintentionally) reflects on the possible consequences of Saint Benedict's venerable injunction, 'Let all guests be received as Christ.'

Years later, Hayley Mills recalled working with Alan:

He was wonderfully pleasant to be with, and during our scenes he was a living lesson in movie acting. He kept so much of the man's character hidden in his performance – he held so much back, which was entirely right. He let the man remain a bit of a mystery, so that the children in the story could impose their own idea of him *on* him. The man doesn't try to win Kathy over, but rather accepts her presumption of his identity. That gives the picture its richness, because Alan allowed the audience into it – he didn't give it all away or reduce it to something simple. It's a remarkably restrained and subtle performance.

Much of that subtlety and restraint may be seen in the shading of his gaze – dark and haunted, alternately filled with incomprehension, fear, bewilderment, tenderness and even, at times, a veiled threat of violence.

'It was my first major part,' Alan said. 'The children really were the star of the film – the *focus* of the film, and the character I played became *their* focus, and that's why it was such a good part. It was very naturalistically shot, done with a very conscious realism.' To his surprise, he often had to defend this small gem of a movie against sophisticates: 'It's not a windy children's tale. It tells of treachery, of the whole area of credibility and faith. It's quite a strong film, and I think it stands up very well.'

Praise for his performance came from none other than Claude Gibson, who wrote to Mary Bates that summer with a perceptive comment on *Whistle Down the Wind*:

> Do congratulate Alan most heartily. His playing of the part was brilliant, and I feel that the direction of the whole thing was very good. But I think it might have been indicated that the man was not quite the desperate character the police considered, so that a happy ending *could* have been contrived in some way – which would have been by no means impossible, and in keeping with the gentle appearance of the man. Alan was not directed as a desperate character, but as one at the end of his tether, and very finely he played it. If one has to look at a fairy tale, let it end as a fairy tale – happily!

Filming in Lancashire and in the studio was completed in early April 1961, and Alan returned to his role in *The Caretaker*, which he played up to its closing on 27 May. On 18 June he appeared in a television comedy – *Duel for Love*, his first time out as a suave young lover. He portrayed a man pursuing a beautiful but remote young woman (Susannah York) who does not look favourably on his amorous attitude until she learns that he is to duel at dawn; after considerable romantic teasing, there is a predictably reassuring conclusion. The critical consensus was summarised by Clifford Davis in the *Daily Mirror,* who cited the teleplay's 'unerring tenderness, with two sensitive performances [providing] a memorable evening'.

Harold Pinter and Donald McWhinnie wanted even more memorable evenings from Alan – in the New York production of *The Caretaker,* scheduled for autumn 1961. A lucrative deal had been put in place with a troika of veteran producers (Roger Stevens, Frederick Brisson and Gilbert Miller), who insisted that the show come over with the London cast intact. Peter Woodthorpe withdrew, but the Americans gracefully accepted his defection, as well as Robert Shaw as his replacement; after all, they could still count on Donald Pleasance and Alan Bates.

By late June, Pleasance had signed, and Philip Pearman (by this time an enthusiastic champion of Pinter and his plays) expected his client to do likewise. But Alan temporised: he said he would sign, then he reneged without giving a reason, then he said yes, of course, he would go to New York. In early August he was still uncertain, telling Pearman he was departing for a holiday and would make his decision when he returned.

Earlier, Alan had discussed with Gibson the matter of the New York production. 'Has Alan made up his mind yet about going to the USA with *The Caretaker?*' Gibson wrote to Mary in August. 'It is a difficult decision to make. On consideration, I rather hope he goes to America. The film [*Whistle Down the Wind*] may go over there – and then, who knows!' In September Pearman was avoiding the demanding telephone calls from New York, while the rapidly approaching October date for the American première caused him, Pinter and McWhinnie – not to say the New York producers – considerable anxiety.

Alan's procrastination, his playing for time while he made up his mind, had nothing to do with demands for higher wages or greater privileges. In fact, his hesitation to give a timely answer became a habit that vexed producers and harassed his agents for decades. That their tempers did not flare, that they were actually grateful if he agreed – and that they were willing to return later with another project even if he did not – is easy to understand. Everyone enjoyed his company, socially and professionally: there is no evidence that Alan Bates was ever moody, volatile or difficult during a stage or screen production; that he made unreasonable contractual demands; or that he sought perquisites denied to others.

From youth to death, his reputation was consistently that of a completely prepared colleague, a team player, and the most good-humoured companion for a director and cast. Bright and articulate, he rarely tried merely to impress; he was known to offer encouragement to other players; and he was never mocking or sarcastic (at least not in another's presence). Unassuming natures are perhaps not found abundantly in the acting profession and, in this regard alone, Alan was one of a few. But his failure to give timely answers to his agents was indeed maddening, and they often had to deal with producers, directors and writers as best they might.

For almost two and a half years, Alan had worked with no respite longer than a weekend. Apart from his time in New York and one brief excursion to Paris as a student, he had seen little of the world. Peter, too, had worked constantly, and had recently concluded one of his most memorable roles – the terrifying ghost of Peter Quint, in Jack Clayton's film *The Innocents*, based on Henry James's novella *The Turn of the Screw*. Peter and Alan had never taken a holiday together further than a weekend at Kilndown and so, that summer, Peter suggested a motor trip. They drove down through France to Spain, then across the Riviera to Italy, where Alan particularly loved the distinctive charm of Venice, despite its August heat and humidity.

Finally, in early September, Alan telephoned Pearman that, yes, he would go to New York. *The Caretaker* opened there on 4 October – again, at the vast Lyceum Theater (on which, as he wrote to his family, he was 'not so keen'), and again, the reviews were extremely favourable. The most appreciative notice came from an unidentified *Time* magazine critic, who praised the cast in tandem and summarised the humanity of the play in simple but not simplistic language:

> Locked in a cycle of self-concern, as playwright Pinter subtly emphasises through individual repetitive speech patterns, no one of the characters can save himself. Each member of this weirdly disparate trio needs the others, but the language of

cooperation is not in them. Their final tragedy is to deny their mutual need and fall apart into isolation. *The Caretaker* represents a high order of aesthetic achievement, the kind of drama that at play's end no longer belongs to the playwright, but to every sentient playgoer.

Despite his good notices, Alan was restless as usual. 'I love *The Caretaker*,' he wrote to his mother, 'but I'm looking forward to something new.' He then added, 'I find America less stimulating than before, and I'm not sure that I like it, after all. I think of England much more affectionately this time. I miss you all very much, and I'm dying to come back!' Notwithstanding his homesickness, 'I've now got a desire for travel worldwide!'

And so, as long queues formed for tickets at the Lyceum box office, the news was announced: Alan was leaving the play on 28 October, and his role was going to Alexander Davion, who played Mick for the remaining four months of the run. His precipitous departure after less than four weeks was not the result of caprice or greed. In London, movie producer Joseph Janni and director John Schlesinger (who had recently won a prize from the British Academy for directing a short film), had seen *Whistle Down the Wind*; at once, Alan was their choice for the leading man in Schlesinger's first feature. In short order Janni paid Stevens, Brisson and Miller the sum of $10,000 for Alan to be released from *The Caretaker*. He left New York on 29 October; it would be more than three years before he returned to stage acting.

The movie in question had in fact been delayed to accommodate his return – 'so I'm a very lucky boy,' as he wrote to Mary. Alan arrived in London on 30 October, met briefly with Pearman, Schlesinger and Janni, and, after a weekend in Kent, departed on 6 November for location shooting in and around Manchester. Even before the deal was signed, Janni issued a press release ('When Actor Is a Property'), identifying his new contract player as 'one of the most important properties in British movies today', which may have given Alan a bad stomach.

A Kind of Loving was the story of Vic Brown (Alan), a cheerfully randy draughtsman in the industrial north of England. Still living agreeably with his parents, he develops a powerful attraction but no great affection for a pretty, somewhat ordinary and half-deliberately seductive co-worker named Ingrid (June Ritchie). She becomes pregnant and he is forced to marry her, and so begins the conflict. The marriage becomes difficult when they move in with his meddlesome mother-in-law, the ultimate termagant; Ingrid miscarries their baby; they separate; and, in the final scene, they attempt to reconcile. A kind of loving, the film implies, may be better than no love at all. The ending is decidedly bitter-sweet.

'It had a lot of human understanding,' Alan said of the film, 'a lot of awareness of young people's problems and their blindness and the whole pot-luck chance of life. It wasn't brutal; it was absolutely life as it was lived. It wasn't about exceptional folk; it was really about everyday people and their struggles.'

As Schlesinger said, he wanted to make a film about 'human difficulties and the illusions of love'. Although it shared some of the British new wave characteristics – working-class people in ordinary settings, as in *Room at the Top* (1959) and *Saturday Night and Sunday Morning* (1960) – Vic is not a rebel, nor is he off-putting. He is simply a selfish, immature young man, however charming, and he evokes almost as much sympathy as the benighted girl. Like several Schlesinger films to come, *A Kind of Loving* is an exploration of a certain portion of authentic adult experience; it was also astonishingly frank in its language and depiction of sex.

In this regard, it was indeed to be expected that the Board of British Censors would rattle their sabres when it came time to grant a seal of approval for release of the picture. 'The secretary of the Board was a man named John Trevelyan,' recalled the agent Gareth Wigan, who, with his business partner Richard Gregson, represented Schlesinger and was later to become Alan's agent. 'On *A Kind of Loving*, it was John Schlesinger's or Joe Janni's idea to bring Trevelyan on to the set during filming, to secure his approval then and there. As the film-makers anticipated, Trevelyan was so flattered by this, and so intrigued to watch a movie in production, that he said he would gladly visit the set at any time – and so there was no problem when it came time for him to approve the finished film.'

Working agreeably with Schlesinger, Alan composed his performance with small, revealing gestures and covert glances to reveal thoughts contrary to his actions. '*A Kind of Loving* was my big break, of course, since it was my first major part,' Alan said. 'It was a wonderful experience. I remember the sheer joy of it. There was such a sense of promise then – such a sense of fun. Of course, John wasn't always confident. Once the first few days of shooting were over, he started in: "Oh, God, I can't do this. It's all terrible. What was I *thinking?*" But of course he *could* do it, and he did it brilliantly' – so brilliantly, in fact, that the picture won the Golden Bear, the highest honour at the Berlin Film Festival. With that, John Schlesinger's career shifted into high gear. He regarded Alan as 'such a good, intuitive actor. I love working with him.'

Schlesinger's direction was crisply unsentimental, and he clearly felt the story deeply. Alan found the appropriate complex of feelings for Vic, an attractive young man who is alternately lusty, reckless, hopeful and yet surprised to find that life eventually imposes responsibilities as well as pleasures. This could have been a one-dimensional portrait, but Alan's gaze was never blank, the smallest movements of facial muscles were always telling something, and his scenes with June Ritchie survive as classic images of youthful confusion. Decades later, the film has neither aged nor lost its sharp edge.

There was a brief but thorny complication early in production, when the director developed a romantic crush on his leading man. 'Had Alan been willing, John would have jumped at the chance to have an affair with his star,' according to Schlesinger's biographer, but Alan was 'fundamentally unavailable' and 'smitten with another young man'. The latter reference may or may not have been to Peter Wyngarde, who was still a significant presence in Alan's life. But it was not gallant fidelity that restrained Alan from yielding to Schlesinger: Alan did not want to assume the risks of an entanglement with his director and the chemistry was unilateral. In any case they finessed some initial awkwardness and formed a lifelong friendship that endured through three more collaborations.

A Kind of Loving was completed in January 1962 and released in April; for the first time, Alan was given star billing, before the title of the film. Produced for a modest £180,000, it grossed three times that amount and was nominated by the British Film Academy in the categories of best picture and actor. It was indeed his 'big break' and it quickly secured more film offers. Years later he confided that the part 'wasn't really far away from my own experience – a boy from the Midlands works at an ordinary job but feels that there is some other area of life he hasn't yet touched, and he is very rooted to his family.' He was entirely credible as a kind of man's man who is also a mama's boy, 'and he goes back to his mother,' as he added.

Similarly, Mary never stopped being a robust presence in Alan's life. When the film was released, he was quite concerned that much of it would offend her, but to his surprise she was unfazed by the sexual frankness. Martin recalled attending the Manchester première with Alan and their mother, after which the theatre manager approached her: 'Well, Mrs Bates – your Alan's going all the way now, isn't he?'

'Well, we hope so,' she replied hesitantly.

'Oh, no doubt – he will, he will!'

Alan had another reason to be up north that spring – to condole the widow of Claude Gibson, who had recently died. The news had touched Alan deeply, for Gibson had been more than teacher and guide: he had been a warm mentor, an advocate in the earliest days and an enthusiastic follower of Alan's success. 'I hope letters are not an intrusion at this time,' he wrote to Mrs Gibson.

I know you must be feeling very sad. I shall miss Mr Gibson a great deal. He always kept in touch with me and was a man of such life and energy, and was interested in all and everything around him. I don't need to tell you how much he did for me. He gave me encouragement, knowledge, and a very strong background to my work. He was the first influence and help to me. When I come to Derby next, I will come and see you. Remember me to your family. I feel this letter expresses very inadequately my feelings. I am sure you understand.

 With great sympathy,
 Alan Bates

On his return to London, there was a screenplay waiting and the offer of an indifferent supporting role in a picture called *The Running Man*. Uncharacteristically, he accepted at once.

There were two reasons for his alacrity: the director was to be Carol Reed, whose films he much admired – among them *Odd Man Out*, *The Fallen Idol* and *The Third Man*; and the picture required him to be twelve weeks in Spain for exterior filming and a month in Ireland for studio work. This not only appealed to his 'desire for travel worldwide', as he had said; he also found his return to life with Peter increasingly frustrating, although he could not simply say so and leave

Earls Terrace and Kilndown. Alan avoided confrontations when he could, especially in personal relationships; he expected things to sort themselves out. Hence he sometimes unintentionally made situations more difficult, and finally more distressing, both for himself and others.

That summer, Peter took Alan's departure at face value: Alan had to go where his work required. But it was not good work at all, and Alan knew that from the start: 'I didn't think it was good when I read it, and I didn't have a good feeling about it when I was doing it.'

After preliminary sequences set in England, *The Running Man* followed a crook (Laurence Harvey) who plots to stage his own accidental death so that he and his wife (Lee Remick) can flee the country with his life insurance money. Alan played an investigator who comes to interview the wife and later, by chance, meets her and her husband in Spain. They believe he has followed them to unmask their scheme, but in fact he has changed jobs and is on holiday. There is a predictable romantic complication and, at the end, crime does not pay.

This was Alan's first colour film, and the camera tests during pre-production showed that his skin tone, hair and eyes presented no problems for the lighting cameraman, the make-up artist or the costume designer. He had little to do in the picture except to look darkly handsome yet innocent – contrary to Harvey, who had to look darkly handsome but menacing. Amid the summer heat and humidity of Malaga, Algeciras, San Roque and La Linea, the cast and crew became a kind of travelling sideshow, coping with noisy bystanders, demanding police officers and lumbering trucks crammed with electrical generators, cables, lights and props.

The Running Man was the most arduous of Alan's movie assignments thus far. Worse, during filming, the cast and crew realised that the project was much less than it had seemed, and yet they had to be present for long periods with nothing to do while set-ups were completed and contingencies negotiated. 'I felt I was working for commercial reasons, because it seemed a good thing to be with a famous director and a famous actor and actress – a promise of international success, you know. It's really the only time I worked with that motive, and I didn't think it was going to be very good. Then, when I saw the final cut, I didn't think it was good at all! I think the film tried to follow a conventional line. No film should try to follow a trend and do what people think the public wants.'

★　★　★

Before the end of 1962 he began work on his third movie that year, a screen version of *The Caretaker*. Convinced that this would not be a popular or lucrative film, banks, studios and distribution companies had not been forthcoming with financing. With great dedication, producer Michael Birkett and director Clive Donner joined Harold Pinter in forgoing a fee unless and until the picture turned a profit, and the cast of three (Pleasance, Shaw and Bates) also forfeited their salary upfront. The budget – a remarkably low £30,000 – was then covered by investments from a short list of the play's admirers, including Richard Burton and Elizabeth Taylor, Noël Coward, Peter Sellers, and Peter Hall and Leslie Caron. 'It was done out of pure love of the piece,' Alan recalled, 'to record it and make sure people could see the cast that had done it.'

Filming began on 10 December and was completed in six weeks. Apart from a few exterior shots, the entire picture was filmed during one of London's coldest and snowiest winters, in the cramped, unheated attic of an abandoned house at 31 Downs Road, Hackney; renouncing studio interiors, there was room only for the actors, the director and two technicians. With Donner's approval, Alan had the idea to wear a false upper plate of teeth over his own, which gave him an eerily menacing overbite and a slightly grotesque aspect for his many close-ups. But the effect of his portrait was primarily due to his almost static gaze and unnerving glances at the other players. 'The scenes between Donald Pleasance and me became more sinister – the closer you are, the more sinister [Mick] is, because you see much more of his mind.' With this picture Alan again demonstrated his mastery of the differences between stage and screen acting – the size of gestures, the variety of tonal nuance, the need to convey character by inference.

The silences surrounding the characters and the jumble of objects in the attic seem properly enlarged in the film – like the odd intrusions of sounds both natural and synthetic; there is no musical score. *The Caretaker*, which is not so much heard as overheard, has no equivalent in the history of filmed plays.

In early 1963, Alan followed the lead of several friends and colleagues. Although his work had not brought in any princely emoluments, higher compensation was theoretically possible. For tax purposes, therefore, he set up Cyrano Productions Ltd – named after his pet corgi

– and legal papers were signed on 15 February; his father, the designated secretary of the corporation, received one of the hundred shares. Then, as if on cue, Clive Donner rang Philip Pearman with an offer for Alan to appear in his first comic role, as an unscrupulous, even murderous, clerk in *Nothing But the Best*.

Among his co-stars was Millicent Martin, of whom the director and producer were uncertain. 'I was called to Merton Park Studios to do a test for the film,' she recalled,

> and Alan came along just to help me through the ordeal. I arrived in a terrible state of jitters, and there he was – all dressed and made up for his part, in order to make it all as painless for me as possible. He was perfect – he always is – but he pretended he wasn't quite sure of his lines and asked the crew if we could go through them a few times to get them right. It was all for my benefit – and it was the same all through filming. He never made a show of teaching the new girl her job, but in his own quiet way he taught me more in that one picture than I could have learned from most other actors in half a dozen pictures. He can be tough when there's a need to be, but he's not the kind to chuck his temperament about between shots. He saves all his temperament for his acting.

Also in the cast was Harry Andrews, a veteran of stage and screen, who played Millicent Martin's father. 'I don't want to be a star,' Harry said to Alan one day. 'I want to be a good actor in good parts.' That season he became a good friend of Harry and his partner of many years, Basil Hoskins, also an actor. Alan was comfortable in the presence of this male couple, precisely because Harry himself was always and everywhere at ease with Basil. 'Harry was the first person I met in my career who represented stability, security in himself, and self-awareness,' Alan recalled. 'He was a man who knew who he was and where he was, and had no false ideas about anything. We meet a few people like this in our lives, and we do not always realise until too late just how significant they have been. I learned from him how rewarding it can be to have close friendships with people who are not your contemporaries.'

The script for *Nothing But the Best*, by Frederic Raphael, had elements of *Kind Hearts and Coronets* and *Room at the Top*, but there was far more of a class satire in this mordant attack on what might be called social capitalism. As a lowly clerk in a firm of London property agents, Alan played greedy, resourceful Jimmy Brewster, eager for wealth and all the pleasures it can provide. He hires an aristocratic spendthrift to teach him the fine arts of forgery, then kills him – and blithely goes on his way with the nubile daughter of his boss. For him, crime pays, and handsomely.

Alan's Jimmy was 'a really ambitious little creep', he said, 'ruthlessly determined to get to the top.' He played the role with an amalgam of oily charm and malicious exploitation, and so was credible precisely because the actor did not follow the character and go too far. His comic timing was finely controlled even for the most manic scenes, and his hilariously exaggerated Oxbridge diction seemed completely natural. When the picture was released, journalists in England and America declared him to be a major leading man and scrambled for interviews. 'Bates is attractive, personable, popular and in demand,' announced the *New York Times*, adding that *Nothing But the Best* was 'the most delightful British comedy of several seasons'.

With that, Hollywood producers besieged Pearman's telephone, but Alan was in no hurry to return to the United States. His salary for the second Donner film was £20,000 – ten times what he had received for *The Caretaker*. He would mark his thirtieth birthday the following February; it was, he reasoned, time to consider buying his own home.

5

Enter Three Women

The house-hunting had to be delayed, for late in 1963, Alan had two good reasons to hasten to New York. The Greek theatre and film director Michael Cacoyannis was there to stage *The Trojan Women*, and he wanted to discuss a movie project with Alan; and the producer Roger Stevens, who had brought *The Caretaker* to Broadway, had a new play on the horizon and also wanted Alan. In short order, arrangements were made for Alan to appear in a movie called *Zorba the Greek* and then, later in 1964, to return to New York as the leading man in a comedy by playwright Jean Kerr.

He accepted Cacoyannis's offer of a supporting role he might otherwise have rejected, for on paper the part was overwhelmed by the flamboyant title character to be played by Anthony Quinn. As he told his agent, Alan anticipated the stout effort he would have to make if his part was to be both memorable and moving. He even relished working with the redoubtable Quinn, who had a reputation for delivering bombastic performances and for being difficult with co-stars and directors. Already the recipient of two Oscars, Quinn expected to be the centre of attention and could be ungenerous with other players. Still, for the challenge, the work and the adventure of living and working for four months on an exotic island far from home, Alan signed the contract.

Based on a popular novel by Nikos Kazantzakis (that was itself based on incidents and characters in the life of the author), *Zorba the Greek* tells of an Anglo-Greek man of letters (Alan) who somewhat diffidently returns to his roots on Crete. Hoping to revive an abandoned mining site that once belonged to his family, he employs Zorba (Quinn), his opposite in every way – a sensual rather than an intellectual man, guided by raw instinct and not by clear reason. The narrative presents two very different men coming to know and learn from one another; it is not merely (as often misconstrued) about the one-sided education of a timid, perhaps virginal scholar by a lusty, mythic old tiger. Instead, the picture explored the need of each for the other, of what might be called a spiritual balance in natural man.*

On 9 March 1964, the film company arrived on the hard and barren island, where many of the locals were happily herded in front of the camera for crowd scenes. Cacoyannis and his cinematographer, Walter Lassally, fully exploited Crete – its rocky coastline and sun-bleached houses, its windswept hills and the faces of aged natives, lined by weather and marked by poverty. Filming continued through mid-July.

Working with Quinn was never less than challenging. 'At his best, he's a marvellous and very instinctive actor,' Alan said a few years later. 'He has a sort of animal quality, although I think he's got a bit stuck with that aspect of himself. He's not the easiest man to work with, by any means. He's quite temperamental. He gets nervous very easily.' Alan paused before continuing: 'I think bombastic behaviour is a sign of nervousness.' He then modified what might have sounded like mere criticism of a churlish colleague: 'The part you play affects your state of nerves while you're playing that part. So if you're playing an extrovert, as Quinn was as Zorba, your nerves will probably reveal themselves in that way. When I'm acting, I tend to *contain* a nervous tension, which works in certain parts [like this man] very well.'

But during the filming that season, Quinn was so imperious and high-handed that even Cacoyannis often could not control him. Uncharacteristically, Alan felt a complete loss of control over what was already a fragile and difficult part. Reduced to a cipher and almost in despair, he sent a telegram to Peter Wyngarde, who came at once

---

* Alan's character had no name in either the book or the film. In the novel he is simply the narrator, while his dialogue in the printed script was indicated by the letter 'B' to distinguish it from Zorba's. During one scene, Alan was photographed in close-up, writing a handwritten letter: he begins the signature with 'B' and the scene then fades out. Seeing this in the first cut, a publicist at Twentieth Century-Fox christened the character 'Basil' for a press release – which was a surprise to Cacoyannis and Bates, among others.

to Crete to offer Alan moral support. Peter also worked with him on certain sequences, the better to help find a subtext that might counter Quinn's dominance.

According to Cacoyannis, Alan made no exceptional demands during the production and refused to be riled by Quinn's arrogance. 'Alan was easy to direct, but I didn't always get on with Anthony Quinn,' said the director. 'He often overacted, and I had to confront him quite a lot – he was always going over the top. But I must say, Quinn became totally Greek: he lived simply on the island, and he became Zorba inside and out.' Quinn's virtuoso performance was indeed impressive – 'towering' and 'monumental' were the terms most frequently used by critics – but Alan somehow managed to bring a remarkable palette of shadings and emotional nuances to a potentially thankless role. Effective at moments of awkwardness and vulnerability (as in *Whistle Down the Wind* and *The Running Man*), Alan completely merged into his character.

Years later he said of his part in *Zorba*, 'He's rather an extreme product, but then there are such people in English society, indeed in every society – closed, locked-up, longing to break out. And Zorba is meant to be the great romantic free character we all want to be. They're extremes, both of them.'

A chain of scenes lifts his ordinary character out of the ordinary. As he watches a sympathetic old courtesan sing and dance and later die (the role touchingly played by Lila Kedrova), his attitude is at first one of embarrassment, then of admiration and finally of compassion. His love scene with a lonely widow (Irene Papas) was performed with credible sensuality; and his character's final affirmation of life's unpredictable jumble – even of violent death – made his last dance with Zorba on the beach a celebration of hope in what was to come, not merely a passive acceptance of what had been.

'It was something new for me,' he recalled later of the role, adding that the character 'felt and thought more than he was able to say or do. It was a difficult part – so ambiguous, you had to suggest a great deal of complication, not actually play it. It was marvellous to make that effort, even if at the end it was not so rewarding, as it wasn't a firework part.' In addition, Alan found it 'an incredibly difficult thing to suggest someone who is in a permanent state of doubt. The part of that man was a problem for me – he just didn't know himself.'

At the time, Alan saw that the character in both book and movie stood in for the author – 'and you can never get to the bottom of things when that's the case – you can never explore those characters fully, because the authors haven't been able to do so with themselves.' Even with the advantage of time and distance, Alan felt that he was 'miscast in *Zorba*, which made me nervous . . . [and] it was a double agony, because the character felt as I, the actor, did – longing to do all the extrovert things Tony's role required! Still, I suppose there was some satisfaction in keeping myself under control.' Michael Cacoyannis neatly summed up Alan's achievement: 'For most actors, it is enough that they manage one mood with competence. Bates reflects three or four moods at the same time.'

Zorba the Greek received Oscar nominations in seven categories, including that of best actor (Quinn) and director, picture and screen-play (all by Cacoyannis); in the event, the statuettes were awarded to Lila Kedrova (best supporting actress), Walter Lassally (for achieve-ment in black and white cinematography) and Vassilis Fotopoulos (for black and white art direction). But Alan's performance was widely ignored: his role was that of a man 'easily pushed around, a smirking straight-man', according to the *New York Times* reviewer, who may have stumbled into another theatre. 'It was a great stroke of luck to be in it,' Alan insisted. 'It seemed like a wild idea, but it turned into one of the most famous films I ever made.'

Notwithstanding his role and the unpredictable Anthony Quinn, Alan savoured the experience. 'Living on Crete during the filming of *Zorba the Greek* was my most memorable time,' he said a year later. 'Just being on the island, living there like the islanders, eating the same food for four months, was a wonderful experience I'll never forget. It was like being in a different life.' From this time, he trav-elled to Greece and its isles many times, alone and with others, accu-mulating friends, acquaintances and the sorts of immediate, unplanned and often raw experiences Zorba encouraged. Alan learned, like the nameless character he played, that life required taking calculated risks. But also like his character, he spoke of the experiences tersely, only generically, never in detail: in Greece, he acquired a taste for retsina and for the occasional attractive and available companion to alleviate lonely evening hours, of which there were very many in his life-time.

★   ★   ★

After visiting his family in Derby for two weeks that summer and stopping briefly at Earls Terrace, Alan hurried to New York. Apparently he had not yet told Peter of his hope to purchase his own home in London, nor could he indeed negotiate for that at the moment.

In Manhattan, thanks to producer Roger Stevens, Alan found an apartment he could afford to rent on a month-to-month basis, in the Murray Hill area, not far from the Helen Hayes Theater, where the play *Poor Richard* had been booked for a December première. Jean Kerr had completed the rewriting of her new comedy some months earlier but was still polishing the dialogue here and editing scenes there when she met privately with Alan for a reading. He thought the play vastly improved from the version he had read earlier; with consummate tact, he made some suggestions.

That year, Jean Kerr was regarded as one of the two or three most entertaining humorists in America, the author of books and essays as well as plays; her husband was the distinguished drama critic Walter Kerr. As she and Alan turned the pages of *Poor Richard*, discussing the timing and the new emendations, theatre patrons were still forming long queues at the Morosco Theater, to which Jean's hit comedy *Mary, Mary* had relocated after more than 1,500 performances and almost four years. The move was made to accommodate *Poor Richard* at the Helen Hayes Theater, so Jean Kerr was about to have two plays running simultaneously on Broadway.

As part of his preparation, Alan saw several performances of *Mary, Mary*, which he thought was a perfectly constructed light comedy. Jean Kerr was justly celebrated for a kind of humour that was not simply a chain of jokes, and for a wit that was never vulgar, bitter or cruel. Hers was not the comedy of invective, and she gave her work a humane yet hilarious tone and attitude about recognisable characters in credible situations. *Mary, Mary* had already set the Broadway record for a non-musical comedy. The title character's rapier wit has alienated her husband Bob to the point of divorce and imminent remarriage; as he tells a friend, 'I married Mary because she was so direct and straightforward and said just exactly what she meant.' The reason for the divorce: 'Because she was so direct and straightforward and said just exactly what she meant.' The friend is a fading movie star who is leaving Hollywood – or, as he puts it, 'the sinking ship is leaving the rats'.

Poor Richard, set in Manhattan, tackled more serious matters. Richard

Ford, 'poor' because he is a boozing widower with a muddled life, is a visiting English poet as famous for his revelries as for his career. His American publisher aims to reform Richard's life, and a temporary secretary has just the solution, which will also make her permanent. Gene Hackman, then thirty-four, had the role of publisher Sydney Carroll, and twenty-two-year-old Joanna Pettet was making her Broadway debut as Catherine Shaw, the lively, vivacious secretary who admits, quite early on, that she has adored Richard since she was fifteen and now intends to marry him.

'*Poor Richard* was billed as a comedy, but it was really very serious,' recalled Joanna Pettet. 'That was clear when I went for my audition and heard Alan rehearsing his very long speeches.' She knew that her first reading with an actor substituting for Alan (so he could watch and listen to her) had gone badly – most of all because she was aware of Alan's presence. Director Peter Wood invited her to return next day for a second audition with the substitute actor. This time Alan went backstage, out of Joanna's sight line. 'He listened to me, spoke with Peter briefly – and I had the part.' As he often did with actors new to the craft and with those who were anxious, Alan encouraged Joanna and, after rehearsals, went over their scenes together. During October and November his behaviour was friendly and thoroughly professional, with no indication that he had any romantic agenda.

On 16 November the director, cast, the crew and playwright proceeded to Boston, for two weeks of performances at the Colonial Theater; pre-Broadway try-outs were standard procedure at the time. Fully staged before an audience, the play now revealed some infirmities, and Jean Kerr radically rewrote it over one weekend. Most significantly, she changed the ending: originally, young Catherine walks out on the embittered, solipsistic Richard; in the revision, Kerr provided a traditional romantic-happy ending – doubtless because everyone wanted to please the audience, and also because it was unthinkable that any young woman would leave a man with the looks of Alan Bates.

While in Boston, Alan and Joanna strolled through the galleries of the Museum of Fine Arts and had long talks about the play, the theatre and their careers. But as they prepared for the New York opening on 2 December, the cast was in a state of confusion, trying to learn new lines as they jettisoned many of the old.

The Broadway critics were divided. John McLain, writing in the New York *Journal American*, stated directly that Jean Kerr had

> another winner. I was concerned and captivated. What really makes the piece is the writing of Mrs Kerr and the brilliant performances of Alan Bates, Joanna Pettet and Gene Hackman. Mrs Kerr's lines are riddled with wit and wisdom: she has the facility of bursting into the most serious scene with a remark of miraculous nonsense without losing the essence. These people talk and behave like living and breathing humans, and so I became seriously concerned with what was going to happen to them. I guess that's about all you have to do, as long as you keep them interesting, and Mrs Kerr never lets them go dull.

But another contingent, led by the *New York Times*, was less fervent and, for one of the rare times in his career, Alan received a few negative notices. Howard Taubman recognised that the comedy had high aspirations and a serious subtext about the complexities of the writer's life, and he admired the playwright's refusal to buttress her work with easy laughs. But he found the situation and character development unbelievable – and the play failed because of the acting as much as the writing. 'Alan Bates is so poised and sure-footed an actor that one does not believe the tales of his frailties, and the things he is asked to say and do are no more persuasive.' *Time* magazine suggested that, as *The Caretaker* showed, Alan brilliantly conveyed menace, 'but as a charmer his signals are garbled.'

'Even when both our disappointments had surfaced,' said Jean Kerr of the generally lukewarm reaction to her play, 'Alan was still sweet, honourable, decent, generous, and enormously kind.' As for Joanna, *Time* hailed her as 'an indelibly enticing ingénue'. Almost all the reviewers agreed that the final moments of the play were irresistible, made (thus Taubman) 'especially moving by Mr Bates's range as an actor, for he and Miss Pettet play the scene with disarming airiness and an ingratiating manner'.

Among the visitors to Alan's dressing room was Noël Coward, who came to express good wishes and to ask about the photograph of Alan in the theatre programme. 'I chose it myself,' he replied somewhat defensively. 'I thought it was – well, rather boyish.' Coward, never one for overstatement, replied in his clipped and quick style with a single word: 'Girlish.'

As usual after performances, Alan welcomed ordinary theatregoers backstage as well as celebrities. One evening before Christmas, a few young women who worked for *Sports Illustrated* and *Time* magazines were waiting after he changed from his costume to street clothes. He signed autographs and bantered politely with them and, as they were departing, one of the girls turned and asked if he would accept an invitation to a party at the apartment they shared – the date to be determined after the holidays. She would also like to interview him for *Time* magazine. It was easier for him to accept than to find a ready reason to decline something so vague, so Alan bade them goodnight and promptly forgot the invitation.

He could not, however, put from his memory the pale, slender blonde who spoke for the group – she of the warm and adoring gaze, the long hair and the ankle-length dress with a floral print. She had a British accent, and she seemed almost a kind of water sprite, an insubstantial creature, willowy to the point of not belonging to this world. She might have been a figment of someone's romantic imagination, he said later; actually, it was his own fancy that shifted and became active in her presence and for some time to come. In just a few moments that evening, she had managed to say that she had seen *Mary, Mary* too . . . and that she was reading poetry like that of his character in *Poor Richard* . . . who reminded her of Brendan Behan . . . who, she said, was 'a great thinker and gorgeously irreverent' . . . who made her think of another Welshman, Richard Burton. Although she was a lively thing, she seemed lonely and even a bit forlorn, needy of comfort and perhaps even a good meal. She was, in other words, irresistible to him.

Victoria Ward, as she announced herself, was twenty-four. She had little formal education but read widely and had many interests. She was also a prolific and elegant letter writer to friends and family: until she was in her thirties and there were drastic changes in her life and health, her dedication to correspondence was remarkable; even the briefest of her letters was stylishly composed, rich in vocabulary, literate, witty and perceptive.

As Alan soon learned, Victoria worked not as a staff writer or even a researcher but rather as a secretary to the director of promotion; hence she had neither the position nor the authority to contract Alan for an interview, which would have had to be arranged through the play's publicist in any case. Their meeting was a matter of minutes and that, he was sure, was the end of that.

★　　★　　★

Invited to visit the Actors Studio as an observer that season, Alan watched a student perform her first scene under the tutelage of the controversial teacher-actor Lee Strasberg. 'It was marvellous,' he recalled.

> But then Lee Strasberg said, 'That was absolutely terrific – do you know what you were doing?' And she said, 'No,' and I thought, Please, Mr Strasberg, don't say anything else. She mustn't know. She must find out – don't tell her what she's doing, she must find out for herself. Give her a lot more class work, give her a lot more space, give her a lot more stuff to do – but don't tell her what she's doing, because that would spoil it.

But that day Strasberg, as usual, proceeded to tell the young lady in agonising detail precisely what she had done and why, and what she should do otherwise.

Alan was adamantly opposed to this method of teaching or even this way of proceeding on one's own:

> I'm afraid I get very nervous when people move in on people who are doing something good. You trust your instincts, you trust your responses, you trust your imagination. You have to be free. There are actors who are not, who haven't found a way to be free and daring, to follow their instincts fully. For that you need what in the old days would be called technique.

Perhaps to his surprise, he then received an invitation from the young woman who worked for the magazines at Time, Inc. On Saturday, 23 January 1965 Alan went along to the apartment she shared with a colleague named Jaffray Cuyler; the occasion was Victoria's birthday. 'Alan Bates rang, which excited and alarmed me,' she wrote in her diary on 29 January, 'since I'd assumed he might not remember the offhand invitation I'd extended him.'

He arrived at the apartment, already crowded beyond capacity, and before long, Victoria gave him all her attention. 'Alan's hair pleased me much,' she continued in her entry, 'dark, curling tendrils falling over his forehead and lying low at his neck, but his misty green eyes of vaguely oblique gaze and far-seeing vision won me.' Jaffray had the impression that 'they fell in love with each other' very quickly.

Eventually, Alan and Victoria sat together on a sofa already occupied by another couple, 'and then Alan got up to fetch more mulled wine, and when he returned, there were four of us squashed on the sofa – which I found rather nice, as it made talking to Alan much easier.' He was, however, on the alert for a telephone call, or he expected a friend to arrive there. Victoria remembered that he 'seemed anxious about the phone call, especially when it didn't come. While he was wondering if perhaps his awaited caller was lingering downstairs, I marched towards the door purposefully, to discover what was happening downstairs. Alan caught up with me and we both heard an ascending tread. At last the latecomer had arrived, accepting on the stairs the offer of coffee rather than mulled wine. He told Alan he was leaving, and the latecomer and I had a staring match which I couldn't maintain.' Alan then departed with the young man.

The following Tuesday, Alan rang Victoria between the acts of *Poor Richard* to thank her for the evening; he said nothing about the young man. But on Friday, 29 January, he reciprocated by taking her to lunch at P. J. Clarke's, a famous watering hole on the East Side. 'Absolutely fabulous [time],' she wrote in her diary on 30 January. 'Dim corner table – mushroom and spinach salad and wine. Strolled back through freezing streets, my hand in Alan's pocket.'

The cosy meal, the walk along the wintry streets of Manhattan, the budding intimacy between them – it all seemed like something from a movie. But her next two days were very different, as she confided to her diary. She was to meet friends at a jazz club, but she 'wandered in next door by mistake. Jazz blaring and not reaching me.' She then went by taxi to another club: 'Night of woes,' she wrote, without elaboration. 'Sunday ghoulish but bearable.' She then noted something ominous: 'I've eaten almost nothing today or the day before, nor much in the week. Must be a disease. Monday [I looked] hagridden . . . [Tuesday:] Felt strong today. Chores and thoughts and tears and calm.' She gave no details, but soon Alan recognised what Victoria's friends all knew: she was a self-absorbed creature, sometimes subject to wide mood swings, and she often ate nothing at all – especially if she thought that the meal set before her might not be of high-quality, or contain artificial colours or preservatives.

For the most part during the 1960s, Victoria was an irresistible social companion with many friends and constant invitations. In America co-workers liked to be with her; in Europe they often gladly opened their homes to her rather than allow her to register at an hotel. She had a quick sense of humour; she could converse on a wide variety of topics; she did not take drugs and drank moderately; she knew the latest novels and films as well as the classics; and she was always reading – in other words, she was no mere hippie.

There seems to have been no more contact between Victoria and Alan during the first half of 1965; in any case she had decided that ten months at *Time* were enough – after all, it was longer than her previous secretarial job, when she had worked for a British diplomat in the Bahamas. In early February, she prepared to leave New York for London and she knew not what.

By that time *Poor Richard* had posted a closing notice, and the final curtain rang down on 13 March. In a curious example of life intersecting art and making it more complicated, there was another attractive young blonde hoping for Alan's attention. His co-star, Joanna Pettet, like her character in the play, had fallen, as she said, 'madly in love with him. I was just besotted. He was my first and greatest love.' With these sentiments she accepted Alan's invitation to accompany him on a holiday, to the warmth of the Caribbean island of St Thomas.

He had booked one room for them at a simple but romantic hotel, where, that first night, they dined quietly before retiring. 'We slept in the same bed,' Joanna recalled, 'but nothing happened.' She remembered that she was too nervous to ask if something was suddenly wrong, 'and I was not old enough or sophisticated enough to be aggressive with him – it just didn't seem right. Then we heard the couple next door making violent love, and Alan got out of bed and turned on the air-conditioner, to counter the noise.' The holiday ended as chastely as it had begun, without any discussion of alternatives.

At the time Joanna quite naturally thought it odd that Alan had invited her to share the same bed in the same room without the likely consequences of such an arrangement between a handsome thirty-one-year-old man and a conspicuously attractive and evidently compliant twenty-two-year-old woman. To her credit, and however disappointed or perplexed she felt, Joanna did not want to lose Alan's friendship just because her expectations were unmatched by reality during their holiday.

He may, of course, have intended another outcome to the evening. Perhaps he expected her to make the first move; maybe, too, he simply changed his mind. He seems never to have spoken of the incident to anyone, but there would be similar occurrences in future intimate relationships with women. Otherwise, Alan was invariably genial, amusing and at ease, and no one would have exchanged his company for another's. A platoon of women and men loved him and loved being with him, including some who wanted and were denied carnal compensations.

'From our first week of rehearsals for *Poor Richard*, I thought he was the most beautiful man I'd ever seen in my life,' Joanna said. 'Then I learned that he was fine and good and beautiful inside, too. I didn't ever want to lose his friendship.'

'Joanna was talented and fun to be with,' recalled Arthur Laurents. 'Back in the sixties, we all went dancing in a group.' Eventually Joanna married, had a son and was divorced; her career continued, but then her only child died. Although there were long intervals when they did not meet, she felt that Alan was the great constant in her personal life, a loyal friend on whom she could always rely.

Alan left New York in late spring and went to Rome, where he appeared in a brief television drama, one of an ongoing series about United Nations humanitarian activities. The Argentine director Leopoldo Torre Nilsson engaged him, the American actor Melvyn Douglas and the English actress Diane Cilento for something called *Once Upon a Tractor*, which was subsequently broadcast in the United States on the ABC network on 9 September 1965; it then vanished until its accidental recovery on a UN library shelf was rumoured in 2002. Whatever the *Tractor*'s fate, Alan readily accepted another humanitarian project – to narrate a documentary called *Insh'Allah*, about Oxfam's volunteer efforts in Algeria. He took neither payment nor credit for these two short films.

While in Rome, Alan met a young Israeli dance student named Yardena Harari. Strikingly attractive, with dark hair and eyes, an expressive voice and a wealth of cultural and artistic experience from both education and travel, Yardena was introduced to him through her friend Yael Dayan, daughter of the Israeli general. 'A small group of us went to dinner and then on to a nightclub for dancing,' Yardena recalled, 'and at the end of the evening, Alan said to me, "I may see you again – or perhaps I may not see you again."'

He did, and soon. On 28 June, he took her to a concert by the Beatles in Rome, and a few days later they flew to the south of France, where they checked into the Colombe d'Or Hotel, then owned by Yves Montand and his wife, Simone Signoret. As with Joanna, the intimate accommodations for Alan and Yardena were not a prelude to anything; the relationship remained chaste for the time being and Yardena was, predictably, as confused as Joanna.

Everything changed, however, when they arrived back in London that July and went to Earls Terrace, where, officially, Alan was still living with Peter Wyngarde. 'He never wanted to discuss Peter – it was the time of a dark cloud in his life, he said, or a poison.' With Yardena's encouragement, they soon relocated to a small flat in Bayswater; soon afterwards, he signed papers for the purchase of a house at 122 Hamilton Terrace, St John's Wood, for which he paid £18,000. 'We never really furnished the place at all,' Yardena recalled, 'and for a while there was no water in the house – just a table and our bed.' And with this turn in his life, Alan had what may well have been his most enduring and passionate sexual relationship with a woman.

His first and greatest attachment, Yardena soon learned, was to his work – 'and when he came home, he expected to find me there, for he hated to be alone. When I said I had to have something to do with my life, he suggested I study medicine or nursing – but I had been trained in the arts.' In that regard Yardena was an excellent companion for him and perhaps the most aesthetically sophisticated woman in Alan's life: they went to galleries and museums, concerts, plays and operas. 'And nothing was left unspoken in our relationship – we discussed everything: my past, his past, and his former lovers. There were no secrets.'

By midsummer Alan was rehearsing Arnold Wesker's two-character play *The Four Seasons*, whose troubles became apparent when audiences and critics fidgeted during preliminary performances at the Belgrade Theatre, Coventry. When the play transferred to the Saville Theatre, Shaftesbury Avenue, on 21 September (under the author's direction), things seemed doomed. The co-star was again Diane Cilento, but together they could neither charm the London critics nor enliven a play that followed a couple from wintry stillness to springtime blossom, through summer's peak to autumnal decay. 'Pretentious and utterly ineffective as drama,' huffed one journalist, summarising the general reaction. In recalling the play's brief run, Alan remarked that he enjoyed only the part when his character was required to prepare and bake a spectacular apple strudel right onstage. To make matters worse, he and Cilento clashed from the start, remaining completely at odds and scarcely speaking to one another offstage.

The onstage cookery demonstration was much enjoyed by at least one ardent playgoer, Victoria Ward, who went to a preview at the Saville. In a letter from London to a New York friend, she wrote of her disappointing romantic experiences and asked, 'Why am I bitchy with most men?' At once she pulled back: 'Not so with Alan. I tore over to see his play, to which he'd invited me and left a ticket with the manager. I was lucky as there was, unaccountably for a wet Saturday afternoon, an enormous queue. He took me for a brief meal between performances.' But their friendship was not a romance, nor did she, for the time being, expect it to become one. They enjoyed talking about theatre and the latest movies. She considered it odd that she was not invited to his home, and for the present she knew nothing of Yardena.

At the same time, Victoria was closely involved in the planning for an historic motion picture, and Alan found her conversation about it fascinating. She had parlayed her typing skills into a position as personal assistant and secretary to Stanley Kubrick, then in the midst of a long pre-production phase for his epic *2001: A Space Odyssey*. Listed as 'Vicky Ward' in the Kubrick files at Warner Bros Studios, she worked at Kubrick's Shepperton and Borehamwood offices, where, among other duties, she prepared transcripts of interviews he conducted as research for the movie – conversations with, for example, Isaac Asimov, Margaret Mead and Freeman Dyson.

'What's it like making a film?' she wrote rhetorically to a friend that November.

> Wonder whether I'll ever know. Still in the pre-production stages and shooting has now been postponed until January 3rd. Spend my life answering telephone calls, sending cables, filing, occasionally meeting interesting visitors – obtain prints of films and books that strike Stanley Kubrick's interest, read the papers, write letters, mull over my fate, look over the sets, glean the latest fashions from the magazines, make tea, coffee and mix scotches for the producers. Have a chauffeur-driven car every day to and from the studios, but beginning to hate this and longing to drive my own car and it's just up to me to pass my driving test.

To another friend she wrote of her boredom with her job and her discontent with the men she was meeting:

> Trouble with a mammoth production like '2001' is that months of preparation are necessary before shooting starts – and honestly, whatever secretarial job you do, it all boils down to answering phone calls and correspondence and umpteen routine chores. Unless any jobs exist where you do the boss's work – I mean don't answer letters – but actually make decisions. And if you're making decisions then presumably you'll land up being the boss. Robert Beatty [who had the role of Dr Halvorsen in *2001*] wandered in this afternoon and I spoke to Peter Sellers on the phone this morning who sounded nice, but doesn't particularly mean anything as not much chance of contact. Anyway this discontent in my soul will only be assuaged by new horizons. Haven't seen Alan since I saw his show. Feel not so confident lately and that if there are gonna be any men in my life, they'll have to make me feel they're interested. Think my ego must have taken a battering lately and just can't muster up any ammunition.

Among the men she had attracted in New York was Gordon Parks, the pioneering photographer, novelist, poet, musician, journalist, civil rights activist and film director. Almost thirty years her senior, Parks was a man of prodigious energy and talent who courted her from Manhattan to London, although he was married and simultaneously involved with a friend of Victoria.

'I dined with him on Monday [13 September 1965] at a fabulous restaurant also called Parkes [in Beauchamp Place, Knightsbridge],' she wrote in September, 'the most magnificent meal I've had in years. But I'm not smitten with Gordon. He called twice yesterday from Claridge's but I missed him. Felt none the loser as he's not my cup of tea . . . Tries to get you into bed in a soft, subtle manner. One shouldn't be annoyed if a man tries this, but the situation was that he was my friend's boyfriend, and he was treating her affections lightly.'

In Kubrick's offices she also met a much older man – the associate producer Victor Lyndon, who had worked with the director on *Dr Strangelove*. 'He's gentle and intelligent and kind,' Victoria wrote to a friend in New York.

Lay on my bed last night and this morning aching and vaguely longing for him. Mad. He's married, we work closely in the same unit, and I'm also excited in Stanley's presence in a different way, which isn't diminished by these new love buds [for Victor] . . . But I would be crazy to leap into it, because he's very much married and can only see me on Sundays (or at least only needs to then) . . . Trouble is, I need every scrap of affection I can scrounge and will probably melt into his arms at the first snatched opportunity. If, however, we become lovers and he still doesn't need to see me save for just a few hours on Sunday, then I'll collapse in defeat.

Victoria's employment with Kubrick, once he began filming, might have led to greater responsibilities and to work in his future pictures. But as usual, she was very soon bored by the very people with whom she had longed to work: 'As usual, I'm utterly discontented with my lot. Have the wanderlust. Think I'll join a friend in France.'

She was bright, talented, articulate, and utterly without focus, discipline or patience; she was also an inveterate drifter from address to address, as she was from job to job; her letters to friends reveal that she moved almost once a month over the course of three years. Victoria wrote that she had lived 'in a pad with girls unfriendly and shallow', for example. 'Wonder whether to take a bed-sitter or hazard another share with idiots.' Then she moved to a tiny space, 'a cupboard with a window but without kitchen or bath, a semi-derelict room at the top of a house' in Kensington that she selected that autumn. At twenty-five, she was as incorrigibly restless as Alan, but without his creative outlet and sense of purpose.

'You must think that I'm bordering on melancholic madness,' she wrote that October to a friend in New York. 'I won't deny it, but like most people, I'm immensely dissatisfied with what I've carved out of life or life's carved out of me, and strongly despairing of ever discarding my sloth and taking a running jump at some impossible dream.' Were 'most people' she met, most people in their twenties, already 'immensely dissatisfied' and in despair?

That was not true of her friends, who had many interests. About this time and like many people she knew in the 1960s, Victoria became more and more concerned about the purity of food: 'I don't feel like I am what I eat,' she wrote to a friend. 'Yesterday I determined to try and buy unchemically produced food. Feel that untampered-with food tastes miles better, but funnily enough, this week's *Sunday Times Colour Magazine* prints a rather telling article on how extreme and unrealistic a food fad or health nut can be.' She would soon learn that for herself.

During a long telephone conversation in late October, Victoria told Alan that she had applied for a bizarre new job – with a documentary film-maker in the jungles of Central and South America. The funny thing, he said later, was that she really believed she could do something like that. He did not tell her that he was already trying to make his way through no less tangled and thorny situations – with both Peter Wyngarde and Yardena Harari.

6

'Mr Bates, are you a swinger?'

I n her letter of application for a new job with a documentary film-
maker, Victoria described her work history.

Dear Sirs,   27 October 1965

I have recently returned to England after two years abroad and
was keenly interested to see the position you advertise in today's
TIMES.

Although my present assignment is a promising one working
for a dynamic film director on the pre-production stage of his
latest film, I'm marooned in the same four office walls for ten
hours each day, and long for the chance to breathe some occasional fresh air and rough it a bit. I'm not a seeker after the
softer comforts of civilisation and would eagerly welcome an
opportunity to assist in anthropological and archaeological
studies.

My first year abroad was spent in the Bahamas where I worked
for a Cabinet Minister – another nine or ten hour day – but I did
manage to swim every day before breakfast and explore the fish
life around the coral reefs, mostly with the aid of a snorkel although
I have done some scuba diving.

I moved to New York from the Bahamas and spent a year at Time
and Life magazine assisting the Promotion Director. My main occu-
pation was coping with floods of visitors, telephoning the ends of
the earth, arranging cocktail and dinner parties and helping to organise
a department of about 40 people.

Before living abroad, I did a stint of photographic modelling but was gradually drawn into free-lance secretarial activities as my photographic assignments were not sufficiently engrossing.

I am 25 years of age, have studied high-speed shorthand under a court reporter and have a working knowledge of French. I'm enclosing a photograph of myself, and look forward to hearing from you.

Yours very truly,

Victoria Ward

She sent Alan a copy of her letter, which impressed him, but he could not imagine her in the Amazon jungle as a technical assistant with motion picture cameras and sound equipment. He and Victoria met for occasional suppers, but contrary to her request, he refrained from playing the role of vocational counsellor. He did, however, gently put some questions to her about the job; more to the point, he was affected by the tone of despondency in her telephone calls and by her evident inability to shape the contours of a stable, happy life for herself in London. 'I've been miserable in loads of exotic places,' she said with marvellous hyperbole, defending the idea of working in the wilds – but there had been nothing more exotic than the Bahamas and the isle of Manhattan.

Alan always had a compassionate ear for those in distress and often devoted time and effort to people who were confused or in trouble. He did not usually give presents to those outside his family, nor was he known as a lavish dinner host at home or abroad – but if he saw someone in even transitory anxiety, he could rarely ignore the situation and instinctively took time to help. His unexpected assistance to Millicent Martin during her audition for *Nothing But the Best* was but one example of his consideration for a nervous colleague trying for a job. There were many such anecdotes from his time in New York, when aspiring young actors came to him for advice and he invited them for coffee, listened to their complaints of unemployment and recommended professional contacts when he could.

And so, for about three years beginning in early 1966 – even when he was busiest at work – Alan tried to respond to Victoria's telephone calls and letters. He admired her gumption, her broad intellectual curiosity and wide reading; most of all, however, he worried about her physical and emotional frailty. When she endured a series of fainting spells ('feeling fuddly', she called it), he asked about her diet and gently scolded her habit of extreme abstinence when she could not obtain what she considered unadulterated organic food. Soon, Victoria began to have suspicions about soap and water, too, and she occasionally avoided bathing for as long as a week. 'I can't be bothered to wash my hair, bathe or wash my clothes,' she wrote to a friend. 'I'm not crawling with lice or smelling to high heaven, and I just can't see the point of overhauling myself each day for no one to appreciate.'

More important: 'I have a great need to unburden myself to someone before I explode or go mad,' she wrote typically, which must have sounded pathetic from one so young. 'What do you do when you have no one with whom you're simpatico or no one who cares what happens to you? If you find my letters bordering on melancholia or insanity, take no notice, it's just frustration. The film studio is in a pool of apathy at the moment, and I feel no point in working here. I wish I could have faith in something, in someone. Nothing else to offer you save my thoughts, negligent and aimless, but drifting towards you. Ripples in a pool.'

Thus it was that when Alan showed up at Shepperton Studios for costume fittings and rehearsals for his next movie, he invited Victoria to the employee commissary for lunch. He was at first anxious when she announced that she had given her notice of termination and that she was leaving her job with Kubrick, but he was simultaneously relieved that she had not won the position of a new Jane, assistant to the documentarian Tarzan of the jungle. Instead, she was heading for Paris before Christmas – not the most auspicious time to relocate, perhaps, especially without employment prospects and with no French friends. 'Common sense won't stop me,' she insisted stubbornly.

That December, her journal entries focused on daily minutiae and chores, interwoven with odd fantasies; only later did she give the pages to Alan, who never discarded them.

> Tomorrow I will arise at a decent hour and faithfully concentrate on body exercises for a good half hour. Attend to my face, then a light breakfast and some French [lessons] on records. Shopping for bra, petticoat, Christmas cards, to the bookshop

to browse. More exercises and bath. How does one shake off sloth? relieve the mind's torpor?

This entry, on 8 December, was at once followed by:

She stood at the closed office door one early winter's morning. Public Relations consultants. Pale mauve coat, loose red-brown hair, dash of lipstick, eyeliner and mascara. To work for a woman, a girl. Typing. First letter, 'Dear Mr Sinner' – no – 'Dear . . . Mr Sinner . . .' – ominous slip, she was affairing with him.

It is impossible to know what Victoria had in mind as she wrote those lines: an idea for a story? a lightly veiled account of an experience at Shepperton? She continued:

Today, exercises, shopping in supermarket, breakfast, long French record session. Bank. Drifted through Kensington Gardens up to pond where squealing wheeling pigeons beat the backs of their fellow floating on the water who upwheeled in panic flight, two girls spraying bread. Stood amidst storm of wings, the pigeon wheel flapping through its watersky axis.

And so began the conflict between, on the one hand, Victoria's ordinary and quite free lifestyle, with its innocent but unfulfilled poetic aspirations; and, on the other, a vivid fantasy life. Whatever their source, her conflicts then and later did not originate with drug abuse, as her friends and acquaintances attest and as her letters witness: 'Everyone I meet lately', she wrote in June 1966, 'smokes hash – which doesn't appeal to me, not even a drag.' There is no evidence to the contrary; as for alcohol, she drank only red wine and not to excess.

Alan worked at Shepperton from the end of 1965 until early spring 1966, rehearsing and then filming interiors for his next movie. *Georgy Girl* was to be a sprightly contemporary comedy (the jaunty title song would establish that), directed by Silvio Narizzano, whom Alan knew from *A Memory of Two Mondays*. The script by Peter Nichols certainly suggested fast-paced fun: Georgy is a plain, ungainly young woman (Lynn Redgrave) who tries to duck the unwanted advances of her father's middle-aged employer (James Mason). At the same time she envies the amoral life of her room-mate Meredith (Charlotte Rampling) and one of Meredith's many lovers, Jos (Alan), by whom Meredith becomes pregnant and whom she reluctantly marries.

When Meredith furiously rejects her newborn baby girl, Georgy and Jos take the infant – but Jos is too much a fun-loving rogue for earnest fatherhood, so Georgy and the baby head for her father's boss, the wealthy man she thoroughly despises. 'You're rich, Georgy girl!' hails the pop group in the last moments of the soundtrack, as if this were the ultimate panacea. It is extremely difficult to sympathise with Georgy's final decision to marry so inappropriate a man, even for the sake of the baby; the audience has not been led to expect this disturbing compromise.

Generally remembered the way it was advertised – as a mad whirl of a screwball comedy – *Georgy Girl* is an acute and bitter indictment of irresponsibility, the frenzied pursuit of self-interest and the refusal to mature. But Alan at last had several opportunities to indulge his penchant for improvised comedy, which had been muted for *Nothing But the Best*. Here, he gradually sheds his clothes in a tumult of passion as he pursues Georgy along streets and through underpasses; he croons in a bathtub and ensures that she will see him rise naked from the suds; he leaps over riverside barriers even as he disclaims the balanced life he covets.

But despite Alan's merry vitality, the character is neither agreeable nor sufficiently drawn; hence Jos is no one's foil, no one's prize – and the audience does not know how to react to him. *Georgy Girl* did nothing to harm his career, however: it was short-listed for four Academy Awards and as many BAFTA prizes, and Alan was nominated by the Hollywood Foreign Press Association as best actor and most promising newcomer. The critical consensus was that he was 'splendid' as the 'brazen and bumptious mod lover'.

Quite openly, Alan spoke of his association with the character of Jos and his simultaneous dislike of him: 'I didn't think he was funny. I felt he was an infinitely sad character, and I found him easy to play, because he's a bit like me – a person escaping into a fantasy world . . . He was really a bit past behaving like a kid – he needed to grow up, but there was nothing underneath the fun and games . . . He's having this great time, with everybody adoring him – but in fact there's nothing there at all!' Alan himself was frightened by mere public endorsement without a concomitant sense of purpose. 'Jos lives on the surface and ends up with nothing. The minute something big comes along, a responsibility or something to take him out of the road of his own pleasures, he can't cope. He can't go outside his own image of himself.'

Alan did not, however, appreciate some comments about his performance:

'Oh, Mr Bates,' said a woman at a press conference, 'I simply adored you in *Georgy Girl* – I couldn't get over the way you took off your clothes in the street while you were running after Lynn Redgrave. You did it with so much finesse! You're such an artist!'

'Thank you, madame,' he said and moments later he confided to a studio publicist, 'Just think – after years of learning my craft, I get compliments for my ability to take off my pants in public!'

Like those at press receptions, writers for movie magazines were sent to glean interviews or at least titbits for subscribers. *Photoplay* managed to put some questions to Alan that winter:

Q: What was your most hated subject at school?
A: Mathematics.
Q: What are your favourite foods and drinks?
A: Wine and vodka, and plain good cooking instead of fancy – by which I mean no heavy or intricate Continental cooking.
Q: What do you hate doing most?
A: Anything to do with business. Working out finances. This doesn't mean I'm not interested in investments, but I'd make sure I had competent people to handle this side of my affairs and not leave it up to myself.
Q: What is your greatest fear?
A: Illness – being incapacitated and helpless.
Q: What past age would you have liked to live in?
A: The Elizabethan Age, when England was properly alive. But I think you would have had to be either wealthy or very bright to enjoy it.
Q: What is your favourite time of day?
A: Very early morning – there's a feeling of great stillness and anticipation.
Q: What is your idea of true happiness?
A: Working. Work gathers my life together – I'm aimless without it. Nothing has much shape to it or matters if I'm not working.

Alan's father, Harold Arthur Bates (1923)

Alan's mother, Florence Mary
Wheatcroft Bates (1930)

1951

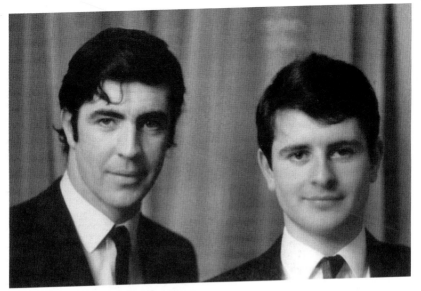

With his brother,
John Bates (1965)

Alan's brother,
Martin Bates (1982)

1957

Mary Bates, Peter Wyngarde, John Bates, Martin Bates, Harold Bates, Alan Bates (1961)

With Harold Pinter, filming *The Caretaker* (1961)

With Anthony Quinn, in *Zorba the Greek* (1964)

With Yardena Harari (1965)

In *King of Hearts* (1966)

In *Georgy Girl* (1966)

In *Far From the Madding Crowd* (1967)

1967

Paul Taylor (1967)

Valerie 'Victoria'
June Ward (1964)

That last reply was virtually a standard. By contrast, Alan saw Victoria the way he regarded Jos: limited by a lack of purposeful discipline, whereas his own dedication to good work provided meaning and structure.

But his intimate relations were problematic. 'One day, to my surprise, he asked me to marry him,' Yardena Harari recalled, 'but I was of course hesitant because I knew about Peter Wyngarde. I told Alan that I had to know if he was a man with a basically homosexual or heterosexual image of himself. He didn't answer, and to this day I don't know. He wasn't at peace with himself, and sometimes I think he took it out on women, who were such a challenge to this confused sense that he had of himself.' Some people advised Yardena simply to become pregnant by Alan, to force him to marry her – 'but I didn't think that was the way to get a man.' And so, during the production of *Georgy Girl*, Yardena thought it better to leave London, at least for the present. She returned to Israel, asking Alan to take advantage of the interval to consider his and their future. 'My life was going by, too,' she added, 'and I had to make decisions as did he.'

He had never confronted Peter Wyngarde, never formally acknowledged what he told a few friends – that he wanted to terminate all contact between them. Finally, when Alan made one last visit to Earls Terrace to collect the last of his clothes, he suddenly told Peter, 'I think I should get married.' But at the time he had no intention of marrying anyone.

Martin Bates believed it significant that the association with Wyngarde ended just as Alan's confidence in his career brightened – and (as he thought) the possibilities of his intimacies with women grew stronger too. The bond between Alan and Peter, according to Martin, 'had become oppressive and stormy – which was a shame, in a way, as I think Alan owed him quite a bit'.

'I thought we had a really important and mutually beneficial relationship,' Wyngarde said sadly many years later. 'We seemed to share the same romantic ideas – that we would be like the Lunts or the Oliviers. I would direct plays for him to act in, and we would have a wonderful joint career together.' But nothing had occurred to encourage such a hope. As for the notion of Alan marrying, Wyngarde thought that was suggested by those who considered it essential for his career. 'And that', he concluded, 'was the end of our dream.' Or perhaps only of his own.

'Alan said that he had been very damaged by his relationship with Peter Wyngarde,' recalled Paul Taylor, soon to come into Alan's life and share his confidence. 'I had the sense that he thought of it as psychologically abusive. It destroyed something in his trust of men.' Alan's report of this era to others was, of course, hardly unbiased, and his perspective on the ten-year relationship was not matched by Peter's, who very much considered it an ideal rudely shattered.

Paul's assessment, however, was essentially that of virtually everyone who knew Alan well, and no one had any reason to prevaricate. Peter Wyngarde gathered Alan up early in his career and became a bit of a Svengali with him, according to the consensus. The artist Gerard Hastings felt that 'Peter had apparently treated Alan in a very domineering way, and Alan found that very hard, of course. Finally, he wanted to escape being "Wyngarde's boy". Alan didn't want that label, but still he had remained with Peter for a decade, and for most of that time, he said he couldn't escape.'

The actress Felicity Kendal, later among Alan's closest friends and colleagues, recalled that 'he talked about his time with Peter Wyngarde as a very unhappy period. He didn't find it easy to make light of – he didn't find the jokes in that part of his life. Sometimes he chose people who tried to organise him. Normally he could extricate himself when it got too intense and people were too demanding; normally he could get out of situations like that. But he couldn't get out of this one for a long time, for whatever reason – so later he didn't dwell on it, and it was never something he joked about.' Conrad Monk was frank in summing up the conviction of many: 'Peter had a catastrophic influence on Alan – he just bullied and dominated him. We knew the relationship was very bad, and we were glad when it was over.'

The last scenes of *Georgy Girl* were completed in late winter 1966. Alan then rushed to his next role, in a French picture called *Le roi de coeurs* – *King of Hearts*, directed by Philippe de Broca, who cast him almost by default. De Broca needed an Englishman for the leading man and photos of Alan (in *Nothing But the Best*, *The Caretaker* and *Zorba the Greek*) were to be seen all over Paris. De Broca hastened to London, told him the story and asked if he could speak French. '*Mais oui!*' Alan replied in one of his few Gallic phrases – whereupon the director, shifting into French, spun a detailed summary of the story. 'He finally looked up and realised I hadn't understood a word, so I had to take a crash course. I didn't even read the script before I agreed,' Alan recalled; in fact, he did so well that no other actor had to post-synchronise his lines.

The story was simple enough. At the end of World War One a genial Scottish soldier named Plumpick is sent to dismantle a bomb left by the Germans as they retreat from a small French town. But he finds that the place has been abandoned: the inmates of a local lunatic asylum have taken it over, and they make him the King of Hearts in an elaborate festival. On the surface, the movie seems to argue that the insane of the world – here presented as merely colourful eccentrics – are not as mad as those who make war. De Broca attempted to go further, when the inmates applaud a real-life army skirmish as if it were a comic performance for their own amusement. War, *King of Hearts* wanted to say, is a spectacle for lunatics.

Years later, some movie fans rated the movie more highly than critics in 1967, when de Broca took a drubbing: 'Nothing about this comedy wears well,' lamented *Time*, recapping the international re-action, '[because] the absurd only looks that way when it stands next to something rational. The movie makes the whole world look crazy, including the babbling hero. Thus the representatives of war and peace appear equally loony.'

Alan agreed. 'The film started off as a comedy, until we realised it wasn't that at all. The mad element of those people should have been more intense, more real – then the moral of the film would really have worked. It was a bit too much of a fairy story – beautifully done, of course, and very light. It was full of smashing things, but they came scene by scene, and one lost the thread.'

With de Broca's encouragement, he had embellished the role of Plumpick with zany bits of comic business. He saw that there was very little in the script for him, and that the narrative was achingly protracted. Practising his French every day and performing his own stunts, he added gestures that were wildly exaggerated, histrionic punctuations of comedy, in which he seemed to step out of the story as if to be part of the audience, even as he remained firmly within its tenacious, tedious grasp.

The final scene revealed Alan nude, facing away from the camera (as in *Georgy Girl*), asking for admission at the gates of the lunatic asylum.

It felt new, I can tell you, and I don't think he shot me all that well, either – a bit too low down and a bit too near. [The actress] Geneviève Bujold was supposed to be nude in one scene but wouldn't do it, and she was full of – well, I don't know whether it was awe at me doing it, or disgust. It was a witty way to end the story and it seemed absolutely right – although it was a bit hair-raising at the time, in the middle of a French town, on location, with as many people watching as could get near enough!

'I worked a six-day week!' Alan wrote to his family from the Hôtel du Grand Cerf in Senlis, France that spring.

It's marvellous! It's been a bit difficult being the only Englishman in a French film of 70 people, but I managed quite well, and it's something I'd like to do again. The French lessons [he had taken before production] were really worth it, because I find no problem in understanding and in being understood . . . The food of course is marvellous everywhere, and I am having to be strong and eat very little. Everybody here is absolutely charming and marvellous – the atmosphere quite different to most English companies. Everyone lives together and does each other's jobs – no union rules which prevent you from doing something for someone else.

He added that Yardena came for a visit, 'but it's been a bit boring for her, I'm afraid.'

Before departing for France, Alan had met Victoria once or twice in London for lunch or tea, but they were still not lovers. He had also invited her to a gathering at Hamilton Terrace, still furnished sparsely but with noteworthy art by his brother Martin, who was establishing himself as a gifted artist and art teacher; as well as paintings by Georges Rouault and John Minton. A large sitting-room window overlooked the thickly planted garden.

'I have always resisted owning things,' Alan told his friends as if he believed it. 'This house is the first thing I have ever really owned apart from a car.' At the gathering that evening, he introduced Victoria to Joanna Pettet, who was in London working in the movie *Casino Royale*. Joanna had rented a house near Alan: 'We had made no commitment, but I wanted to be near him,' she recalled. With puckish perversity,

Alan gave each of the two women the clear impression that he was ardently in love with the other – a tactic perhaps designed to short-circuit the tender inclinations of both. Joanna coped rather better with this than did Victoria.

At the same time, Victoria suddenly fancied the idea that she would launch a career as a movie star; to that end she managed an appointment with Michelangelo Antonioni, then in London to direct his first English-language film. 'I spent three quarters of an hour with Antonioni in his suite at the Savoy,' she wrote to a friend in New York. 'He thought he might test me for his new film, *Story of a Photographer and a Woman on a Beautiful April Morning* [eventually and economically retitled *Blow-Up*]. We had a strange talk, as his English is a little halting and mine always takes off in stilted flight when conversing with a foreigner. He asked me if I would be in England this week, which is why I delay my Paris trip, as naturally I wouldn't turn down a film test.' The test was never made and Victoria – with a ticket to Paris in hand – then paused again, this time to consider an offer to 'dance in a Madrid theatre for six months and in a circus for a month prior to that'.

Once these various chimeras had faded, she at last crossed the Channel and obtained a part-time job at UNESCO's Paris office on the Place Fontenoy – 'sticking labels on Ektachromes of Etruscan sculpture', as she said dismissively; actually, it was a responsible assignment, requiring a keen eye and subtle judgements.

Victoria landed in Paris just after Yardena had quit the scene. 'I've been stuck in Paris for months,' she wrote to Alan in June, when he was working in Senlis. 'I'm slaving away in the Arts Division of UNESCO temporarily but am going to Greece in July. Am wilting away in this Paris heat. If you ever have a moment, do you think you would ring me at UNESCO as I don't have a home phone? I'd love to hear you speak French – it can't be as atrocious as mine – I now find I can't speak English, either!' For her residence, she at first relied on the kindness of acquaintances, hopscotching from one co-worker's apartment to another, from one grimy doss-house to the next, and even from one lover's garret to another's.

But after a short interval of such rootlessness, she had a stroke of true good fortune. Marie Malavieille, a colleague at UNESCO, invited Victoria to share her apartment on the rue Péclet, and in the bargain the two women became lifelong friends, as Marie offered a patient and constructive perspective for Victoria during difficult times.

'She was without doubt one of the cleverest people I've ever known in my life,' recalled Marie. 'I think one of the reasons she eventually didn't function well in society was her outlook on things: she had very deep feelings and different, interesting ways of comprehending life and people. Add to this that she was really a self-made person, and that her background could never have predicted such talents, and one can understand what an unusual person she was.'

Victoria concluded one letter to Alan with a provocative question: '*Comment vont les amours?*' Like hers, Alan's love affairs, such as they were, were not going far at all just then, but in her case it was not a matter of choice: for six months she had suffered from an unpleasant gynaecological complaint and was in the care of a physician who forbade all sexual activity – which was irrelevant in the case of Alan.

Once Victoria had been returned to the pool of available, single young women, she made the most of it, as Marie Malavieille remembered: 'Vicky was a very sexy girl and she attracted men very easily. I recall that she was the only woman at UNESCO who dared to wear things like a lime green or shocking pink miniskirt – in fact, she preferred *very* mini. In or out of the office, that sort of outfit wasn't to be seen in Paris, but Victoria got away with it. And her lovers didn't seem to mind what she wore.'

But that year Victoria was often depressed. 'Why is it', she wrote from Paris to a former colleague in America, 'that some days one is melancholic to suicide, in a black mood of despair, and other days, everything's light and lucid? I feel almost as if I'm floating. Maybe I will drift down to the south of France or Spain or even London.' Drifting, alas, was becoming the essential characteristic of her life, and her sleep was more and more disturbed: 'My dreams are always nightmarish blues in the night.' If awakened, she took refuge in reading volumes by writers as diverse as Ernest Hemingway (whom she found 'slightly stilted, like a schoolboy trying to impress his English teacher with his formalised style'), Mary McCarthy ('a remarkable writer') and Henry James ('now *there's* richness of prose and depth').

But typically, after four months in Paris, Victoria was bored with her job and with France. In July she resigned and travelled with friends to the Club Méditerranée on the Greek island of Corfu, a resort catering to an international set of young people. By August she was back in England, looking for another job.

After completing two movie roles in six months, Alan was also in London, but neither for a holiday nor in search of employment, of which there was a surplus. He quickly dispatched the leading role in a BBC television production of Mikhail Lermontov's novel *A Hero of Our Time*, broadcast on 28 September, in which he earned glowing notices for his performance as a world-weary Byronic wanderer: *The Times* praised his 'sure touch for foreboding and bravado'.

By that date, however, he had been working for a month in Dorset, playing one of the defining roles of his career in *Far From the Madding Crowd*, his second picture with director John Schlesinger. Based on the novel by Thomas Hardy, Frederic Raphael's screenplay neatly captured its spirit and faithfully limned its characters. Bathsheba Everdene (played by Julie Christie) is the strong-willed heiress of an English farm. She is courted by three men: the gentle sheep farmer Gabriel Oak (Alan); a wealthy farmer, William Boldwood (Peter Finch); and the vain and insensitive Sergeant Troy (Terence Stamp). After dramatic and romantic complications that include a tragic sub-plot about a servant girl, Bathsheba finally marries Gabriel.

Philip Pearman had died in 1964, and now Alan was represented by Gareth Wigan, an esteemed agent and later a successful producer and studio executive. 'Alan was very reluctant to play the part of Gabriel,' Wigan recalled.

> He wanted Terence Stamp's role, because he wanted to be recognised as a leading young man. And so he would not make a decision – he kept insisting Troy was the part for him – and this was quite a dilemma for all of us, because the start date for filming [29 August] was drawing near. I agreed with John Schlesinger: I thought he would be much better as Gabriel, because Alan played complex men very well. But Alan wanted to assume roles like Romeo and other classical leading characters.

Gareth Wigan also represented John Schlesinger and Joseph Janni; hence everyone worked to have the contracts in place so that *Far From the Madding Crowd*, with its long and complex shooting schedule on location in Dorset, could begin on time.

On 30 July, Wigan was at home, watching the televised final match of the World Cup. Unexpectedly, Alan telephoned, insisting he had to come over at once to discuss the film; an hour later, they were deep in conversation. 'We agonised over it,' Gareth recalled, 'until Alan finally agreed. But I don't think he ever actually signed a contract – he just showed up and did the picture, with his usual charismatic presence and complete professionalism.'

'I didn't want to play that part,' Alan said, 'because I felt it would come as no surprise to anybody that I *could* do it – it called on certain qualities that I'd used before, and I think it's necessary to surprise people – and to surprise myself.' But it is difficult to know which 'qualities' he was referring to: Gabriel Oak is a far more sympathetic character than any he had so far played – and one who was more of an 'action hero' than he had yet been. In each of his previous movies he had been very much a supporting character (*The Entertainer* and *Whistle Down the Wind*); an ungrown-up roustabout (*A Kind of Loving*); dangerously minatory (*The Caretaker*); an appealing foil (*The Running Man*); a cad (*Nothing But the Best*); a man in need of some kind of maturation (*Zorba the Greek*); or a mod anti-hero fearful of romantic commitment (*Georgy Girl*). On the other hand, *Far From the Madding Crowd* gave him an opportunity to project a kind of quiet nobility and, like it or not, he had to seize that chance and make it work.

From the end of August 1966 to February 1967, the cast and crew – working mostly outdoors – coped with England's unpredictable weather. Rain, sleet, snow and fog alternated virtually daily during the twenty-four-week schedule, which the director described as 'a jolly difficult and ambitious undertaking'.

Everyone connected with the production lived on location in the south-west – in countryside cottages or in small rented homes. Alan arrived looking the part of a rumpled farmer – his thick, wavy hair unparted and uncombed, his beard slightly wild, his sideburns widening at the jaw, his eyebrows unclipped and shaggy. His blue-green-gold eyes (depending on the light) were sometimes lively, his glance kind but somehow wary, his face strong, his expression vulnerable. He learned to ride a spirited mare, and he took lessons on the flute, which the script required. Alan then settled into the North Mill, in Broadway near Weymouth – a creaking old mill house, but he loved its weathered atmosphere. There was only one problem, as he confided in a letter to his family and in calls to a few friends – he was unutterably lonely.

No matter his initial indifference to the role of Gabriel Oak, his performance managed a delicate balance of the heroic with the romantic sensibility, precisely right for Hardy's honourable farmer – a determined man of the soil, uneducated but no simpleton, and simultaneously one able to love and be loved. 'What's good about the film', he had to admit, 'is the atmosphere, the period, the whole sense of that farm at work, and the distance and elements of nature – all these things put pressure on the four characters and their passions.' That was a fair summary of Hardy's literary ethos, which exploited a certain social readjustment of the pathetic fallacy linking man and nature.

When Gabriel says to Julie Christie, 'At home by the fire, whenever I look up, there you will be – and whenever you look up, there I shall be,' Alan's delivery sounds neither cloying nor doubtful. As shooting progressed, he perhaps came to see that indeed his role might not have had Sergeant Troy's explosions of temper or swordplay, but that Gabriel was (his words) 'a strong, direct man who sees at once through everything and everybody. Nature parallels his emotions and his life . . . It's a rather difficult role, really. Hardy is speaking through Gabriel, so it's very personal. On paper, he seems very simple but he's really more wry – the sort of man who knows a situation so well that he can afford to laugh at it a bit.' Gabriel was, in the final analysis, the moral centre of the story, and the film – contrary to some international indifference on its release – is entirely agreeable and entertaining, magnificently photographed by Nicolas Roeg, directed with a sure hand by Schlesinger and acted without mannered exaggeration by a first-rate cast.

Critics and the professional film academies in Hollywood and London ignored *Far From the Madding Crowd* and so, for the most part, did audiences. But the venerable National Board of Review, a respected consortium of 150 New York filmgoers and critics, chose it as the year's best film and Peter Finch as best actor. Otherwise, the spotlight and prizes in 1967 went to more incandescent movies like *Bonnie and Clyde, The Graduate, In the Heat of the Night* and *Guess Who's Coming to Dinner.*

At the time Alan seems to have readjusted his perspective, or at least re-examined it. With his lengthening list of movie credits, he was more often asked if he preferred theatre to cinema acting: he admitted that the former had immediate rewards – both commanding the stage and enjoying an audience's favourable reaction. That was all forfeited to a movie director, who could cut, adjust or even delete what an actor thought his best scene. Schlesinger and Alan had no significant disagreements on which shots to hold on screen, but this camaraderie was unusual.

'Sometimes you do have to fight with a director for a choice of takes,' he said after returning to London from Dorset in February 1967. 'In the end, one finally wants to have complete control – I mean, it would be great to direct and to act in a film at the same time, simply because one wants that control. But only if it was a part I didn't have to go out and find – something that just came along, as it did for Albert Finney in *Charlie Bubbles*.' That said, he dashed to a television studio, and on 15 February 1967 was seen in *Death of a Teddy Bear*, written by Simon Gray, a young playwright with whom he would enjoy an historic association and a deep friendship.

At the same time, thorny negotiations were in process. Michael Langham, artistic director of the Stratford Festival in Ontario, Canada, offered Alan two roles for the summer of 1967 – the title character in *Richard III* and Frank Ford in *The Merry Wives of Windsor*. Christopher Plummer was to have played Richard, but he withdrew for a movie role – a detail unknown to Alan when Langham rang to offer the part. A Stratford press release, picked up by *The Times* of London, then reported that Alan was the Festival's second choice for Richard and that he would assume only 'a minor role' in *Merry Wives*. With unusual spleen, Alan fired off an angry message to Langham, complaining that the press announcement, which he read with astonishment, made him appear as a stand-by and that he just might not come to Canada at all. He received Langham's wired response at once:

MOST DISTRESSED BY MESSAGE RECEIVED – PLUMMER ORIGINALLY CAST RICHARD BUT THAT PRODUCTION AND ALL CASTING WHOLLY ABANDONED BEFORE CHRISTMAS – I PHONED YOU NOT TO FIND QUOTE A REPLACEMENT UNQUOTE BUT TO SECURE IF POSSIBLE AN ACTOR IN WHOM I DEEPLY BELIEVE AND AROUND WHOM I WAS PREPARED [TO] BUILD ENTIRELY NEW PRODUCTION THAT WOULD

EFFECTIVELY SET YOU UP [AS A] MAJOR STAR OF THEATRE – WHEN YOU AGREED I EMBARKED FULL RENEGOTIATIONS TO ACHIEVE NEW AND APPRO-PRIATE CAST AND IN PAST 48 HOURS THIS ALMOST COMPLETED – AS BALANCE FOR RICHARD [IT] SEEMED YOU SHOULD PLAY SOMETHING COMPARA-TIVELY FRIVOLOUS IN WHICH [YOU CAN] LET HAIR DOWN – HENCE FORD – NOT PRACTICING DECEP-TION WHEN I MADE NO REFERENCE ON PHONE TO PREVIOUS PLUMMER RICHARD INVOLVEMENT BECAUSE TO ME THAT PLAN ALREADY DEAD – SECURING YOUR TALENTS HERALDED SOMETHING TRIUMPHANTLY NEW – OFFER MADE DID NOT REPEAT NOT PLACE YOU SECOND FIDDLE [TO] PLUMMER HOW COULD IT WHEN YOU'D BE HERE SIX MONTHS LEADING IN 2 PLAYS WHILE PLUMMER HERE FOUR IN ONLY ONE – AS PROOF [OF] GOOD FAITH [I] UNDERTAKE NOW THAT ONE OF YOUR PLAYS WILL BE PUT ON ALSO AT THE MONTREAL WORLDS FAIR – YOUR APPEARANCE HERE RECEIVED GREATEST EXCITEMENT IN NORTH AMERICA AND YOUR PROPOSED BACKTRACKING PUBLICLY HUMILI-ATES ONE OF YOUR GREATEST ADMIRERS – FINALLY AND PRESUMPTUOUSLY YOU NEED THIS CHANCE AND YOU KNOW IT AND YOU'RE A BLOODY FOOL ALAN TO TURN IT DOWN FOR WHAT ARE CANDIDLY UNIMPRESSIVELY SUBURBAN REASONS – ANYTHING REPEAT ANYTHING I CAN DO TO ACCOMMODATE YOUR NEEDS PROFESSIONALLY AND PERSONALLY ONLY A MATTER YOUR ASKING PLEASE COME TO YOUR SENSES – YOURS IN REAL BUT CONFUSED ADMIRATION – MICHAEL LANGHAM

Alan drafted a handwritten response:

Dear Michael,

Please regard situation exactly as it was except for the thought on Ford. Sorry for panic but *The Times* announcement came at vulnerable moment. Rich[ard] III is enormous prospect for me. I had not really got used to the idea and was in any case not expecting any announcement of any kind. Please do not make a Montreal commitment that you are not ready to make, nor do anything especially for me that would not normally do. Nobody cares if they're 25th choice for a part, but it's a bit of a shock to see it in print when one is also ignorant of the fact. Can only reiterate that I'm very excited and look forward to seeing you in March.

He was further mollified by a press release issued by John Hirsch, the director appointed for *Richard III*: 'The part is absurd, the melodrama grotesque. Richard is a monster on a huge scale. As wicked as Ivan the Terrible, as satanic as Lucifer in Milton's *Paradise Lost*. How do you make him human? Only a charmer like Alan Bates can do it.'

In late March, Alan met with Hirsch in New York, where he was directing a revival of Brecht's *Galileo* for the Lincoln Center Repertory Theater. During a long and animated discussion about Richard at the Ginger Man, a West Side eatery, the two men downed copious amounts of beer and, when the bar closed, they stumbled outside to continue the conversation. Trying out the crippled king's limp, Alan shambled along, beer mug still in hand and oblivious to the stares of late-night pedestrians in the busy district. Hirsch was rather more formal next day when he told a reporter: 'Alan's a thoroughly dedicated craftsman. Malleable. Like human plasticine. He can hardly wait to be moulded into a state of fixity for his next characterisation.'

Several weeks after arriving in Toronto that spring, Alan appeared at a press conference for the Festival, where he wore a black pin-striped suit with a white shirt and dark tie – an ensemble he had worn in *Nothing But the Best* and had bought cheaply from the studio. 'He radiates a certain sensual quality,' remarked David Williams, director of *Merry Wives*. 'Part of it is in the way he moves – lithesome, with a kind of feline grace. Mostly, it's the expressiveness of his warm green eyes. Whether in a film close-up or on the dark stage of a large theatre, they shine like beacons.'

For all that, Alan's glances in public that day seemed guarded and defensive, and reporters noted that he was 'nervous and uncomfortable'. As Gareth Wigan recognised from the time of their first meeting through the long years of their friendship, 'The shutters were usually down with Alan – he was very suspicious of people. But when the shutters were drawn up, with those he trusted, they remained up forever.' They were not up, however, for the press, nor for casual acquaintances – and Alan could be pointedly impatient with unimaginative questions from reporters:

Q: In today's swinging London, Mr Bates, are you a swinger?
A: I hope I fit into swinging London.
Q: What do you think of Shakespeare, Mr Bates?
A: They're plays, just like any other.
Q: No better? No worse?
A: Well, perhaps a bit better.
Q: How's a handsome guy like you going to tackle the evil hunchback that is Richard III?
A: I'll be unpredictable. I'm opposed to type-casting. I'm all for *mis*casting. But really, doing Richard will pose no special problems. He's rather like the character in *Nothing But the Best* – ruthlessly ambitious. Out for all he can get.

Warming a bit, Alan acknowledged that he had visited the National Portrait Gallery in London to gaze at paintings of Richard. 'The face is like granite – but it's not an evil face. In the context of his own times, he probably had his virtues.'

After opening night at Stratford, Ontario that June, he met with the press at an inn; this time he wore a trendy fawn-coloured suit with high Edwardian pockets and a chartreuse cravat with a floral pattern – a costume purchased after he had worn it in *Georgy Girl*. 'I buy most of my clothes from the wardrobe department of my films. Why not? They're measured and cut to fit me.' After vodka and lemon, he ordered a filet mignon and a vintage bottle of Château Pontet-Canet. 'But I thrive on honey and watercress,' he volunteered, thus implying (with some subterfuge) that the rich dinner was a rare indulgence. 'Usually I live on organic health foods' – a regime encouraged by Victoria at a recent lunch in London – 'because one must keep in trim.'

But reporters were more interested in the more intimate life of a bachelor than in his diet. 'Speaking of love,' asked one journalist, although no one had been, 'why is it that you've never married?'

There was a momentary pause, then, 'Oh, I am too involved in my work. I had a big romance about a year ago, but I'd rather not talk about it.'

He may have been thinking of Yardena Harari, as he wrote to his mother during the so-called six-day war that June, 'I think about Yardena quite a lot with the war that has been going on, and I hope she is all right. We have not been in touch, which I think is much the best. It's awful to think of Yardena deciding to go home and walk straight into all that!' When Yardena returned to England later that year, she found Alan's romantic feelings for her – such as they may have been – much changed. 'As usual, his work was an escape hatch for him,' she said later, 'a way of avoiding the challenge of intimacy in any category.' For a long time there was to be little communication between them.

That evening, any elaboration on past romance was quickly forestalled when Alan rose from the table: 'I really must dash to catch a performance of your Royal Winnipeg Ballet on the telly!' With that, he neatly averted any potential reference to a newly minted romance that was beginning to attract some public attention. Alan had been enchanted by a visitor from London who had come backstage to meet him after a performance of *Richard III*. Almost at once, he invited the young man to share his quarters.

7

Women and Others in Love

B orn in Lancashire in 1947, Paul Taylor was twenty years old
when he met thirty-three-year-old Alan Bates. Slim and blond,
with a warm smile, ready wit and expressive eyes, Paul had attended
drama school and the National Youth Theatre, England's leading
company for young people studying performing arts. On a brief
holiday in Toronto, he bought a ticket for *Richard III* and joined other
admirers backstage afterwards. 'There was an immediate rapport,' he
said years later, 'and almost at once, it seemed, Alan invited me to live
with him. I accepted.'

Paul was no gushing, subordinate fan. He and Alan shared many
interests, from the fine points of tending an English garden to the
spate of recent movies, from healthy cooking to theatre history. 'Alan
taught me a great deal, and we had a very intense and loving sexual
relationship.' They set up quarters in an old farmhouse fifteen miles
out of Stratford, amid the Canadian countryside. For Alan this arrangement was preferable to that in Weymouth, where he had been quite
alone.

Always the archetype of discretion and the most vigilant custodian
of his privacy, he took a long time to confide in anyone about Paul.
To his mother, who not only welcomed but expected frequent communications in his absence, he wrote apologetically, 'I am horrified to learn
that it's a fortnight since I spoke to you over the phone – I'm sorry,
I really am. The plays are quite heavy, but I will *not* make excuses.'
And to his father: 'The work is very tough here but rewarding. As
soon as the film is through that I'm doing afterwards in Hungary, I

shall have to stop work for three months, I think!' He was already planning a long holiday with Paul for late 1967.

A dozen years earlier, callow and perhaps overconfident, Alan had been an effective Romeo in the provinces and, disappointingly, he had played Richard II at RADA. That summer of 1967 he went onstage as the third Richard in a far humbler state of mind, eager to dig beneath the text, constantly refining gestures, asking other cast members for reactions and suggestions on how they might together improve a scene. He was at his best learning a difficult and demanding part, and he was energised by the summer's work and by Paul. 'I'm going to do a role like this every year, either winter or summer,' he told a visiting journalist. 'It's probably impossible, but I'd like to.' It was a pledge he could not keep.

Alan's Richard received indifferent notices. Senior drama critics, who knew the text and its history and had lively memories of other memorable performances, were perplexed by Alan's strange interpretation. However one conceives Richard, the man is neither dispassionate nor unsure of his goals – nor can he be indifferent to lust, ambition or pleasure in the fate of Hastings. In a way, Alan's performance was of an alienated antagonist, 'clear, cool, self-contemptuous, observing', according to Walter Kerr, 'as he slips unemotionally out of sight'. Kerr and others had no doubt about Alan's intelligence, but he was put off by the detachment: 'the center of the stage goes unoccupied in this production . . . [and] the central void in the play is due to a reserve in Mr Bates himself.' *Time* was blunter: Alan was 'singularly miscast'.

Where the stage says to the actor, 'Fill me,' Alan preferred to walk around in this case, peering in, studying sceptically – and most of all (thus Kerr, perceptively), 'preserving his privacy by refusing the invitation of the stage to become as public as thunder'. The majority of critics agreed with this assessment, several of them also pointing out that Alan seemed not to believe that Richard was a leading role – that instead he was the supporting character to which he was accustomed. He did not take full command.

No artist, musician, dancer, actor, singer or writer can leave the self outside the theatre, the studio, the recital hall or the study. That truism stated, it well may have been the combination of caution and excitement, at the time of a new affair, that prevented him from going onstage with the kind of attack that Richard required and that Kerr, one among many, longed to see. Alan's Richard was too much Alan – a wary man. 'The kingdom of this play needs a masterful Richard,' complained *Time*. 'This Alan Bates lacks.' In private, he gave himself without restriction to the first throes of passion; in private, he could be and often was the most open, forthright and direct of men, and was certainly never a tentative or vacillating lover. But in public he preferred to keep his feelings in reserve.

This may help to understand why, in his best performances onstage and screen, it was the characters with interior conflicts, the men struggling with themselves, those making their way through a wild, unacknowledged or even terrifying process that evoked his deepest sympathies and hence those of his audiences. He may have kept back so much from his Richard, in other words, because that summer the programme of his life required him to proceed with extreme caution. Indeed, that summer Alan described his own existence, for a journalist, as 'fragmented'.

There had been a gap of more than three years between his last stage performance in *The Caretaker* (October 1961) and the première of *Poor Richard* (December 1964), and recently there had been almost two years since *The Four Seasons* (September 1965). Meanwhile, Alan had learned well the powerful effects of bringing things down for screen acting – of substituting less for more. Of this he seemed very much aware that summer at Stratford: 'I hadn't actually lost confidence in acting, but your mind gets very oriented to the camera. You can't be half-hearted about Richard – you've just got to go on and do it . . . When you go between theatre and film, you have to be very careful that you're not bringing one into the other, that you're not being too subtle for the theatre or too big for the screen.'

This is one reason why, years later, viewers feel so much from his multivalent glances and his understated gestures on film. In the theatre the part of Richard required much more and – that summer at least – something in him could not convey it. A certain passivity was present where it should not have been – not weakness, not lack of depth, but an absence of bold attack, for which there is sometimes no substitute.

Most often that passivity as an actor made for profoundly human characterisations: viewers recognised the mirror held up to nature. His best performances, which meant most of his performances, were remarkable for their ability to make dramatic passivity much more than inactivity. In this regard 'passivity' can perhaps be a component of very high praise, for actors like Alan presented not themselves, but the characters. At his normal best, he was a bright prism, a conduit. But at Stratford that summer there was a momentary dimness, a temporary barrier in the otherwise smooth mystery of his capacious talent.*

That summer in Canada, his life with Paul forestalled a repetition of the loneliness he had felt in Weymouth during the making of *Far From the Madding Crowd*. And their excursions in and around Stratford distracted Alan from the negative response to his Richard, with which (to his credit) he later agreed. As Paul afterwards recalled, they had much to discuss, including various plans for the immediate future and the possibility of an autumn holiday. What to do after Stratford?

They did not have to wait long for an answer. In July a screenplay arrived by express post, with an offer for Alan to assume the leading role in a movie based on the best-selling novel, *The Fixer*, by Bernard Malamud. Published the previous year, it had recently won both the National Book Award and the Pulitzer Prize in America, and Metro-Goldwyn-Mayer had quickly purchased film rights for John Frankenheimer to direct a picture based on a screenplay by Dalton Trumbo. 'I was on my knees playing Richard when I got the script,' Alan recalled, 'but I knew it was my kind of subject.'

Set in Russia early in the twentieth century and based on an actual incident, *The Fixer* told the grim story of a Jewish handyman, wrongly accused of the ritual murder of a young boy. The case comes to trial – and there the script (like the book) stopped; the point, for Malamud, was not the outcome of a judicial procedure but the moral involvement of the reader and the audience. That was an admirable conceit, but *The Fixer*, on the page and on the screen, became an unfortunate victim of artistic indecision.

Alan at once accepted the role – not only because it was a challenging movie lead, but because it would spring him free from Stratford before the end of the season, an escape allowed once again by his contract. Hence, although the Stratford Festival was scheduled through

---

* Alan's performance in the role of Ford in *The Merry Wives of Windsor* was ignored by the press.

mid-October, Alan's resignation and his replacement were announced on 23 August. He and Paul returned to London, where Alan gave him keys to the house before departing for the filming in Hungary.

Production began in and around Budapest that October and was completed before Christmas; the cast included Dirk Bogarde, Carol White and Elizabeth Hartman. While there were scenes of epic action – a Cossack charge through a Jewish ghetto, for example – the stress was on the enormous struggle of Yakov Bok, whom Alan played with almost terrifying and unbearable intensity. 'It was totally different from anything I'd ever tried before,' he said later, 'totally new, and undoubtedly the hardest bloody thing I've ever done in my life, both physically and mentally.'

Alan's many prison scenes were shot in a cold, damp and abandoned castle high above the Danube, used for a jail up to 1960; on the walls of the cell he had to inhabit for hours each day of five weeks he could read the names of Stalinist prisoners. 'We did it all in real dungeons,' he said, 'and we worked every day except Sundays . . . I think it made me aware of what persecution must be like. After the filming every day, there was only time to have something to eat and get a bit drunk. It was completely absorbing – I was hardly aware of doing anything except that.' To his family he wrote, 'If I ever had a part that made me probe beneath the surface of a character, it is that of Yakov Bok in *The Fixer*.' In a sense, the real-life victim on whom Bok was based becomes a second Job, and in Alan's depiction he grows equivalently, through suffering to nobility.

'He is the finest young actor I have ever worked with,' according to Frankenheimer.

> Bates was an angel – getting up at three in the morning for scenes in below-zero weather, behaving in an exemplary and professional manner at all times, remembering all his lines. What made Alan all the more admirable was the fact that two of his colleagues were such rotters – [one of them] couldn't or wouldn't learn his lines, and, worse, Dirk Bogarde flatly tried to sabotage Alan and the film by missing cues and reading his lines badly. Bogarde is an impossible human being. But Alan? He always knew his lines, and generously did his off-camera lines [to other actors, for their close-ups] with all the care and brilliance of his on-camera lines.

Frankenheimer was perceptive about his leading man: 'Alan Bates was divine. He guards his personal relationships and is not close to many people. And if there's one thing wrong with this paragon, I'd say it is that he is too afraid of hurting people – of not being liked. I think that he has got to assert himself more.' That was an opinion shared by many colleagues and friends. Alan did, however, assert himself artistically in *The Fixer*, and the performance earned his only nomination for an Academy Award. (The statuette for best actor went to Cliff Robertson, for *Charly*.)

Alan was working congenially with a meticulous director on a difficult role he built gradually, from bits and pieces of small business. 'He doesn't understand what is happening to him,' he said of Bok, 'and slowly, slowly, through the awful pressure and humiliation, it dawns on him who he is and what circumstances he is in. It's only at the end that he knows, and he doesn't care whether he lives or dies, as long as it's truthful.' His astonishing delivery of one line, in a tone of almost unbearable anguish, may have been enough to convince even a casual moviegoer of this actor's extraordinary depth: 'Suffering I can gladly do without, I hate the taste of it – but if I must suffer, let it be for something.'

Paul arrived near the end of filming, and when the picture was complete, they took three months driving back to England in the red Ford Mustang Alan had bought in America and driven in Canada. They were in London for the first days of spring.

While driving through the Derbyshire countryside, Alan saw an old grey stone farmhouse for sale – a country cottage, actually – situated on a generous tract of land, on the edge of a valley and close to the Peak District; there were two detached buildings as well. The setting was irresistible to him, with nearby mountain streams, windswept hilltops and fields dotted with low stone walls. He made a down payment, which was no complicated task, for the place had been vacant over two years and required considerable upgrading to be habitable. But the property was not for himself alone. For several years his mother had been longing to move from the family home in Allestree, but she had found no suitable place – and her husband, who disliked anything to do with change or uprooting, saw no need for relocation at all. 'So this had led to deadlock,' as Martin recalled. 'Father always held back, seeing problems with *every* property [Mary found].'

All three sons had tried to mediate the issue and to find a compromise, but to no avail.

Alan was keen on the new place, however, and he drove his father to see it and finally persuaded him to sell the house in Allestree and to put the proceeds into a fifty-fifty joint purchase: the idea was that Harold and Mary would have it as their new home. That year their house was sold and they moved to the new one, at Bradbourne. 'And so started a long period of stress – and happiness – for all three of them,' according to Martin. 'Our parents were too old – she was sixty-four, he seventy – for a move to a tiny, somewhat remote village,' and they faced a long period of refurbishing, refitting of the house and general work on the property. The move also meant making new friends and having to travel further for doctors or shopping. In addition, the builders were slow and, as it happened, incompetent; sheep often invaded the garden; and at least once the heating system broke down and the place was flooded.

But Alan never yielded. 'He was a Derbyshire man to the core,' as Paul Taylor said. 'He was close to nature, he had a love of gardens that was both practical and poetic, and he loved everything to do with country life. He rebuilt the drystone walls, for example, and he saw that all the traditional styles and processes were put back into the rebuilding of the barn and the main house.'

Gareth Wigan spoke for many: 'His roots in Derbyshire were very dear to him and going back to visit – and eventually having a second home there – was an enormous pleasure, because it was important to him not to lose touch with the non-actor's life and world. Alan's way of both sensitising himself and of dealing with any subsequent exhaustion was to go back to Derbyshire. There he could recover from the exposure that had tapped all that sensitivity.'

Hence Alan began to visit more often than ever – for his own refreshment and also to see how his parents were (or were not) coping. Despite the problems, Harold liked the quiet rural life of Bradbourne, while Mary – initially captivated by the romantic setting – soon became frustrated with the lack of social and cultural life, especially during the winter.

Over the next several years Alan worked an almost frantic schedule. He travelled a great deal, and his personal life was to be greatly transformed, to everyone's astonishment and his parents' hushed but obvious disappointment. From 1968 there was a long period of uninterrupted professional success, countered by severe personal pressures.

With the properties under management, contracts signed and work under way, Alan agreed to play a role in a television drama. On 28 August 1968 he was seen briefly in *Spoiled*, another short play by Simon Gray, filmed several weeks earlier; on the same day Alan began twelve weeks of work on the movie *Women in Love*, a project set up by Gareth, who negotiated Alan's fee of $100,000 plus an additional $150,000 and 7.5 per cent of the net profits, to be paid after the movie recouped its expenses. Alan's name appeared as the first star credit, above the title.

Based on the controversial 1920 novel by D. H. Lawrence, Larry Kramer's screenplay for Ken Russell's *Women in Love* aimed to be high-culture movie-making; this it partly achieved, along with a box-office-winning notoriety for its several unusually candid sexual episodes, male nudity and frank dialogue. More character study than narrative, and more a Lawrentian reflection on sex than a character study, both the novel and the film are a series of lushly symbolic, often disconnected sequences. In it two men – a school inspector named Rupert Birkin (Alan) and Gerald Crich, a wealthy industrialist (Oliver Reed) – try to understand modern marriage, the complexity of their relationships with women and the meaning of intimacy between the men themselves. At the same time, the two sisters they marry, Gudrun and Ursula Brangwen (Glenda Jackson and Jennie Linden), long, respectively, for unfettered passion or idealised romance.

'I think', Alan said later, 'that the movie was slightly excessive here and there – but apart from that, the whole thing was a wonderful reflection of the spirit of the book.' Part of that spirit, as the cast knew from the outset, was to explore the nature of love between two men. The production, therefore, had an ironically apt timing at this point in Alan's life for, in the role of Rupert Birkin, he was required not only to articulate a man's need for some kind of same-sex intimacy, but also to appear nude in two sequences. Russell made clear from the start that he saw the character of Rupert as 'sexually ambivalent'.

In the first nude scene, Alan is seen alone outdoors, a kind of primal man at the dawn of a new creation; in the second, he engages in a wrestling match with Oliver Reed. 'Not only did he want to be drunk to do this scene,' Alan recalled of his colleague, 'but he wanted me to be drunk, too. We weren't.' Reed was more anxious about the nudity than Alan, who had already disrobed for *Georgy Girl* and *King of Hearts* (which had led one critic to remark that he had 'one of the most exposed behinds in cinematic history').

'That was of course a very awkward scene for both actors,' recalled Gareth, 'and it was deliberately left to the end of the schedule to be filmed. Actors are vulnerable in any case, and all the simulated mechanics of the scene, the wrestling, the many cuts and angles, the repressed sexuality of it was difficult for them to handle.'

'We didn't think too much about it before we came to the wrestling scene,' Alan recalled. 'I suppose we thought, "When it happens, it will just happen and that will be that." But of course it wasn't. When we shot the scene, it hurt [because of bruises caused by wrestling and falling]. We were OK, but the task was quite shattering.' The sequence was carefully choreographed in advance, with the added expense and lighting complications of four cameras running simultaneously. Alan and Oliver performed the scene in sections, over a day and a half.

They then sat in a screening room with Russell and in a way that was more difficult, 'staring up at yourself in glowing colour. You get to see only a few moments of it in the film, but we saw hours of it. It seemed to go on forever, and it was torture. I thought at the time it all looked so – well, so *wrong*, and that I looked so hideous. I suppose it's a great lesson in humility. If you can get over the awfulness of yourself in the flesh, you can get over anything. I was slightly nervous about the reaction when the film was released, but hardly anyone paid any attention to the wrestling scene. Some of the love scenes came under attack as being too sensuous, but people seemed to accept the stark nudity without too much shock. My worst fears were about my mother's reaction – *that* I really dreaded – but it never bothered her in the least!'

As always, Alan wanted to do something different, something new, to be recognised as an actor who could surprise. He also wanted to be entirely of the moment in the self-consciously audacious style of the late 1960s – to prove that, at thirty-four, he was physically and temperamentally among the daring young men of film and theatre, taking advantage, with his director, of the new freedoms permitted. At the same time Alan was unwilling to risk being branded a frank exhibitionist, nor did he wish to lose a serious audience in the future; unlikely though that seemed years later, it was very much a possibility at the time. Nor was the filming made easier by the director,

whom Alan (not given to speak in such terms) called 'very uncommunicative, very hard to get on with . . . I don't think Ken Russell
would listen to anything an actor said.'

Notwithstanding the tension between them, Russell offered Alan
the lead in his next picture even while they were filming: 'I had him
earmarked for the homosexual composer Tchaikovsky in *The Music
Lovers*. He read the script and was suitably impressed. It was one helluva
part, calling for another virtuoso performance of a complex character
tormented by his sexual hang-ups. In retrospect, I think that was part
of the problem. I guess Alan didn't want to get typecast as a sexual
deviant – heaven forbid!' Typically, Alan delayed his reply to Russell
until well after the filming of *Women in Love* was completed: 'After
leading me up the garden path for some time, I eventually learned on
the grapevine that he was about to turn me down. He did!'

Because he knew that total undress was required for two scenes
in *Women in Love*, Alan requested and was granted the right to preview
the finished film as well as to approve the advertising for it, so that
(as a letter from Wigan to the co-producer confirmed) 'he would be
protected from unfavourable publicity . . . and would not be shown
frontally, full length and nude'. In the film as released, and as re-
released for private viewing years later, there is not so much of Alan
exposed as people may remember: Oliver Reed was much the more
revealed.

'When you were around Alan, there was always laughter,' according
to Glenda Jackson, who recalled that the rigours of filming in
Derbyshire, Durham, Yorkshire and Northumberland were leavened
by his irrepressible humour and by his quite unselfconscious brilliance. 'It seemed to me then, as it did years after,' she continued, 'that
he got better and better as an actor with each picture – he never
remained in the same place, never took his talent for granted – and
I always learned so much from watching him act.' Although she was
known and respected in England before this film, Glenda Jackson rose
at once to international stardom with the release of *Women in Love*.
Nuanced, provocative and layered with complex feelings, this performance won for her the Oscar as best actress, and she was similarly cited
by the National Board of Review, the National Society of Film Critics
and the New York Film Critics Circle. (Alan was nominated as best
actor by BAFTA; the award went to Dustin Hoffman, for *Midnight
Cowboy* and *John and Mary*.)

Alan's wit and joking with colleagues during production was perhaps not unrelated to an important element of his performance. As D. H. Lawrence's alter ego and the spokesman for much of his thinking and questioning, he was deliberately presented as a visual analogue of the writer – the same beard and hairstyle, the same clothes, the same slightly superior demeanour. But generally unacknowledged at the time was the ubiquitous veneer of humour he gave the character of Rupert.

> I gave him a certain lightness. Perhaps I could have made him at times more bitter or dark – perhaps more unpleasant, just at times. Lawrence does have a side that is unpleasant. But I took my cue from reading about him, and learning that he did have a terrific sense of humour, and he liked playing practical jokes. And that went into my mind, and I think the degree of light-ness I gave it is quite valuable to the film. It could have been a heavy and ponderous performance if I'd thought about it in any other way.

Alan's careful pre-production study, his invention of this touch of 'lightness', was the perfect seasoning to the role. The counterpoise to Oliver Reed's sullen, glowering rendering of Gerald, it also provided the hint of buoyancy that prevented both Rupert and the story from sinking under the weight of the film's frequently gaudy self-importance.

Women in Love was completed in early December 1968 and – as he was contractually obliged to do – Alan hastened to New York to do interviews and publicity for the American première of *The Fixer*. At his hotel he promptly went down with the season's strain of influenza but continued with his schedule. 'All I do is eat fruit,' he told a reporter as he munched red grapes and a tangerine. 'Oh, I meant to have pancakes this morning!' Recovering enough to indulge his love of opera, he hurried off to the Metropolitan Opera House for Joan Sutherland's performance in *La Sonnambula*: 'Bliss, sheer bliss!' was his high praise for such artistry.

From New York, Alan continued the press junket in Los Angeles. Invited to a private, men-only party high in the Hollywood Hills, he was reunited with the movie star Rock Hudson, whom he had briefly met at a New York gathering in 1958; like Alan, Hudson ferociously guarded his unconventional private life. There was, Alan said later, a strong mutual attraction between them, but the wine and champagne flowed like wine and champagne, and as the evening progressed, Alan – still taking alcohol-laced cough syrup for his flu – became more and more inebriated. Hudson, who lived nearby, offered to escort Alan back to his room at the Beverly Hills Hotel, but what subsequently occurred did not make for a titillating story. Hudson guided him to the hotel, where Alan became suddenly and violently ill. Rock did the necessary tidying up, set out a bottle of water, ensured that Alan was feeling better, then quietly withdrew without so much as a farewell kiss. Some encounters do not turn out as the principals and the gossips expect.

On his return to London early in 1969, Alan found several cards and letters from Victoria awaiting his attention. Replete with clever literary allusions and the occasional short poem, her letters captivated his imagination, and her style he found delightful; Victoria was certainly an original. Over two months, they met irregularly but often, and rumours of romance began to swirl in certain theatrical circles. 'Oh, he's back with women again, is he?' said Peter Wood, the director of *Poor Richard*. 'Really, he is so tedious!'

'Alan was soon madly in love with her – or so he said,' recalled Joanna Pettet, who worked hard to maintain her friendship with him. 'She had a sharp mind – almost too sharp for this world – but she was also very odd.' Alan and Victoria were not yet sexual partners, but there was no doubt that he was keenly attracted to her fey spirit, her intellectual curiosity and her infectious energy. She could quote lengthy passages of poetry from sources as diverse as Shakespeare, Donne, Shelley and Coleridge, although her recitations were frequently inaccurate. But what Victoria lacked in scholarly accuracy she supplemented with a kind of zestful style, and with a touching vulnerability that Alan found irresistibly appealing. He also preferred to be the caregiver in any relationship; he liked feeling necessary to someone; and he was eager to be a kind of older brother or father figure, no matter the partner.

Alan felt that Victoria relied on him, and he was not off the mark – but she had a certain independent spirit, too, and this he found a safeguard against possessiveness. She was, in other words, a welcome presence in his life that season – and, as she said, apropos of nothing one afternoon, she longed for children, as did he. Alan was thirty-five and some friends – even those who were gay, like John Schlesinger – were urging him to marry for the sake of his public image. He heeded this counsel and, as winter melted into spring, he spent more time with pretty, quirky Victoria, whose hippie charm seemed more whimsical at each meeting, and whose working-class background appealed to him. Their rendezvous were respectable meetings in public places – hence Paul Taylor, who was virtually living with Alan in the cottage, had no reason to think that he might soon be supplanted.

Responding to Alan's questions, Victoria described, over the course of several months, the contours of her life up to the time they had met in New York in 1964. She began by telling him her real name, which thus far she had not revealed.

Valerie June Ward was born in London on 20 January 1940 in a deprived area of London's East End. Two years later a baby sister arrived and was named Patricia. When Valerie was three and Patricia one, her parents, who had neither the financial nor psychological resources to be parents, deposited the babies in an East End orphanage, one of the Barnardo residential homes. There they remained throughout the war, unvisited and deprived of anything like a normal home life. As the Barnardo homes later acknowledged in their history of this time, 'Residential care emphasised children's physical and moral welfare rather than their emotional well-being. The homes housed hundreds of children, and staff were sometimes harsh and distant. Many adults who grew up in the homes look back with affection and believe the charity was a true family. Others remember loneliness, bullying and even abuse.' Valerie and Patricia were among the latter.

How Valerie became Victoria is not entirely clear. Some claim that, one day in her childhood, someone wrongly addressed her as Victoria and this name so appealed to her that she at once claimed it as her own, although now and again she responded to the less formal 'Vicky'. Others insist that she herself assumed the name some years later.

Their mother May – thirty-four when Valerie/Victoria was born – evidently never formalised her cohabitation with Roland Ward, who worked occasionally as a printer. Nevertheless she found it convenient, in light of motherhood, to call herself Mrs Ward. In 1954, when she married a bricklayer named William Catchpole, May testified that she was an unmarried spinster and that the marriage to Catchpole was her first; he died in 1968. Of Mr Ward nothing absolutely certain can be determined, although Victoria later confided to Alan and to a few friends that he had sexually abused her during childhood. Whatever the case, he subsequently left, or May dismissed him.

After the war a cousin of May paid for Victoria to attend school in the countryside, a period that inspired some poetic reflections:

> My home was pictureless: though in one room,
> Sepia amidst the omnipresent brown,
> My father's photo on the mantelpiece
> Between two Chinese vases, did suggest
> A world of imagery just out of reach.
> I loved the infant school: in time of war
> Its songs and spelling bees: its plasticene
> And sugar-paper and bright powder paints
> Were vivid joys: the teachers made the world
> Alive with tadpoles, plants and poetry.
> Then once a month the magic moment came
> When, like a conjuror, Miss Bottomley
> Would shift a sliding blackboard and reveal
> Upon the board beneath a masterpiece
> In glorious and incandescent chalk
> By Rubens or Van Gogh or Constable,
> Copied with a skill beyond imagining.
> We never saw her work or heard the squeak
> Of secret chalk: perhaps she drew at dawn
> Or after hometime in the gas-lit hours.

After a few years up popped May, with the news that Mr Ward had died or left home (ambiguously, she said he had 'departed'), and now she wanted her girls back. They resumed a life of grinding poverty until May decided that she had, alas, made a big mistake, so she promptly returned the girls to Barnardo's, where they remained from about 1949 to 1951. Patricia seems to have coped with this rather better than Victoria, who from her earliest years was prey to profound depressions, irremediable insecurity and a deep distrust of affection, even though that was of course what she most of all needed and desired. Her refuge was books, to which she turned with an almost manic need for distraction. She acquitted herself well at school, and by the age of nineteen had done some photo modelling and learned some secretarial skills.

On Alan's thirty-fifth birthday that February of 1969, Victoria consigned to paper both her desire for Alan and her fear of his rejection; she placed the poem in an envelope along with sprigs of rosemary, the traditional herb for remembrance.

> I never heard of a more cowardly plea
> Or a defeatist so inclined to grasp
> That strange negator, Death
> Where neither fire nor ice
> Disturb his sleeping mask
> Do what you will
> Embrace an ease in life
> Cast your chill breeze on a more sturdy flower
> But smile at least if there be no ill will
> Or else I'll faint from sight
> If more exposed to that forbidding glower!

That month, perhaps to have some distance from the accumulating complexities of his relationships with Victoria and Paul, Alan agreed to perform with the Bristol Old Vic in Thomas Otway's seventeenth-century tragedy *Venice Preserved*.

On his return to London he met Victoria's mother, the recently widowed May Catchpole, a feisty sixty-three-year-old eccentric who lived in not very genteel poverty in Hackney. A colourful character who rarely censored her speech, she rattled on amiably about her earlier 'marriage' to Mr Ward. Alan, who hated artifice and liked people who wore no masks and did not affect counterfeit emotion, thought she was a tonic; during their visit at teatime, Victoria puttered ineffectively at unnecessary chores.

With perhaps guileless impertinence, May Catchpole then stopped the conversation when she suddenly asked if her daughter and Mr Bates had fixed a date for their forthcoming wedding.

8

Going to Town with Butley

Alan and Victoria met more frequently during the run of his next engagement. From 22 April to 17 May 1969, he performed at the Royal Court Theatre in David Storey's *In Celebration*, as one of three sons who return home for their parents' fortieth wedding anniversary. The play explores the characters' current and past problems, their deeply repressed emotions, the tragic early death of a fourth son, and the sense of love celebrated but perhaps betrayed or at least never fully realised. Storey had written a remarkable theatre piece, partly in the tradition of domestic dramas by Ibsen and O'Neill, but composed in his own pure, deft style, with a unique voice and a keen North of England sensibility that was also universal in its scope, its reach and complex of feelings.

As the playwright acknowledged, the work was inspired by his own personal experience, just as it coincided remarkably with Alan's. Written in a white heat of creative genius in just three days, the play concerns a family based on the author's: like the brothers of *In Celebration*, David Storey, too, was one of three surviving sons after the death of a fourth, and his father, like the one written, was a coal miner. Alan recognised analogous correspondences. 'Lindsay [Anderson, the director] sent me the play,' Alan said years later,

> and I saw that it had parallels to my own experience. I'm one
> of three brothers, and my parents were ordinary, sweet people
> who dedicated themselves to their family. My father could have
> been a considerable cellist and my mother a considerable pianist,

but they didn't have either the opportunity or the final bit of drive to do it. The social parallels [of the play] aren't the same [as my family's], but the fundamentals are the same – especially the wife who always wants a grander life, a more refined life, a well-mannered and courtly life.

At first, director Lindsay Anderson suggested that Alan take on the role of the youngest and most repressed son. But he preferred to play the oldest, for which he was in fact far better suited and which was, indeed, the leading part. Rehearsals proceeded smoothly – too much so, Alan suspected after a week. Hence he asked for reactions and suggestions from the director, who had nothing to say; everything was just fine, thank you, and the cast should move on to the next scenes. This both gratified and unsettled Alan, whose intuition told him there were indeed things that needed improvement – but very well, he would continue to do what he had been doing. 'And then, once I was at ease in the role, Lindsay began to direct. He was brilliant and enabled me to find even more nuances. Not all directors are so aware of actors – to allow them first to feel at ease in a play, and then to build on that, rather than to impose an interpretation from the first day.' For the present, Lindsay and Alan were cordial collaborators.

The evening of the dress rehearsal coincided with the annual Oscar awards in Hollywood, for which Alan had been nominated best actor for *The Fixer*, but he felt he was missing nothing by remaining in London: 'Americans have a neurosis about success that is depressing,' he told a reporter. 'It doesn't have much to do with anything.'

His presence in the play guaranteed a healthy box office, and his performance was enthusiastically praised for its nuance and vibrancy – the range of his voice, the unexpected emergence of comic business alternating with a bottomless well of pain. 'At one point in every performance,' David recalled, 'Alan went downstage, lay down with his back to the audience and leaned his head on one hand, while he listened to the other players. This was entirely his own idea, and it was thought to be very daring at the time – it was also quite brilliant, because of course the audience listened with him.' The film of *In Celebration*, produced five years later with the same cast and director, skilfully adapted everyone's stage technique to the more subdued requirements of cinema, and Alan was one of a memorable ensemble.

Onstage, his rumpled and dishevelled charm and his frightening anger created a ferocious alchemy that, as London critic Harold Hobson had observed about the London stage première, 'made the play vibrate with life'.

Lindsay heartily agreed, as he wrote in a note: 'Thank you, Alan, and congratulations – I don't think this play and above all this part, could be, or ever will be, done better!' David felt that Alan's character had come to life in ways he had not anticipated: 'He played the maverick, renegade lawyer, the outsider – and the most injured brother, expelled from the house as a child, while the mother tried to cope with the death of one son and the birth of another.' Alan was the ideal exponent of the role, and the playwright much admired the final grace notes he played out onstage: 'In the end, he achieves a kind of recon-ciliation [with his parents], so that they can all go away separately, bearing their wounds – but the presumption is they have found a way of dealing with them.' Audiences that spring found *In Celebration* suspenseful, mysterious, amusing and profoundly moving.

As for Alan's co-players – Bill Owen, Constance Chapman, Brian Cox, James Bolam and Gabrielle Daye – 'they stayed in touch like a real family over the years and remained on very friendly terms,' as David remembered. 'That was directly due to Alan's influence, because one remarkable part of his character was that he was very good company and very loyal to colleagues. He never acted like a star and it was natural for him to induce a sort of bonding with members of a company.' That became both habit and tradition throughout Alan's stage career.

One evening during the run of the play, Princess Margaret attended with her retinue of minders and friends. It was expected that her party would leave the theatre after the first act, but they remained to the end, when Her Royal Highness went backstage to greet the players. One of her friends, however, remained behind, and when the hall was empty, it was observed that the woman was still sitting and weeping copiously. An attendant approached to ask if she were ill or required help. As the lady brushed away tears, she said in a choked voice, 'The play – it is so like the Royal Family.'

Backstage, meanwhile, the cast was being presented to the princess, who had an eye for Brian Cox, then twenty-three (she was thirty-nine). As usual when she fancied someone, Margaret quite directly proposed a rendezvous: would he dine with her privately at Kensington

Palace? Cox did not, however, accept the royal invitation. Very soon afterwards the Princess turned her attention to Alan and a similar invitation was forthcoming – but he, too, declined. Although Her Royal Highness continued to pursue Alan over several years and with dogged determination, she never succeeded.

In addition to any other reasons, Alan refused to be drawn into the royal circle; perhaps quite perceptively, he saw that any sort of relationship with the capricious Margaret would be only an unwelcome entrapment, as disastrous for his reputation as it had been for that of other young men – especially when it came to his inevitable exclusion. In the decades to come, his closest friends and many theatre colleagues felt that his long-expected, much anticipated, consistently proposed and mysteriously delayed knighthood was the result of deliberate interference by HRH The Princess Margaret, who was unaccustomed to having her invitations rejected and never forgot what she considered an intolerable snub. (His knighthood was eventually bestowed just months after her death.)

Requiring a new agent when Gareth became a successful producer, Alan was subsequently represented by Judy Scott-Fox at the London branch of the William Morris Agency. She took a call from Laurence Olivier's office at the National Theatre in early August: a scheduled film version of their production of Chekhov's *Three Sisters* had hit a snag when cast member Robert Stephens, as Vershinin, fell ill. Would Alan replace him in the picture? Not only would Alan do just that, he told Judy with unusual alacrity, he also offered to travel to Brighton, to see the production at the end of its tour. On the basis of that reply Olivier went further still, offering Alan the chance to join the cast during the final week, the better to relieve Stephens early as well as to prepare for the film that was, said Olivier with his tongue impishly planted in his cheek, 'a somewhat highbrow-sounding enterprise'. Indeed.

It was also something of a surprise to Alan, who was not a member of the company, hence the curious title card announcing 'The National Theatre of Great Britain – and Alan Bates', which much amused him. Early that autumn he went down to Brighton, where he stayed at the seafront home of Olivier, the star and director. 'During rehearsals for the play,' Alan said, 'it was I who had to fit in to their established staging. But when we began filming, we all had to rethink everything – in addition to the fact that Chekhov is notoriously difficult to film in any case. I don't think anyone has ever cracked it.'

The movie version was shot quickly late that year and is perhaps the finest film of a Chekhov play. Alan understood Vershinin as 'a figure almost of fantasy', as he said, 'a mirage for three sisters. He plays up to an image of himself, almost drifting through life – indeed, he plays the role circumstances give him. He actually lives out someone else's idea of him – and that's the difficulty with the part, the mystery, the ambiguity.' Wearing a spruce military uniform, his hair and beard styled like the last tsar or King George V, Alan cut a dashing figure and as usual used his voice like a musical instrument tempered with octaves of colour. Just so, he is the quintessential figure of fantasy when he yields to Masha's illusions: 'I love,' he whispers three times, almost as if the direct object of that love were fading into the gauzy trees. 'It's a play about people trying to fulfil one another's dreams,' Alan told an interviewer, 'but they cannot.' A typical review hailed his performance as 'spectacular in its subtlety and effectiveness'.

While he was immersed in the formal, melancholy elegance of the Chekhov play and movie, Alan had an offer of a radically different project – the film version of Peter Nichols's controversial play *A Day in the Death of Joe Egg*. The story of an English couple who struggle to care for their severely handicapped daughter with whom they cannot communicate, it is both daring and effective in its use of humour as refuge from and resistance to a heartbreaking situation. As usual, he was at first hesitant – but for a good reason. 'With that subject,' he said, 'one is treading on very thin ice indeed and constantly asking oneself, "Am I making a sick film?" . . . I felt more uncertain where to tread in *Joe Egg* than in almost anything else I've ever done.'

Pre-production began in January 1970, even before Alan signed a contract: he, his co-star Janet Suzman and director Peter Medak spent several days visiting a hospital for spastic children – an essential and difficult element in the preparation. 'The great lesson was the staff,' he continued. 'They accept these children as part of everyday normality. When you first go in, you are struck dumb – appalled – but within an hour or so you reach out to them and you can suddenly cope with it. At that point I knew I wouldn't be making a sick film . . . We took care. We had to. The story made us want to care.'

Deeply moved by what he saw and by what he had to bring to

the film, Alan forever after claimed that his love of children and his desire to be a father became almost an obsession that winter: 'I hope to God it's not just something temporary I've got from living with this film, and that I can keep it.'

Despite the emotional and physical rigours of a wintry, twelve-week filming schedule in Bristol and London, Alan drew fresh energy from working with the director and cast, and he was disappointed that the movie went unreleased for two years: 'I think they [the distributors] were afraid of it – they weren't sure what they had and they didn't know what to do with it.'

As for his concurrent desire to be a father, he did not have to wait long for that to become reality. By springtime he and Victoria were meeting almost daily. 'I had the impression', said Elizabeth Grant, a neighbour and soon a close friend of the couple, 'that Victoria had made an enormous play for Alan – and succeeded where others hadn't.'

In April 1970 Victoria informed Alan that she was expecting a child, but to her modern way of thinking that did not necessarily mean marriage. 'I gather', said their son Benedick, 'that she got pregnant unintentionally – but perhaps intentionally.'

Nickolas Grace, soon to be a close confidant of Alan and his family, had a similar impression of divided intention:

> Victoria wanted Alan Bates, but she did not want to be the wife of Alan Bates, the actor. As for him – here was a man who had many sexual affairs, but her pregnancy gave him the moment when his middle-class upbringing required a conventional decision in favour of a conventional life – and he may well have thought this would be possible for him. But he did not consider what it would lead to – it was really an idyllic dream world. And when things became difficult, he thought they could just go on as they had before.

And that was the dilemma affecting everything to come. Friends and family are unanimous that, despite his diffidence about marriage, Alan never urged Victoria to submit to an abortion. 'They talked about marriage for some weeks,' continued Benedick, 'but no quick decision was made. Then, one day, Mum apparently said to Dad, "Maybe we should get married," and he replied, "OK" – just like that.' As Nickolas recalled, 'He followed through, he did the honourable thing, he married her almost as soon as she thought out loud, "Maybe we should get married."' It was as Yardena had said: Alan let the circumstances and events of life lead him, or force him, to act. Martin had the impression that Alan and Victoria were both dubious about marriage: she liked her own gypsy lifestyle, and Alan was fearful of commitment. 'He loved the wandering life of an actor, moving from company to company and forming [new] bonds each time.'

But some close friends sensed dark clouds on the horizon. 'Victoria was actually very ambitious in her own quiet way,' recalled Ian White.

> Marrying Alan was her step to stardom, and he wanted a pretty creature to hang on his arm and to charm people. But she wouldn't do that. She was determined to get Alan as a husband, and she went about it just the right way. Although he and I both knew the truth about our sexual orientation, we were certainly not flagrant about it, and this was no time to be 'out' in the theatre. In a sense, Alan was an easy victim for her. He certainly wanted the children, and when they arrived they were the great pride and joy of his life.

There was one awkward task that Alan had to dispatch and there was no easy way to do it. 'One evening, Alan came home,' Paul Taylor recalled, 'and he said very quickly and simply, "I'm going to have to ask you to leave, as I'm going to be married."' I was taken completely by surprise.' And so, without recrimination or harsh words, Paul left the house – but not Alan's life.

Conrad Monk, then marking almost twenty years as Alan's close friend, understood the problems:

> I could sense that this was a hard time for him. His star was very much in the ascendancy, he was in constant demand onstage and screen, and of course he had an image to maintain. It would have been a terrible story for the press to get hold of in those days – that she was pregnant, first of all, or worse, that she was pregnant and he refused to marry her. Apart from that, I could never understand the marriage. He wanted her to have the children – he wanted the children perhaps more than she did – but the marriage was not something he wanted.

David Storey spoke for many: 'It was a big mystery to me why Alan chose her – it was an inappropriate union right from the start.' But he, too, knew that it was important for Alan to be a caregiver and, however severely she protested, Victoria certainly required care.

Then – and for the rest of their lives, it certainly seemed – things happened very quickly for Alan and Victoria.

About the first of May 1970, he introduced her to his family and announced their impending marriage – scheduled, to everyone's astonishment, for the following week. 'When Alan brought me to meet his mother,' Victoria told a friend, 'she was sitting on the patio, very elegantly sipping a glass of sherry. When he told her we were getting married, she dropped the glass and it shattered into a hundred pieces. I guess I wasn't what she had in mind.'

Victoria could not have been more accurate in her judgement of Mary's reaction. 'The news was quite sudden,' recalled Martin,

> and Mother and Father were not happy about it. Their instincts told them that Victoria was not right for Alan, and this turned out to be the case. My parents' background, values and outlook on responsibility couldn't have been more different to that of Victoria, whose love of freedom [and desire for] creative and intellectual fulfilment appeared to lack any kind of necessary discipline. With a severely troubled childhood behind her, Vicky brought highly unconventional, wayward and perverse behaviour into all our lives – and this was during an era of alternative philosophies, health fads and the general rebellion against anything traditional.

Still, the Bates family had to admit that, in Martin's considered words, Victoria was 'highly intelligent, attractive and at times very charming and stimulating'. And as for any implicit challenge to Alan's decision to marry, Martin was on the mark: 'We must remember that he liked having his own way and that he was a complicated man.'

Everyone put a good face on the wedding – 'it was done almost anonymously,' as Conrad remembered, 'and attended only by a few close friends and relatives.' The ceremony was held on Saturday, 9 May 1970, at the parish church of Bradbourne, Derbyshire. Martin was best man at his brother's side. May Catchpole, smiling and all atwitter, arrived just in time, but Patricia was absent: Victoria had given everyone the clear impression that she wanted her former life erased, her new one entirely separate from the past. Harold and Mary Bates signed the register as witnesses; Alan gave his address as Bank House, Bradbourne (the property recently acquired for himself and his parents); and Victoria signed, legally, as Valerie June Ward, of 52 Balcombe Street, London. 'It wasn't what he wanted,' according to Conrad, 'but he went through with it with his usual good grace, good humour and concern for others.'

'The reasons for Alan's marriage are not hard to understand,' said Simon Gray. 'He was a great romantic, and he tended to fall in love very easily. I think he persuaded himself that he was indeed in love with Victoria. Also, he had very respectable parents in Derbyshire, and part of him wanted that conventional life of marriage and a family. There was certainly no doubt that he had goodwill and very good intentions about her.'

Regarding a union she had hoped for herself, Joanna Pettet was creditably benevolent: 'With Victoria, Alan was so good, so patient.' And Marie Malavieille, who visited frequently, felt that in the beginning of the marriage, 'Victoria was really good for Alan. She read plays with him, she offered some good ideas about them, and she offered him suggestions no one else could.'

There could be no thought of a honeymoon, however, for Alan – 'driven', as he said, to continue his work – had no less than two more jobs on the immediate horizon and told Judy Scott-Fox to send along all offers directly she received them. Some weeks the paperwork accumulated quickly: Kirk Douglas, for example, was producing and starring in (of all things) a pirate movie to be shot in Spain, and he desperately wanted Alan aboard. Judy was relieved to turn this down, however, for just days before, Alan had agreed to participate in something more appealing – Joseph Losey's film of L. P. Hartley's novel *The Go-Between*, with a screenplay by Harold Pinter.

'The script was marvellously economical,' Alan said later, 'yet one knew everything. It was completely crystallised and clear.' Set in turn-of-the-century England, it concerns an adolescent boy (played by Dominic Guard), who is emotionally exploited by a wealthy aristocratic woman (Julie Christie) engaged to a viscount (Edward Fox). The boy's task, which completely galvanises his own embryonic romantic feelings, is to convey messages to and from the woman and her lover, a tenant farmer (Alan).

The Go-Between was to be no facile exercise in nostalgic sentiment, and the glorious look of the picture became a deliberate counterpoint to its bitter core – hence the Norfolk estate and countryside are no prelapsarian paradise but rather a tangled garden of evil. 'The boy, after all, is exploited by these people,' as Alan observed, 'and in this superficially proper society, this innocent is thrown among them all and becomes the victim of their selfishness.'

Alan's role was filmed in Norfolk during late summer, after most of the picture had already been completed. The character he played, Ted Burgess, is in some ways a dark twist on Gabriel Oak (in *Far From the Madding Crowd*), but Alan brought something fresh to his few scenes: 'He's a deeply sensitive and yet unexplored person. All the figures in the film are quite mysterious, and the farmer especially so.'

Unfortunately, as Simon Gray pointed out years later, 'the movie had not much to offer Alan except more exposure and the opportunity to play a character at the romantic centre of the story.' Perhaps because the tone of the picture was so coolly observant, and because Ted's character did not develop, it was difficult for audiences to feel either shock or sympathy for his suicide. Never mind: Alan was generally praised as 'the best of his contemporaries [for] his talent and intelligence, consolidated into one – and he's loaded with sex appeal'. More important to him, however, was a pleasant surprise for his youngest brother, John, then twenty-five, for whom he arranged a silent, brief but important cameo appearance during the movie's final moments.

Victoria waited out the last months of her pregnancy in London, while Alan began rehearsals in late September for his *Hamlet* at the Nottingham Playhouse, where the première was fixed for 4 November – not the easiest of roles in the circumstances. He was glad of the presence in the cast of his old friend Ian White, with whom he could relax off-hours.

'I've done certain parts that expressed a thinker, a man with an intense inner life, but never on the scale of Hamlet,' Alan said that season. 'He is the inner person of all time – faced with a situation he isn't ready to cope with, yet he has to do something about it. It's something I've experienced in various ways – not being able to do what you should have, then making excuses and not living up to your ideals.' He may have been thinking of his diffidence about marriage and his inability to balance his sexual needs.

Alan compared Hamlet with the role he had played in *Zorba the Greek*: 'That was a man caught in a situation which rendered him almost totally immobile. He was so introverted, so analytical, that he couldn't move. He couldn't do anything – not even dance or sing, though he desperately wanted to. Even when it came to someone being killed in front of him [the widow played by Irene Papas], he couldn't make himself react.' The comparison may have seemed odd at first, but he was, as usual, on the mark in expressing his belief that Shakespeare's prince was not, after all, a case of abnormal psychology – and was, indeed, more like himself than not.

Then, in an astonishing, rare moment of public candour, Alan drew closer links between himself and Hamlet:

I think I am rather like Hamlet myself. He is caught in a situation and simply does not trust himself to deal with it. He is completely subject to his emotions and he has this fantastic awareness of the motives of other people and of his own. But this has a stifling effect on him. He believes himself capable of doing something, but he does not trust himself to do it. That's true of me.

The critics were divided. 'Nothing he does is false or unharmonious,' wrote the *Daily Telegraph*'s reviewer. 'Throughout, he has the dignity of a sensitive, deeply wounded boy.' But the *Evening Standard* regretted that 'Alan Bates, virile and handsome, provides a well-spoken, deliberate, persistently brooding Hamlet with few of the shades of humour and grandeur which make this character so eternally rewarding.' And J. C. Trewin lamented that Alan 'had little magnetism [and] no touch of splendour in a correct, rather dispiriting performance'.

Philip Hope-Wallace, on the other hand, was a staunch supporter, writing in the *Guardian* that Alan was 'masterly . . . keenly intelligent and deeply moving . . . Never miss a *Hamlet* – not this one, anyway.' And while Michael Billington in *The Times* did not like the production, he praised Alan as 'admirably dashing and intelligent, [and] strong enough to bear the onus placed on it by Mr [Anthony] Page [the director]. Mr Bates reminds us that Hamlet's tragic flaw was not an inability to make up his mind, but an impulsiveness and intemperateness that rendered his actions ineffectual. He has exactly that racing mind without which any Hamlet is a non-starter . . . [and] he handles the soliloquies excellently, as if trying to release the tensions inside himself.'

Victoria, who did not want to be in London at the time of her delivery, travelled to Nottingham before Alan's opening night. But there were complications when she arrived, as Ian clearly recalled. 'She gave Alan a tough time about everything in his life – his work, his friends, everything – she was just deeply, deeply unpleasant to him.'

Then things became worse. Doctors had warned that because Victoria was so thin and frail and was expecting twins, they would have to schedule a Caesarean section. For three weeks, Victoria flatly refused to submit, until finally Alan was told that he might well lose her and the babies, and they forced him to make the decision. May Catchpole turned up too, urging her daughter to do what was sensible. Finally Victoria was rushed into surgery, and afterwards (as Ian added), 'for some inexplicable reason – perhaps because she blamed Alan's friends for forcing the operation – no one close to Alan was allowed to get near her or her children if she could help it', which of course she could not always do.

And so, on Thursday, 12 November 1970, six months after the wedding, twin sons were born at the Firs Maternity Hospital, Nottingham. Weighing a healthy six pounds eight ounces and seven pounds nine ounces, the infants remained unchristened for two months while their parents sifted through lists of names. Finally the boys were named Tristan and Benedick.

Hamlet moved to the Cambridge Theatre, London, where it ran until 6 February. 'Now I have to look for another house to rent,' Alan told a reporter. 'The one I've lived in [122 Hamilton Terrace, which he had shared with Yardena] is too small for all of us.' A purchase was not sealed until 1973, when he bought Ashdown House, Vale of Health, Hampstead; three years later he also bought Lavender Cottage, in the Vale of Health too. But Alan kept 122 Hamilton Terrace, used it as an office address and even as a residence, and later bought an adjacent coach house at 122A, between which he and his sons moved, from time to time, for the sake of convenience and/or necessity. He also upgraded Bank House, Ashbourne, Derbyshire, a much-loved refuge for him and his friends. 'He liked having property,' said David Storey. 'It had something to do with his provincial upbringing – acquiring houses and land was a solid, sound investment. Each time he bought a new place I refrained from asking, "*Another?*"'

Alan marked his thirty-seventh birthday that February. Until now he was accustomed to fixing his own schedules, travelling at will when between jobs, coming and going according to his needs and desires, and exploring relationships as his fancy led. Now all that had to change, but it was not easy for him to accommodate himself to the demands of ordinary family life with two babies and a wife who was completely ill-suited to household duties and the chores of motherhood. Accordingly, nannies were engaged, cooks hired and housekeepers entrusted with daily tasks. Those additions and the concomitant rise in household expenses ought to have brought some measure of discipline and order to their lives – but they did not, for no matter how many servants were in attendance, it was up to Victoria to coordinate, organise, plan and clarify what she required. Any and all of this was beyond her, so those duties fell to Alan – when he was there to dispatch them.

In the years to come, he tried to supply in his own active responsibility what was lacking in his wife's. 'He also tried, from a practical point of view, to ease Victoria's creative frustration,' as Martin added. 'There were nice homes and clothes, lovely meals out, special family holidays, au pairs, just about everything, including considerable financial help and, later, medical and nursing assistance for Victoria's mother when she was seriously ill.'

While Alan continued with *Hamlet* early that winter, Simon Gray was writing a play called *Butley*, to be directed by Harold Pinter. Alan arrived for the first discussion with the two men – 'and he felt an instantaneous connection and rapport to the person of Ben Butley,' as Simon recalled. 'He was also late, flustered and embarrassed, because there had been some trouble with Victoria.' Alan remembered that meeting too: 'I loved that part from the first day – most of all, because Simon's language is so wonderful.'

In May, discussions and preparations for *Butley* were briefly interrupted when Alan travelled to the Cannes Film Festival, where *The Go-Between* was awarded the Grand Prix. Away from the press and the crowds, in the hills above the Mediterranean at the Colombe d'Or Hotel in Vence, Alan met the theatrical agent Rosalind Chatto. Also present was Michael Linnit, the agent for Julie Christie and Joseph Losey. Later, Chatto and Linnit formed a partnership and, at Alan's request, they represented all his projects exclusively after Judy Scott-Fox relocated to work in Los Angeles. For the rest of his life, Alan counted Ros Chatto and Michael Linnit among his good friends, just as he did their able staff colleague Lucy Robinson. 'I recall very clearly our first meeting that spring,' said Ros Chatto. 'He was carrying a large basket with two babies in it!' Victoria, who avoided stars, crowds and unfamiliar people, was not present.

Final preparations for *Butley* began in London on 7 June. 'I spent the first three weeks of rehearsal kind of bumbling and stumbling around,' Alan acknowledged. 'But then, in the fourth week, it just happened, it came to me.' The action of the play – with which Alan was forever associated if not identified among theatregoers – occurs in a single day, when his wife and his male lover decide to leave university professor Ben Butley. With corrosive and perceptive humour as a defence mechanism, the dishevelled, dispirited and self-destructive Butley alienates everyone as he puffs cigarettes, swills whisky and hurls abuse.

'He's unsympathetic,' Alan said of the character, 'but he's so eloquent, witty and outrageously funny that he becomes sympathetic to a degree.' When Alan told Noël Coward that his agent, Judy Scott-Fox, had urged him to decline the role because of Butley's remarks against women, Coward asked, 'Have you told her to put on her brogues and go for a sharp walk?'

Alan knew that stage roles did not come better than Butley. 'You can go to town with Butley – he's a complete extrovert, wonderfully written. It's a gift to be asked to play that character. Sometimes you know you've met the part, you know that you're right, you know you're in tune and really on to the centre of the part. You have to work quite hard, even when you're excited about it and can see how it should be, to find your own way to it.' As usual, he had few peers in his ability to discuss the nature of his craft and the conjunction of actor and role, without sounding orotund or coyly self-conscious.

Onstage for virtually every moment, Alan was pitched into the most taxing role of his career, with Gray's swift verbal tropes requiring meticulous delivery and flawless timing. 'This is what you become an actor for,' he said as the play began previews in Oxford on 5 July. When it came to the West End on the fourteenth, a few critics found fault with the play, but the response to the star was unanimously favourable.

The opening night, on 14 July 1971 at the Criterion Theatre, London, was plagued with a few technical hiccups that brought a moment of panic to Gray and Pinter. A moment into the play, Butley enters and reaches to turn on a desk lamp that is not supposed to operate – and had not done so during previews. But that night it did. From the rear of the stalls, playwright and director glanced at each other and expected to see Alan's confusion onstage. But as Simon Gray recalled, 'You could count on him in a tricky situation, on the stage as in life . . . He scarcely gave [the lamp] a glance as he Butleyed to the other desk,' where a second lamp, which was indeed expected to work, came on brightly even before he touched it – and when he did so, promptly went off. Alan muttered with irritation, as if this were standard procedure in a college office building; the audience laughed; and the star, never stepping out of character, turned the moment into a bit of brilliant farcical business.

For Harold Pinter, the role was 'a remarkable creation and Alan Bates gave the performance of a lifetime. He took such relish in acting, and he had such a great heart and possessed true dignity – but he could also be mischievous and wicked in a very droll way.' Simon Gray added: 'It was his merriness, I think, that marked him out from anybody I've ever known – his laughter made you feel instantly better. A generous, forthcoming laugh that demanded company.' Years later, he would always remember Alan's 'mischief and the appetite, the exuberance'.

Butley settled in for a long run. 'I find it much more tiring than playing Hamlet,' he admitted. 'I don't even get a breather. In *Hamlet*, you have time offstage for a good rest – and even when he's onstage, he isn't really doing all that much [!], just lolling about. But not Butley – he's up there and at it for the whole time. I shed pounds every night from the sheer hard slog of it all, and it takes me three hours after every performance just to get back to earth.'

There were compensations in addition to his splendid notices. Alan's fee of £250 weekly in London was augmented by a bonus of ten per cent of gross box-office receipts, and when the play transferred to the United States in the autumn of 1972, he went, too, and received

$3,000 each week and yet another ten per cent of the receipts. Inland Revenue subtracted a healthy share, but Cyrano Productions was able to squirrel away some considerable profit. For himself Alan bought a green BMW and for Victoria an orange Volkswagen, but she always preferred an old bicycle.

That summer of 1971, while Alan was busy with a solid hit in the West End and toting a pair of infants in and out of carry baskets, Victoria suddenly announced that she needed time away from London, from England, from daily duties she found increasingly tiresome. With that, off she went for lectures and seminars at the Yeats International Summer School in Sligo, Ireland, where she also hoped to write more poetry. There, for two weeks in August, she shared quarters and formed a lifelong friendship with the writer Niema Ash, a Yeats scholar who remembered Victoria's 'haunting solitary beauty, her face mobile, vulnerable, her eyes surprised, slightly frightened, her mouth controlling a quiver, her body alert, slender, waif-like. She gave the impression of a doe poised to flee.' She was shy, Niema added, but she observed everything.

'But she didn't seem to have any special interest in Yeats,' Niema continued, 'and I never really understood why she came there – except that she said she wanted to get away from London.' At lectures and seminars, Victoria frequently made wistful observations and asked provocative questions. She was a 'strange blend of shy and strident', with a 'mischievous glint in her eye when she knew she was being impossible. She was enigmatic and unpredictable.'

Nor did Victoria say a word about Alan. But one day Niema noticed a postcard she thought was addressed to her but that was destined for Victoria: 'I had lunch with Noël Coward and Zsa Zsa Gabor, who was passing through London' ran the message, with the signature 'Alan'. Victoria then identified him and told Niema, 'I'd rather you didn't tell anyone – I'd rather people knew me as myself and not as Alan Bates's wife.' Awkward, careless of dress and appearance, utterly without glamour, Victoria was nothing like a film star's wife. 'She swore me to secrecy,' said Niema. 'She wanted to be her own person, and so everyone thought she was single. After all, she was on her own.'

'How come you're married to Alan Bates?' Niema presently enquired.

'Accident' was the reply – then came an astonishing remark: 'I didn't want to get married, I never intended getting married. I'm very jealous of my freedom and my privacy. Besides, we come from very different worlds. I didn't like his world, didn't fit into it – and didn't want to.'

When she learned that Victoria had two babies, Niema asked how she could leave them behind for Alan to supervise alone. 'Alan has to learn that just because he's an actor, he gets no special privileges,' replied Victoria flatly. 'He has to learn to change the nappies and care for the babies.'

Returning to London, Victoria found that Alan had engaged a personal secretary – a meticulous, discreet and dedicated woman named Rosemary Geddes, who had worked in the same capacity for Vivien Leigh and for the writer-director Val Guest. 'Victoria was for the most part very nice with me,' Rosemary recalled, 'but she was difficult for most people to be with for any length of time – especially those in the public eye. She seemed to resent them.' That was precisely the impression of Niema Ash, who lived nearby in Hampstead. 'Victoria could be very strident, and she gave Alan a really hard time. She found fault with his friends, especially actors, and more than once I said, "Victoria, don't talk that way – for Alan's sake."'

Perhaps better than anyone, Martin Bates understood the dynamics of the Bates marriage, which was already unravelling:

> It was a problem for Vicky to be married to a man who was so famous. She tried to be assertive and independent, but she hadn't the psychological and emotional equipment to do so. And she was frustrated at not having an outlet for her writing, while Alan was going from strength to strength, having such success in his career. She was always unpredictable – charming and stimulating one moment but withdrawn, silent and reclusive the next – and you never knew where you were with her. She was clever, she read a great deal, she was fascinated by alternative philosophies and religions and the latest in nutritional fads and so forth. There were enjoyable and hilarious moments with her, but things gradually descended into absolute turmoil, and the whole family atmosphere was rocked.
>
> Alan, meanwhile, had the pressure of supporting his family and pursuing his career – travelling, making films, selecting plays

– and he thrived on the energy and liveliness of it all. But poor Vicky's childhood had been very unlike Alan's and ours, and her background – plus her own frustrations and confusions – gradually made life a real roller coaster for everyone.

Unfortunately, the worst twists and turns of the ride were yet to come.

9

Pernicious Interpretations

Beginning about two years after Alan Bates married Valerie 'Victoria' Ward, relatives and friends started to notice that the marriage endured only because he wanted desperately to maintain the image of a respectable middle-class family life and because he felt an obligation to her. 'We were highly incompatible,' he said later, and the terms of that incongruity were many. For one thing, they both desired male companionship.

Friends like Niema Ash admired Alan greatly. 'He was really one of the finest, most gentle and generous people I've ever met. I often marvelled at the patient way he dealt with Victoria's unbridled unconventionality, her wild roughshod manner, her distrust of his fellow actors, her disdain for what she considered their indulged, ego-inflated lives, her exasperating principles, her loathing of what she considered middle-class pampering.' For all that, Victoria could, occasionally, still be warm and amusing with a few friends she trusted, and by common consent she was never dull and sometimes even capable of interesting conversation. But those times grew increasingly infrequent.

Elizabeth Grant, who also lived in the Vale of Health near Ashdown House, agreed. She befriended Alan and Victoria during this time and remained a strong support and ally in the years to come. Highly educated, perceptive and sensitive, Elizabeth had a daughter the same age as the Bates twins.

We women were still in the depths of our hippiedom in the early 1970s, with our long dresses, our interest in everything alternative, our obsession with astrology, our talk of living in pyramids, of organic food, macrobiotics and so forth – we went to some dreadful vegetarian restaurants where everything tasted like mud. No one embraced it all more than Vicky. She was very bright, and she took courses in everything from reflexology to iridology. She was also totally non-materialistic and seemed only interested in people's spiritual worth. But she was strange: I recall seeing Victoria with her twin babies, looking miserable and unable to come to grips with the chores of motherhood.

Elizabeth also recalled that Alan

joined in our excursions sometimes, if he wasn't away working or out seeing some man. That part of life must have been hard for Victoria. She was aware of it, I'm certain, but she never spoke of it – after all, she must also have been aware that she was not the perfect wife. When I visited her, she was sitting with bowls of dirty clothes in bucketsful of water – she didn't believe in soap. She just couldn't manage things, and eventually everything went terribly wrong. For quite a while, for example, she fed the boys nothing but beans, and they were miserable, just miserable.

Marie also saw how 'the children suffered a lot. Victoria didn't know how to feed them – she had such strange ideas about eating certain types of food.' As Niema recalled,

the house was a mess, and her theories about fads were astonishing. She once went to a food guru, and he said, 'If you eat an onion, you have to eat the peels!' More than once, the boys were fed carrots for a week. And when they came over to our house, they were so happy just for a bowl of soup. I don't know how she lived in chaos. A chair was piled high with clothes, and then she said she couldn't find the boys' shirts.

However much Victoria said she loved Tristan and Benedick, however often she insisted that they were at the centre of her life and believed that was so, Niema (among others) thought that 'she always did exactly what she wanted'. With no childhood experience of a caring mother,

Victoria had nothing on which to draw and perhaps saw her own odd style as far superior to anything else.

By 1972 Victoria's ideas of what constituted indulgence and pampering extended to the notion that it was henceforth unacceptable to engage hired help, whom she forthwith and forever dismissed; she did not, however, assume the basic tasks of housekeeping, cleaning or cooking beyond a nearly imperceptible minimum. Laundry accumulated everywhere at Ashdown House; the refrigerator contained stale vegetables and leftovers; the bathroom was left untended. Things improved temporarily when Alan had time for these chores; if, as often, he was away working, the surroundings in which she and the children lived were perilously filthy, and food was scarce and based on fads to which she was committed but which were insufficient for toddlers. The fact that the boys survived at all was remarkable.

For his part, Alan took occasional opportunities to absent himself from it all. According to Simon, 'Although he felt responsible for it, the marriage was not really part of his world. The children were, of course, part of his world – he adored them – but not the marriage.'

Weary as always of spending too much time in the same role, Alan also did not want to become 'inflexible, unreal, tricksy [*sic*] while superficially giving the same performance'. Hence Alan played Ben Butley for only half of its thirteen-month run in the West End. 'In some ways, perhaps I loved that part too much – I couldn't bear to let it go.' But in February 1972 he did, bequeathing it to Alec McCowen when a lucrative offer came along for him to appear in another film under John Frankenheimer's direction. Made in France, *L'Impossible Objet* indeed turned out to be just that – the nearly incomprehensible story of a married English writer living in France, whose fantasy life of hypersexual high jinks may or may not have a correspondence in reality.

Tangled and burdened with a treacly score by Michel Legrand, the film apparently hoped to replicate something of Alain Resnais's 1961 movie, *L'Année dernière à Marienbad* (*Last Year at Marienbad*), but *The Impossible Object* lacked that picture's bold obfuscations (which, for many spectators then and later, were somehow successful where Frankenheimer was not). Potential distributors were unimpressed with the director's finished product and, after a few screenings in Spain in 1973, the picture disappeared.

But that season Frankenheimer made interesting comments to a journalist:

> The leading character in this film is very close to Alan person-
> ally – so is Butley, and in this picture Alan gives the same kind
> of performance as he gave in that play. In *Impossible Object*, you
> have to feel sorry for the character, you have to like him –
> women in the audience have to like him. I need an actor with
> every nuance: comedy, pathos, the chaos of everyday life and no
> self-pity whatever. I saw all these things in *Butley*, and when I
> found the script for *Impossible Object*, I realised that only Bates
> could play it.

Off the record the director went further, citing Alan's resentment that film audiences did not really know who he was: he desperately wanted more recognition. 'He has been upset about the fact that people don't remember him. He may still be shy in interviews, but Bates is determined to come out from behind his own shadow and bask in the fame that's eluded him for so long.' Martin had a lifetime of insight. As Alan's career intensified, he said,

> shrewdness was not only evident in his choice of projects but
> in his choice of career contacts – he was very good at what's
> called 'networking', putting himself about, making himself known
> and popular. I remember him saying to me, '*Use* people, Martin
> – *use* people!' This sounds hard and ruthless, but I don't think
> he was. He simply meant to put oneself and one's work out
> there, to *sell* yourself, and to recognise when to move on. That
> was the way of the world [for him] – the route of ambition.

Back home, Victoria continued to insist that acting was 'no big deal – anyone can do it – even I can do it'. Finally he agreed to let her try and perhaps to challenge her. After acquiring performance rights to D. H. Lawrence's 1912 short story 'Second-Best', he produced a short film of it at home in Derbyshire, engaging Stephen Dartnell as director. The sixty-minute picture, shot mostly in the picturesque countryside, starred Alan and Victoria in the unresolved story of a woman who chooses a simple countryman as 'second best' when she is rejected by her more sophisticated first choice. Broadcast on Dutch television and shown at the London Film Festival, *Second Best* was never released to theatres.

In late September 1972, Alan hired a nanny, packed up the family and took them along for the American tour of *Butley*, to which he had finally consented (as a news correspondent noted) 'after months of driving competing Broadway producers up the wall with his refusal to decide on a firm commitment'. With his salary of $3,000 weekly, he could afford to lease a spacious, well-appointed house at 322 East Fiftieth Street – which, to the owner's chagrin, even the nanny could not keep tidy, given the presence of a pair of playful and undisciplined boys and a mother disinclined to lift a towel or send out laundry. Victoria did, however, read poetry and good literature to Tris and Ben, insisting they could comprehend far beyond their two-year-old aptitude.

Alan occasionally absented himself from the family in order to enjoy a few hours in the company of one attractive young man or another – a pattern of which, wrongly, he hoped Victoria had no inkling. As if for compensation, he was eager to introduce her to his closest American friends. 'The first time I met her was when Alan brought her to Quogue [Long Island],' recalled Arthur Laurents. 'She was wearing bobby socks and sandals and carrying a guitar, and I remember thinking, "What are we in for?" But I liked her. I felt sorry for her, too. I feel that gay men who marry are terribly unfair to women. I loved Alan dearly, and our friendship lasted forty years, but sometimes he didn't think what he was doing. It was really very unfair.'

Butley began a successful Broadway engagement on 31 October and continued to 24 February 1973, the term date to which Alan had agreed; there were fourteen previews and 135 regular performances, most of them sold out. The *New York Times* review was typical: Simon Gray had written a play with 'astonishing compassion' and 'considerable adroitness – a literate and literary comedy with a heart', and Alan Bates was 'nonchalantly superlative'.

The producers insisted that he make himself available for promotional interviews, which he always disliked but for which he sat with undiluted courtesy. Admitting that he found interviews 'sticky', he resolutely refused to discuss his family and his private life – indeed, why should he have done? – but he admitted the need for publicity: 'I can't have it both ways, but the thing to do is play yourself down' and emphasise the work at hand. He would not, however, discuss Ben Butley's sexual orientation with the press, and he tried to avoid the subject in private. 'Alan sat in our living room during the run of *Butley*, insisting the character wasn't gay,' recalled Arthur Laurents. 'But this didn't make sense and we told him it didn't. Talk about denial!'

At first, Simon Gray did not agree with this assessment. 'I could never understand the assumption that Butley is homosexual,' he said at the time of the London and New York premières.

> He sleeps with women, though his closest relationships are obviously achieved with men. But the assumption that he and Joey became lovers strikes me as extraordinary. All I mean is that there are many ways of being attracted and wanting to possess, and the usual sexual way seems to me the least interesting, though for Joey it's the most important, because he's a homosexual and wants to be. The things that Butley wants are far more intricate. It's certainly in some ways bound to be sexual, though the sexual act itself is quite irrelevant. In a real sense I think he loves Joey, but that doesn't mean he has to have slept with him.

But at Butley's psychological centre there is indeed a cauldron of sexual ambiguity.

'You slept with her,' says Joey of Butley's wife. 'You sleep with women.'

'Not when I can help it,' Butley replies.

This exchange, wrote Simon Gray in the published text of Butley in 2002, 'was cut from the production the night before we opened [in 1971]. I am re-instating it because it now seems to me a passage that . . . conveys a great deal of useful information about Butley's relationship with Joey and about his sexual nature.' The dialogue occurs a few moments after a long conversation about homosexuality.

For all his understanding of the role, it is surprising that offstage, and even among friends, Alan refused to acknowledge the compelling and poignant dramatic confusions of Ben Butley, who is more inclined to sexual games with young men than to a stable relationship with a woman. In this regard, it is interesting to note that in the first draft of an article prepared for *Time* the following year, the London researcher reported the well-known affair between Bates and Wyngarde. 'When he married Victoria, she changed him,' the draft continued, 'and now he is completely involved with his family and devoted to domestic life.'

According to none other than Martin Bates, this was sheer nonsense. 'No!' wrote Martin in the margin of the *Time* essay he saved, adding: 'Alan was bisexual. He confided this to me in 1965 – a confidence I always kept. However, very rarely, a passing reference to the fact *was* published in articles.' For Martin,

> Alan's orientation gave him a finer understanding of human nature, enabling him to play so superbly and sensitively such parts as Guy Burgess (in *An Englishman Abroad*), Alfred Redl (in *A Patriot for Me*) and some of the Simon Gray characters. But Alan wanted [his privacy]. How he kept much of his 'switch-back' personal life private, I'll never know – he either had a talent for keeping the media at bay, or they respected him too much to probe too deeply.

'At one point,' Alan told a journalist, 'I really hated [Ben Butley] – but I always loved doing the play. He really is a pig. He's intoler-able, yet you do like him. He watches himself losing his grip. He watches his own decline – and he enjoys it. He hits out at everyone, thinking he's destroying other people, when in fact he is isolating himself out of fear. I feel his despair more now, and that makes me like him more.' As for any similarity to himself: 'I don't deal with it as he does – well, in the end, I do.' And with that, he perhaps revealed more than he intended.

After the final Broadway performance, the Bates family left New York and travelled across Canada by train ('I don't like flying,' Alan admitted), then continued down to San Francisco, where the produc-tion was mounted at the Curran Theatre from 6 through 17 March 1973. The box-office receipts were disappointing, despite the concur-rent announcement from New York that Gray, Bates and Hayward Morse (as Joey) were nominated for Tony Awards. Then, while performing in a nearly empty Shubert Theatre in Los Angeles on Sunday afternoon, 25 March, it was announced in New York that Alan won the Tony as best actor of the year, as he had been awarded the Drama Desk Award for outstanding performance of 1972–1973.

Did he revel in the praise and citations whose absence he had once rued, as Frankenheimer had claimed? 'It's nice – in fact, it's pretty disappointing if they don't recognise you [with an award]. Then you always feel that what you've done accounts for nothing. But I better watch the way I answer such a question. I might give the impression of being vain,' and the proper impression counted almost as much as an award.

'I don't look at praise as just for ego,' he continued. 'You always need people to tell you how good you are –' and not only the critics and the public, but colleagues, too. Sheila Ballantine was acting in the West End during *Butley*, and Alan wanted her to come to his matinée, scheduled two hours after her play began. 'You could come out directly at the end of yours,' he told her, 'then run down Shaftesbury Avenue, cross Piccadilly Circus, pop into the Criterion Theatre and see twenty minutes of my performance!' This was virtually impossible, she replied: 'I told him I went through a lot in my play, I'm stabbed horribly in the end, I look terrible, I've got on a frightful grey wig, and I could not come out into the street that way – no!' Alan could not understand her reasoning.

Notwithstanding his exhaustion after months of performing the demanding role – 'I'm ready to have it over,' he told a reporter that spring – *Butley* was still the favourite play of his career. 'It comes closest to being the perfect part,' as he said years later. 'Everything came together – good script, good cast, and I really enjoyed myself.' By mid-May, Alan, Victoria and the boys were back in London, and at once he began rehearsals with Pinter, Jessica Tandy and a new cast for the film version of *Butley*, which occupied them from 28 May to 2 July.

Although they worked together several more times and the friendship only deepened with the years, Simon Gray felt that Alan's moment with *Butley* was the great highlight of the actor's entire professional life. 'His career actually peaked with *Butley*, and everything after was a kind of holding operation. He thought it was the beginning, but it was in fact a moment of complete fulfilment that never came back. I watched his career with great affection, but the moment, the part and the man never quite coincided again. There was always the hope, but –'

That autumn, after many months during which he could or would not decide to accept the invitation, Alan finally agreed to make his debut with the Royal Shakespeare Company at Stratford-upon-Avon.

'It was always a torturous process as to whether he would accept an offer or not,' recalled his agent Michael Linnit.

> There was no such thing as a quick answer. He delayed responding until the very last moment, and often he tried to extend the deadline for his reply. With the serious offers, which came along all the time, this was not mere indifference: he read scripts, discussed them, asked whether he had to travel, how long he would be on location, whether he could return for weekends and so forth – and this was before any artistic assessment of the project! Alan was always very elusive and altogether hesitant to give a reply one way or the other, and I think he enjoyed this gentle torture – one knew it was a game, and you played it with him because he was really in every other way a marvellous client and a superb friend.

Alan had the role of Petruchio in Clifford Williams's idiosyncratic production of *The Taming of the Shrew* at Stratford that summer. Also in the cast was Nickolas Grace. 'I had met Alan briefly backstage during the West End run of *Butley*,' Nickolas recalled, 'and of course I was thrilled to be working with him in a Shakespeare play. He became a great friend and a brilliant mentor, and I taught him a few stretching exercises that helped him in this hyperactive production.'

The Clifford Williams concept of *Shrew* was a critical disaster but a commercial success, for he conceived the play almost as street-theatre entertainment – a gymnast's fantasy and a box of tricks, with every conceivable joke and gag and a terrific lot of business that included leaning at a forty-five-degree angle every time the word 'Pisa' was mentioned. Actors made entrances and exits by turning cartwheels or somersaults, and there was liberal use of food, tossed across the stage and even floating down on parachutes from above, as, for example, when Petruchio intoned, 'Will't please your honour taste of these conserves?' – a cue for the players to throw about all manner of fruits and vegetables. 'I hated being in it,' Alan said flatly.

Not the least reason for this reaction was a fracas caused one evening by a spectator who, as the food-throwing erupted, stood up and shouted repeatedly, 'Pernicious interpretation! Rubbish!' As the discomfort of cast and audience grew, Alan stepped forward and called to the man, 'Fuck off!' After a moment of awkward silence, the man

loudly rejoined, 'And the same to you, sir!' Somehow the performance continued, and the press gleefully reported that Alan Bates had
taken to swearing at the audience from the stage of the RSC.

There was, however, an important development offstage that
summer, when Alan and Nickolas (who was twenty-five) became, in
the latter's words, 'very close and very loving, in an intense affair that
was one of the most important relationships of my life'. This was
facilitated by Alan's leasing of a cottage in Stratford.

Over the course of almost six months, a deep intimacy was formed
between the two men, to the point where Nickolas also became a
good friend to Victoria and the boys. 'Alan was at ease,' Nickolas
continued,

> as long as he pretended – and he insisted on pretending – that
> our relationship was not what it was, was not disclosed to or
> evident to others. He was absolutely terrified of me saying or
> hinting anything about us, or talking about it with anyone at
> all. He seemed to be afraid that I would be so much in love
> with him and so committed to him that I would try to break
> up his marriage – but nothing could have been further from
> my mind, and he knew it. He was my hero and I loved him
> greatly – and I told him that I would never have jeopardized
> or threatened that part of his life.

Alan always remained terrified of anything like public disclosure
about his intimacies with men, invariably denying, even with his
lovers, that there was even a homosexual component in his nature. 'I
told him labels didn't matter, but that we must be who we are,'
Nickolas recalled years later. 'But he could not accept that. Intellectually
and professionally, he was a liberated man – but not otherwise. In a
sense, there were two Alans – one was free and happy, and at such
times he took me to meet his family in Derby, where we had lovely
weekends. But at other times he was reserved and frightened, whis-
pering to me, "Don't say this . . . don't say that . . ."' If they travelled
by car together, 'he made me lie down in the back – he didn't want
me to be seen with him. That was an indication of the fear that he
had. Sometimes in the presence of others, he would break into a little
French conversation with me – not considering that other people
might understand!'

Martin recognised an additional component. Alan, he felt, was

> so obsessed with working and yet was so attracted to other
> people romantically and physically that he suffered genuine
> dilemmas and inner struggles. He was often lonely in life. This
> is not to say that he didn't have some happy, loving and mean-
> ingful relationships – he did, but they didn't and *couldn't* last.
> And like so many actors, he was a bit in love with himself!

At the same time, Nickolas was solicitous for Victoria:

> I encouraged Alan to tell her what she certainly knew – about
> his relationships outside the marriage, which in any case seemed
> very much over by 1973. But he refused to do so. His back-
> ground required him to make a conventional decision for a
> conventional life, and he may well have thought this would
> always be possible for him, that he could go on putting people
> into various compartments. But he didn't consider what it would
> lead to – it was something of an idyllic dream world, that things
> could go on forever as they had before, uninterrupted.

It was the universal opinion of those who knew him that Alan was
a firm, loyal and unwavering friend to a remarkable array of men and
women. But he was not made for marriage – nor perhaps for any
permanent intimacy, though he protested otherwise – and he was an
inconstant and anxious lover who invariably fled from the implications of commitment. 'He never wanted to be alone,' as Arthur Laurents
said – an observation shared by many. 'But the minute someone got
too close to him, he ran and the relationship ended. Of course there
were exceptions with a few friends, if he felt really safe. He was
comfortable and secure with Tom and me, and so our friendship not
only lasted but got stronger.'

So just as he had done earlier with Paul Taylor, Alan precipitated
the rupture with Nickolas Grace. 'It's been very nice to have known
you,' Alan told him with astonishing coolness one day, 'and I'm sure
I'll see you around in London' – as if they had been but polite
colleagues on a project, or fellow travellers on a journey. But Nickolas
had taken their relationship very seriously. 'Suddenly Alan ended it
and, for a long time, he wouldn't even let me see Vicky and the boys.'

With enormous effort Nickolas tried to get on with his life and career. Invited to travel abroad with the RSC, he contacted Alan, who would not talk to him. After arriving in New York, Nickolas went down with a serious bout of bronchial influenza, and his condition became ever more alarming. Ill and confined to his room, he endured what he later called a time of great '*cri de coeur* – I performed in the play, returned quickly to my hotel and went through a kind of breakdown.'

Slowly his health improved and, after six weeks in America, Nickolas returned to England, where he recuperated with his parents and in time pursued an impressive career as actor and director onstage, screen and television. By the summer of 1974 he was able to ring Alan to suggest they share a meal and secure, at least, a true friendship. 'He admitted that he had acted very badly and we did go on, as friends [not lovers].' With that, and to his everlasting credit, Nickolas Grace forever became (thus Benedick Bates, Martin Bates and Joanna Pettet among others) an enormously attentive and generous friend to Alan and his entire family, in good times and bad.

Negotiating the rocky shoals of intimate relationships, as well as the choppy currents of life with Victoria, Alan took refuge in a busy and demanding career. In early 1974 he began rehearsals for *Life Class*, an ambitious, discursive play about art and life by David Storey, author of *In Celebration*; Lindsay Anderson once again was the director. The production (for which Alan received a mere £50 weekly) opened at the Royal Court Theatre on 9 April and transferred to the Duke of York's Theatre on 4 June.

As an artist dry of inspiration but damp with aesthetic theories, Alan portrayed an unhappily married man in the throes of a complete artistic, mental and moral decline, a teacher whose students are more interested in the nude model of their life class than the pursuit of their art. 'Lindsay Anderson taught me more than most – he showed me that acting wasn't to do with power games or insecurity or trying to prove anything. It's to do with knowing yourself, not hiding behind technique or disguises.'

With Alan as exponent and the play misidentified as a thesis drama, some viewers and critics considered *Life Class* as a dark riff on *Butley*, but the works differed more than stylistically. Whereas Gray's Ben Butley is embroiled in an emotional crisis and his epigrammatic statements are punctuated with acerbic wit, Storey's Allott drowns in an artistic predicament whose allusively expressed confusions are merely theoretical. (Gray had been a university teacher of literature and Storey an artist before they turned to full-time writing careers.) In any case this was not an easy work for the cast – perhaps most notably for Rosemary Martin as the class model, required to remain nude onstage for the evening. It was a different kind of challenge for Alan, who was simultaneously exhausted and exhilarated each evening by the play's complex verbal interplay.

'This was not an easy role for anyone to play,' recalled David.

> But Alan was like a tightrope walker, and he achieved an extra-ordinarily refined balance. He not only projected the part – he physically defined it by a remarkable choice of movements around the stage, which he selected and maintained once he had settled on them. And just as he had done during *In Celebration*, Alan performed the magical feat of drawing all the actors into a kind of bond during the run of the play. Some of them were unknown young actors, who were of course especially pleased when Alan casually and without affectation formed everyone into a kind of friendly confederacy.

Life with Victoria, however, had no such emotional satisfaction. Occasionally, for example, Alan took the boys and their mother for a visit to Derby – anything in an effort to include her in his work or family life. But Victoria was more and more perverse. 'She could affect an innocent look and a childlike manner,' Martin recalled, 'but then came the provocative arguments, when she turned more and more nasty in expressing her opinions. "Don't be sucked into it," Alan warned us and often one just had to ignore her, which was not an easy thing to do.'

Martin recalled how swiftly Victoria shifted her approach to things – as once, when he drove them all to the train station in Derby. 'There was a ticket-taker at an old-fashioned gate, and we went to the platform to see them off. But then Vicky decided she didn't want to go – she went through the gate, came back, went through again and returned another time. It was maddening, and it literally developed into a kind of crazy dance as she said, "I can't go . . . oh, all right, I'll go . . . but I don't want to go . . ." And there were the twins, while she embarrassed Alan by performing this little attention-getting scene. The kids were unhappy and he didn't know what to do – there were many such moments. He could verbally outsmart her and he often did, but then he always had a certain clarity about her and felt pity, because she was really her own worst victim.'

Such incidents seemed more and more to be combinations of ornery self-expression, acted out in an attempt to salvage an identity from a dreadful childhood; of immature, neurotic displays of temper; and of taking revenge.

It is perhaps important to stress that there was no question of frank malice on either side. Victoria had been irredeemably bruised by her early experience, then she found herself trapped in a situation she once thought she desired but eventually despised. 'Our mother said that most women in Vicky's position would have loved it,' Martin remembered. '"What's wrong with her?" Mum muttered. But Vicky was being rebellious about a situation that had nothing to do with her world. And Mum learned how to cope, how to choose the right remark to put Vicky in her place – but very gently.'

Alan, on the other hand, had once believed that a woman he saw as an attractive, intelligent and complaisant wife would be the right one as mother for his sons and public companion to his image. But in fact he had chosen a marriage that could not possibly be successful and this gave him the excuse he needed to absent himself more and more from its demands. 'I think', said Martin, 'that Alan enjoyed a touch of drama, provocation and abrasiveness in relationships.' That, after all, is part of the actor's daily equipment: in a sense, he had to put some drama (or even melodrama) into life so that he could draw on it in his art. It is not likely that this was a conscious programme.

'More and more, she couldn't come to terms with having the babies in her life,' according to Nickolas. 'And she never really wanted to be known as Mrs Alan Bates – but I told her that's what she was. And the more he tried to encourage her interests, the more she gave up on everything.' When that happened, her behaviour could become even more bizarre. Once, when Nickolas was invited to join Alan and Victoria for supper with Lindsay Anderson during the run of *Life Class*, she crawled beneath the dining table – and remained there for the balance of the evening. To cope with this, everyone's subtlest acting abilities were required in full complement.

★   ★   ★

After the closing of *Life Class*, the filming of *In Celebration* and a day spent recording some bits of voice-over narration for a biblical television drama (*The Story of Jacob and Joseph*), there was an offer of $35,000 to work in Munich, in a drearily unfunny movie called *Royal Flash*, that was supposed to be a comedy but failed. 'I was knocked out from filming *In Celebration* all day and playing in *Life Class* in the evening,' Alan said just after completing the assignment, 'and it was . . . kind of fun jumping into a nineteenth-century white costume and fencing. But I've honestly forgotten what the story is.' As did audiences: *Royal Flash* cannot be called the zenith of Richard Lester's directorial career.

In his absence, Alan asked Conrad Monk to look in on the family.

> He often rang me to say he was off to do a film. I took Victoria out shopping or for lunch, and visited the boys – but if I invited her to dinner with friends, she usually arrived unwashed and barefoot, even in wintertime, and with her guitar slung over her shoulder. She was bright, but she had awful mood swings: sometimes she spoke cheerfully with me, but at other times she said nothing. Unfortunately, the children suffered from her negligence.

Evidently planned as a satire on swashbuckling military-adventure tales like *The Three Musketeers*, *Royal Flash* was poorly constructed and crudely edited – a confused parody of Ruritanian romance and bumbling spies, but without an atom of humour, much less a coherent narrative. From the first day, Alan had problems with his senseless (indeed, unnecessary) minor role, which he may well have performed for easy money. 'He's very fast and works quickly – sometimes too quickly for me,' said Alan of Richard Lester. 'A film of that kind is made under such pressure of time and money that they tend to accelerate in the making of it.'

He also resented the white suit he was forced to wear: 'It makes me look fat!' he told co-star Malcolm McDowell, who knew that 'if you wanted to be Alan's lifelong friend, you had only to say, "You look marvellous – you've lost weight!"' McDowell soon had a nickname for him: 'Bounty Bar Bates', after the candy confections Alan squirrelled away in his costumes.

Back in London, he rushed to perform roles in two hour-long television dramas by Simon Gray, filmed in the spring of 1975 and broadcast on BBC Television that October. In the first, *Plaintiffs and Defendants*, Alan appeared as a disaffected lawyer with a lacklustre marriage, a hysterical mistress and importunate clients: he enriched the play's ambiguities with a sweet-and-sour smile and a tense awareness that life does not always offer remedial alternatives to one's problems. In the second, *Two Sundays*, the characters' history moves backwards, with flashbacks suggesting an adolescent crush between the two boys whose friendship endures into manhood, whose marriages apparently prosper, and whose unspoken fears, assumptions and deceptions about past and present are obliquely but poetically explored.

Georgina Hale appeared in both teleplays and formed a friendship with Alan that lasted through collaborations to come. 'We were both always dieting, but we also sneaked off – separately – to a local sweet shop for chocolates. There were two entries to the shop, I remember, and somehow Alan and I arrived at the same moment. That's when I started calling him Bounty Bar Bates.'

Michael Lindsay-Hogg, the director of both teleplays, recalled working with Alan. 'He always took the serious things lightly and the light things seriously. He never had anything like a sense of grandeur, and he was enormously kind. If he thought some younger player was talented, for example, he was quick to promote their work.'

Meeting Victoria, Michael thought her 'very thin-skinned, troubling and troubled. The boys were playing when we all gathered at [the actress] Jean [Marsh]'s home one Sunday afternoon, and Victoria seemed not to pay much attention – she just seemed absent from the scene.' At that moment Michael noticed that Alan was not with them, 'and I went upstairs to find him deeply, profoundly asleep. This was more than a respite – sleep was an escape for him.'

Years later, Michael felt that 'there was in Alan's nature a kind of passivity, and I don't mean that in a weak or disturbed or pathological sense. I think it was connected in a very interesting way to the sense that there was something passive about his acting – he listened, he responded, he reacted, and in that lay his great power. Some tennis players are aggressive – they charge the net – while others are content to play from the back line, and Alan was for the most part like that. When he did charge the net, in his craft and maybe in life too, it was a different brand of tennis and more emotionally charged.'

In this regard Michael Lindsay-Hogg pointed to something crucial – perhaps even essential – towards understanding the genius and character of Alan Bates. This actor had a rare trait directly related to what Yardena referred to as Alan's 'playing the role that life and its circumstances gave him'. For the most part he did not (as the saying goes) take life by the throat. Instead, he let the circumstances of life lead him. This is not as unusual among the most effective actors as may be commonly thought; indeed, it may be one of the reasons why the best among them do not force themselves on a role – they let the role lead them. And they do not play *at* the part: they let the part inhabit them the way they let aspects of life get through to them, and that may be the best understanding of 'playing the part' with active passivity.

These reflections are not tangential to a consideration of Alan Bates as the most effective exponent of the work of Simon Gray, a fact both men explicitly acknowledged. It was easy for Simon Gray to indicate the reasons for his choice of Alan Bates:

> because he's the most human actor of his generation – and because any playwright would consider himself lucky to get him once, let alone four consecutive times in as many years. I recognise in his face so many faces, and there's a gorgeous vulnerability about him which is, I suppose, what I've tried to give some of my leading characters. But I've never sat down and written a script specifically for Alan. It's just that as one goes through the list of actors, one comes back to his name again and again. Besides, I think it may help a playwright and an actor to work together more than once – after a while, in rehearsal, one no longer has to finish the sentences, and you acquire a kind of intuitive understanding of each other.

Once again, Alan was astonishingly articulate in his understanding of his role in *Two Sundays* and *Plaintiffs and Defendants*: '[The character of] Peter is very much in control, albeit unfulfilled and disillusioned. But that's not the same thing as letting go. All Simon's plays seem to have the habit of looking into the reality of people's existence and saying, "This is where we are – isn't it awful?"'

By the end of his career, Alan had performed in a total of twelve works by Simon Gray – six plays, a film based on one of them, and five television dramas; of these, four were directed by Harold Pinter, who wrote six works in which Alan appeared, two of which Pinter also directed. 'I suppose the plays [Simon] writes could be called sad comedies,' Alan continued, 'but through them runs a tremendous sense of separation, of being alone, however much they may seem to be together.' Those words could fairly have described Alan's own marriage – the sort of union manqué of which Gray wrote, and which Bates lived. 'Maybe that's why I like these plays so much.'

He did not have to wait long to appear in yet another. In late spring, preparations began for Gray's *Otherwise Engaged*, which (again after previews in Oxford) opened at the Queen's Theatre on 30 July under Pinter's spare, uncluttered direction. Alan portrayed Simon Hench, a publisher who (unlike Butley) will not allow himself to be known. Apparently longing to be otherwise engaged – for enough solitude to appreciate his new recording of *Parsifal* – he is constantly entrapped by the importunate demands of others – his lodger, his unfaithful wife and his brother among them. Alan played with a keen sense of self-protection and even selfishness that somehow found ambiguous, sympathetic human notes in the character – hence he drew even more critical raves than he had received for *Butley*. The actor was, according to a typical notice, 'at his most magisterially comic, even better, deeper and funnier than in the earlier play . . . In fact, Mr Bates is terrific. It is an exquisitely judged performance.'

Cool, detached and rueful, Alan's portrait of this slightly sinister, passively manipulative but recognisably human character – the gestures punctuated by the signature Pinter pauses – suggested that this man lives in a world so hermetically sealed from feeling that he will never be as alive as any of the fictional characters he publishes. A man 'who only gives permission to little bits of life to get through', he has the sort of sanity 'that causes people to go quietly mad', as his wife says. *Otherwise Engaged*, like *Butley*, implies that some people of education and high culture miss both the point and the value of it all. In this case the play and its star deftly employed a kind of demonic voice, affirming the good by showing the dreadful state of its absence. Playwright, player and director, in other words, presented a state of chronic emotional disengagement that begged to be replaced by its opposite.

But unexpectedly and at the height of its success, Alan left the cast of *Otherwise Engaged* after six months, turning over the role to Michael Gambon, who also thrived in it: the play drew audiences for another year and a half, for a total of 1,029 performances. The reason for Alan's sudden departure in February 1976 had nothing to do with the play and everything to do with a family crisis.

10

Towards a Demi-Paradise

Harold Bates began to suffer a debilitating illness late in 1975. At the kind suggestion of Harold Pinter, who knew that Alan wanted to be closer to Derby, Laurence Olivier invited Alan to appear in the inaugural production of a drama series he was producing for independent television. Alan immediately accepted, precisely because the filming of *The Collection* (based on a 1962 Pinter play) was to be in Manchester, much closer to Derby than London, for four weeks during April and May 1976. Chatto & Linnit Ltd had prudently arranged for Alan to receive, in addition to his acting fee of £2,200, a share of the programme's worldwide royalties, which eventually brought him another £4,000.

All that year, Alan was a frequent visitor to home and hospital, arranging for his father's care, comforting Mary and effectively helping Martin and John, to whom, hitherto, most such duties fell. 'His parents were always a strong presence in his life,' according to Simon Gray, 'and he was always very much a family child, attached to them and to life in Derbyshire. That was the soil in which much of his talent was nourished.' As Harold and Mary aged, therefore, Alan wanted to be more attentive, at least as much as was allowed by his career and the situation with Victoria and the boys. Alan was pleased to see that, even during his last year, Harold somehow managed to summon strength to pick up his cello on his best days. Nickolas retained a vividly moving image of him, playing music outdoors on a beautiful summer day.

An economical hour-long teleplay, *The Collection* is a spare, witty but disturbing treatment of people suddenly caught up in suspicions of infidelity and the tangle of a gay relationship. Did the young hustler Bill (played by Malcolm McDowell), rent boy of the businessman Harry (Olivier), have an affair with Stella (Helen Mirren), wife of the jealous James (Alan)? In hands other than Pinter's, this might have been mere soap opera; here, however, the emphasis is not on what actually did or did not happen, but on what everyone has to gain or lose from what they think happened, or what they may want to have happened. The ensemble playing under Michael Apted's direction was allusive, quietly suspenseful, gravid with unspoken fears and absurdist humour; as one critic wrote, Alan was called 'the quintessential Pinter menace: if looks could kill, the rest of the cast would be dead'.

Offstage, there was yet another sort of family crisis as the marriage of Alan and Victoria reached critical mass. 'I remember that during our early childhood, my mother dressed nicely most of the time,' according to Ben, 'and I think she did when she first met my father. When she was happy, life was OK. But then there began a long, slow deterioration and even her physical appearance declined.'

It is impossible to blame the collapse of this ill-advised marriage on one side or the other – either to fault Victoria's pathetic self-absorption, which was certainly neurotic and which co-existed alongside an increasingly pathological illness, or to criticise Alan's refusal to face the consequences of his other engagements, both professional and romantic. In any case, by 1976, Victoria's loneliness and heartbreak had taken a sharp and disturbing turn: she now tormented and teased Alan mercilessly.

Instead of countering her attacks with further skirmishes, he chose retreat and decided to move back to the house he had kept in Hamilton Terrace. 'He told me later', Ben continued, 'that my mum simply became impossible to live with, and he had come to the point where he felt he didn't have to.' There was no talk of divorce and, because the boys were about to begin pre-school in Hampstead and Alan's career often took him away from London for more or less protracted periods, the decision was made to have them remain with their mother for the present.

As Ben recalled:

> It was a very mean and frugal life for my brother and me. She
> had strange ideas about what was healthy food and what wasn't,

and we were put on bizarre diets – nothing but beans for a while, then nothing but a certain organic vegetable. She wouldn't have a working television. When she became more and more depressed and detached from life, she refused to seek help – and no one forced her to – nor was she offered any kind of medication. And so the house deteriorated, things were broken and never mended, she didn't wash our clothes. My mother wouldn't have central heating, and I remember having to go to bed in a sleeping bag, my fingers shaking with cold in the winter. It was a very strange way to live.

Ros Chatto, among others, recalled that sometimes Victoria would appear at supper with the children, and their meal would be 'just a pot of cabbage, or something like that'.

When Alan was not travelling the twins spent weekends with him, raiding his refrigerator out of sheer ravenous hunger, as they often had to do when they visited Niema and other friends. 'Alan hardly ever came round to visit her or us at Lavender Cottage,' according to Ben, 'and he said later that he had no idea what was going on.' Simon Gray recalled that Alan 'often popped round and held forth, usually comically, on the state of his marriage. This was his way of dealing with it – to make it into a comedy.' When they were six and seven, the boys had no basis for comparison in life; they simply showed up at Alan's door hungry and needing a bath. Had their father taken these visits for what they were, he might not have turned it into a comedy.

Although he returned frequently to London, Alan decided to remain as much as possible near his father – hence after *The Collection* that spring, he agreed to perform in June in the Derby Playhouse production of Chekhov's *The Seagull*, which then moved to Leeds, Wilmslow and Birmingham before arriving at the Duke of York's Theatre, London for a limited engagement beginning 11 August. With perhaps a bit too much charm for the role, Alan played Trigorin, the poet with whom the capricious Nina runs off. That role was undertaken by Georgina Hale. 'I was something of a novice at Chekhov, but Alan never used his experience with, for example, Olivier's production of *Three Sisters* to tell me what to do or how to play a scene. He accepted whatever I wanted to do and he gave me breathing space.'

In several interviews that season, Alan was questioned about his intellectual analysis and interpretation of playwrights like Chekhov, but he conveyed the impression that he avoided conscious analysis and simply did what he felt worked. Well, then, what about creative affinities? 'Affinities?' he repeated, politely impatient with such high-toned talk. 'I don't know really what these things are. You have to behave the character rather than act it. It's vital that the part sits well on you, and that you don't have to reach out for it – because then you kill the lifelike quality . . . Acting is too mysterious to describe exactly. If it's anything, it's an identification with something instinctive.' Once again avoiding self-conscious, arty rhetoric about the mysteries of acting, he knew what he knew, he knew what he could do, and he did it – without trickery or fancy, self-centred showmanship.

'Not only was the pressure of Alan's work becoming more weighty for him,' as Martin said, 'but so were the pressures on [our] parents – and Alan's need to provide for fast-growing twin sons, not to say life with their very troubled mother, which was becoming badly disorganised.'

With considerable patience and understanding, Alan's Derbyshire family – as well as Victoria and the boys – were obliged to come to terms with Alan's fame, his obsession with acting and the long spells away on location. 'There were happy family gatherings in Derbyshire,' Martin recalled, 'but generally, these were troubled and stressful years. Alan did not deliberately neglect the boys, but he did feel a certain guilt about being away for long periods, especially beginning in the late 1970s.' In addition, he generously took on many of the problems of Victoria's mother, who also began to endure a series of ailments; he bought her a house in Kentish Town, furnished it, saw that she was deprived of no necessities and subsequently undertook those basic nursing duties from which many people would instinctively recoil.

Finally, after enduring a series of more paralysing strokes throughout 1976, Harold Bates died in December at the age of seventy-eight. According to Martin, their mother was once again the family's tower of strength; at seventy-two, Mary was in superb health, and she managed the final details with extraordinary grace and restraint.

On his forty-third birthday in February 1977, Alan found a torn piece of paper in his post box – a hastily written poem delivered by his wife, with the prefatory note:

Ally – happy happy birthday!
much much love
Vic

and then her lyrical present:

raindrops cling to the orchard bough
branches wet and bare of leaves
will soon sprout green and new with spring
the willow leans down to limpid pool
and the song of the birds stirs my heart again

It was just such occasional bursts of simple feeling that made Victoria's condition all the more tragic for her, for Alan, their sons and their friends: beneath the wearying eccentricities and psychological derailment was an alert and sensitive soul.

She had good reason to be in fine humour early that year, for at last she had an opportunity she had long coveted – to visit the museums and monuments of Washington DC, which she had somehow missed during her American sojourn in 1964. After the usual protracted indecision, Alan had finally agreed to appear in writer-director Paul Mazursky's film *An Unmarried Woman*, to be made entirely in New York. That would be the first of no less than four major assignments he accepted between April 1977 and May 1978 – three feature films and a seven-part television miniseries. The volume of work was crushing, but it subsidised his several homes, his high lifestyle and the expenses incurred by his wife, sons and mother-in-law. It also satisfied his professional need to be needed.

Mazursky had sent the screenplay for Alan's consideration in September 1976. 'He read it and saw he didn't come in until the story was more than half finished,' recalled Michael Linnit. 'But I convinced him that could be remedied and that it was important for him to do an American film. Otherwise American producers would not know he was on the radar – they often didn't watch foreign or British films.'

Like Michael, Simon Gray understood that 'in the United States, they knew about Peter O'Toole and Richard Burton – but not about Alan Bates. *Lawrence of Arabia* had transformed O'Toole's career, but Alan never had that kind of major international role. You can start with a great splash, as did O'Toole, but at the time it was very rare for someone to work his way up to international stardom in the movies. Most of the time actors worked their way along on the same rung.' Hence Michael's constant efforts to find important American roles for his client.

That was not always easy – not because Alan was not in demand, but because he so often temporised. In addition, as Michael emphasised, 'When he was making a film, he thought he should have been doing a classic play. And when he was doing a classic play, he thought of new films he should be doing, or that new plays were passing him by, and so on.'

In late March 1977, Victoria and the twins joined Alan on Concorde from London to Washington, where they made a whirlwind tour before heading for New York and the filming of *An Unmarried Woman* – his twenty-second feature but only his first American movie. This was the story of a vulnerable but resourceful woman, suddenly abandoned by her husband and forced to construct a new life – a character appealingly brought to life by Jill Clayburgh. Alan had the role of a handsome artist who offers a fresh perspective on and opportunity for love, a man who is virile but not macho, sexy but not domineering.

When filming began, the part had indeed, as subsequently promised by the producers, been expanded from the original screenplay – but it was then mercilessly cut for the final release and, as the *New York Times* critic noted, 'Mr Bates's role is no challenge to an exceptional actor.' His scenes did, however, provide an opportunity to show his gift for comic mimicry and, with only his expressive eyes, he made a double take the equivalent of an ironic speech. In this regard some friends often asked why Alan did not undertake more comic roles in his career. The reason may have been that he took what good things were offered; in addition, he may have feared that if he did too much comedy, his reputation as a serious actor might suffer.

With his adoring gaze, quiet assertiveness and darkly undulant voice in *An Unmarried Woman*, Alan found that he was very quickly considered a movie heart-throb in America, especially after *Playgirl* magazine included him on a motley list of the sexiest men alive, along with Calvin Klein, Woody Allen and O. J. Simpson!

Immediately after his last day's work in New York in late May, Alan gathered up his brood, returned to England, visited his mother in Derby, then hurried down to North Devon at the end of June for four weeks of work. He had often spoken of his preference for a wide variety of roles, and that of the unstable Charles Crossley in Jerzy Skolimowski's mostly incoherent picture, *The Shout*, certainly filled the bill – it was the story of a man with a shriek so powerful it could be deadly, a feat of magic he supposedly learned in the Australian outback. Whether the director intended a horror story, a social metaphor or something else was a challenge to the cast and to audiences. The picture was eminently forgettable, and Alan's portrait of full-blown wackiness seems at least partly tongue-in-cheek. As he said, 'I have been in rubbish, as there was the matter of school fees.'

The weeks in Devon had one social benefit, however: the sealing of a lifelong friendship with his London neighbour, Elizabeth Grant, who happened to be on holiday there with her daughter. As she recalled, there was a moment when Alan seemed to want more than a platonic relationship with her, but she wisely declined that complication; instead, he gained her trust forever after, and he often benefited from her sympathetic understanding of the thorniest aspects of his life.

> I really got to know Alan when he, Victoria, the twins, and I and my young daughter went down from London to a hotel on the beach at Devon in the summer of 1977, when he was filming *The Shout*. I first noticed his exquisite manners and politeness when he introduced me to everyone as a good friend and neighbour and made me feel quite at home with his colleagues. Somehow, he and Victoria both still believed they could have some kind of relationship, which was very odd – not only because of Alan's double life, but because at that time a Scandinavian painter fell very much in love with Victoria and she was going to move in with him. But Alan ended that affair.

Victoria's time with the artist that summer was apparently not her only romantic diversion: over the course of about three years, she had (according to inferences in her letters) brief liaisons with other notably creative men, including a composer, a playwright and an architect. Because of his own scarcely concealed expeditions with this or that male companion, Alan could hardly object; in any case none of her affairs endured long enough to threaten their public image as a stable family.

With only a week's interval after *The Shout*, Alan began an ambitious job – the title role in a seven-part television drama based on *The Mayor of Casterbridge*, Thomas Hardy's brilliantly gloomy novel of guilt, deception, missed opportunities and unutterable loneliness. The series was produced rapidly in Dorset, where Alan was housed from August through November; the first broadcast occurred in January 1978, to coincide with the fiftieth anniversary of Hardy's death.

On first consideration, it may seem difficult to understand why he so willingly undertook to play the profoundly tragic and deeply unsympathetic Michael Henchard, a singularly charmless figure of murky motives who is wounded as much by his own habit of self-absorption as by the story's sense of impervious fate and ineluctable destiny. More to the point, Dennis Potter's script softened none of the novel's dark bitterness – this was the uncompromising tale of a man who, in a drunken fit, sells his wife and infant daughter for five guineas. He spends the rest of his life within the increasingly narrow choices possible for a man in the grip of his own somewhat cherished remorse, in a world disinclined to forgiveness.

There may have been several reasons for both his choice of this role and his lasting regard for its place in his career. For one thing, Alan had enjoyed the rustic roughness of *Far From the Madding Crowd* a decade earlier. Additionally, he saw that to humanise Michael Henchard, to find the grain of sympathetic humanity beneath such fatal weaknesses of character, would be a major challenge for any actor. But Alan also recognised that at the end Henchard becomes a figure of almost penitential humility. His guilt, the steps wrongly taken to forestall suicidal loneliness, the desperation of his deceptions – all this leads Henchard to admit the depths of his selfishness and to accept its consequences. As in the sexual ambivalence of Rupert Birkin and Ben Butley, as in the calculated disaffection of Simon Hench, as in many more parts to come, just so here: Alan had opportunities to explore a character not always offered to him because of his appealing presence and attractive appearance. Henchard is an expert at the fine art of placing his own needs above those of anyone else, and this is the source of his undoing.

Although Alan's emotional greed was not as extreme as Henchard's, he was acutely aware of his primary dedication to himself, his career and his desires. That was certainly not the sum of his character, but it was a part of it. Indeed, Henchard was, he said at the time, 'such a full character – in each crisis, he makes a worse decision, and in the process he puts himself through every emotional experience. He's so touching, so rich, so wonderfully self-destructive.' Later he elaborated with remarkable frankness:

> I don't know whether the parts I've played have affected who I am or how I live, but I know that when I did *The Mayor of Casterbridge*, I had a huge identification, sympathy, empathy. Someone who made a hideous mistake in his life, couldn't recover from it, went through parental love, love of wife, rejection of wife, love of someone else, obsession with a protégé, ambition. It's the human condition, a fantastic story of how we can't fulfil the ideals we set up, or be this wonderful thing we want to be, or some ideas that youth gives you, and I thought, 'This is really wonderful.' And how he ends up, saying, 'I don't want anyone to know I was ever here. Just bury me and don't mark the grave.' I found the whole beginning, and coming to that end, so moving – because we all fail, somewhere. None of us is a hero, really.

As late as a month before his death, Alan called *Butley* his favourite play and *The Mayor of Casterbridge* his favourite screen performance: 'I could identify with the mayor's journey.' It was the role of a lifetime and he knew it; more to the point, he could not shake it off. Was the character's 'hideous mistake' not in fact like Alan's own marriage from which he could not extricate himself? Had he not gone through both 'love and rejection of wife' as well as 'love of someone else [Paul Taylor]' and 'obsession with a protégé [Nickolas Grace]'? Did he not feel the sting of ambition as both blessing and curse?

That he asked these questions of himself, however inchoately and interiorly, is indicated by the fact that Michael Henchard haunted Alan Bates for more than a third of his life. And herein lies a clue to the essential humanity and dignity of the actor himself, for his understanding of Michael Henchard was linked to his own sharp self-awareness. That he took nothing for granted, that he worked at a role, that he was always a dedicated team player and a gracious collaborator with directors, writers and actors – all this was already established. But then, in his early forties, his decisions about how he would conduct his passional life, his marriage, fatherhood and career, were more and more revealing consequences he could not have foreseen; like Michael Henchard, he saw that he could not escape the results of much that he set in motion. Like the mayor of Casterbridge, he wanted it all – marriage and independence, success and esteem, publicity and privacy, honour abroad and love at home. None of these alternatives is necessarily an ignoble goal, and none is easily achieved; pursued in tandem, however, they make for impossible illusion.

'He lived quite dangerously, both in his personal and professional life,' said Martin.

> He took risks, and usually they worked for him. His appetite was keen, not only for work but for discussion of ideas in the arts and politics, for food and sex – his sweet tooth was famous. You could say that, not least because of his charm, he got away with things – though he certainly had a few wobbles. He was a master of the metaphorical tightrope.

Doubtless there were practical reasons for his choice of Henchard, too. *The Mayor of Casterbridge* was a major leading role, larger than any he had played, and it would have significant worldwide distribution; he would certainly be seen in more homes, in more countries, for more evenings and by more people, than perhaps he had in all previous projects combined. The negotiated fee of £10,500 substantially raised his agents' bargaining power for the future; and of course he loved the months in Dorset, however demanding the daily schedule.

For these and perhaps other reasons, Alan insisted that Michael Henchard was the most satisfying role he ever had – sometimes, he said, even more rewarding than Ben Butley. It was the only one he occasionally showed to friends at home on a video recording: every one of his hundreds of scenes was a small masterpiece of understated feeling; even his scenes of drunkenness avoid clichés and have a deep emotional referent.

'What was so impressive', John Schlesinger wrote to Alan when the series was broadcast, 'was how extraordinarily you have grown in stature as an actor since we first worked together. You know what affection and respect I have for you as an artist, and how terrific I feel it is that you have taken so many risks with your career. I think your *Casterbridge* is quite marvellous, quite spectacular.'

Unfortunately, the final cut of *The Mayor of Casterbridge* resulted in several episodes of glacial lethargy rather than majestic deliberation. Most scenes were played far longer than necessary; every point of mood and plot was italicised with a grave sense of solemn purpose; everything that is discussed is then shown, and scenes are too often diluted by excess – there was simply too much of the muchness of things. And because the pace of television production, as usual, was hasty, sometimes there was scant attention given to continuity. In some sequences, for example, Alan spoke in a crude, nasal, roughneck tone that was entirely appropriate, while seconds later – in the same scene but in separate shots, for close-ups and/or post-dubbing – his speech pattern was suddenly quite educated and polite, and we almost hear Butley replace Henchard.

But nothing detracts from the almost unbearable intensity of Alan's gaze and the rightness of his gestures, nor from his finding complexities in a character not always so rich on the page. What finally burns in the memory is the look of haunted guilt, the awful astonishment at so wide and deep a trough of loneliness.

Back in London before Christmas, he spent time with his boys, who marked their seventh birthdays in November and were enrolled at the King Alfred School, Hampstead. About Alan and Victoria, Simon Gray was as usual on the mark: 'He was born to be a father, not a husband, and his marriage was really a sort of flawed adoption. He was honest and sad about the ways in which he'd failed [Victoria], but then she was always, in a friend's phrase, a reluctant incarnation, and I doubt if anyone could have given her what she needed in life, or even known what it was.' In the matter of fatherhood, Alan also rejoiced in that of his friends, as Michael Linnit (among others) recalled: 'Alan was the first one through the door when my son Ben was just six hours old. He was wonderful to him – he came to our country house, he always got on famously with him.'

By the beginning of 1978, the Bates marriage was a stalemate, with cool politeness defining the distance and Alan, for the most part, hoping that his wife's difficulties would be resolved if they were simply ignored or precluded by diversion. The offer of a Hollywood picture seemed to provide just that for the family.

In February 1978, Alan read the screenplay for *The Rose*, scheduled to be singer Bette Midler's debut in a major feature film loosely
based on the life of the feisty, doomed Janis Joplin; he was to play
the pop singer's smoothly ruthless manager and lover. 'The main attraction of the picture', recalled Michel Linnit, 'was Bette Midler. He had
admired her from afar, and he knew it would be good – in fact necessary – for him to work in Hollywood.'

In late winter, Alan, Victoria and the boys were again heading for
America. During a ten-day sojourn in Manhattan there were meetings with executives from Twentieth Century-Fox, a tour of several
rock-music auditoriums and a read-through of the shooting script
with Midler and director Mark Rydell. 'She was very exciting to
work with,' Alan reported. 'She'd never attempted to play a part before.
Her great genius is in her one-woman show, her songs, her patter,
her comedy. She's a great clown and an extraordinary entertainer. She
was quite nervous, but charged with it, and she really gave a terrific
performance' – for which eventually Bette Midler received an Oscar
nomination.

But Alan noticed, as they went through the script, that his role had
been abbreviated since the first draft; never mind, the producers said
– he would certainly be pleased with their plans. As it happened, they
had no clearer idea of what they meant by this than did Alan. The
company and crew then proceeded to Los Angeles, where production was completed during April and May.

While negotiations were concluded for the rental of a convenient
and child-friendly house, the Bates contingent checked into an appropriate hotel – the Chateau Marmont on Sunset Boulevard, the preferred
venue for the likes of Jim Morrison, Bob Dylan, John Lennon and
Mick Jagger. On a visit with Victoria and the twins to the home of
friends, the English writer and comedian Marty Feldman and his wife
Lauretta, Alan confided that his wife was 'driving him mad – she will
not allow me to take the children to the doctor or dentist!' After she
had heard Alan elaborate on his unhappy marriage, Lauretta told him
she had always assumed he was gay – 'and he replied without any
hesitation, "I am!"' The moment was both unexpectedly funny and
pointedly sad, and Alan's mood that day brightened only when he
spoke of the work at hand. 'He was a real thespian,' Lauretta said years
later. 'He made movies and he did them brilliantly – but he was really
of the theatre, and he knew it.'

Finally, Alan and his family settled for almost two months into Benedict Canyon, in a house that belonged to actress Sarah Miles, then out of town. 'I hadn't met his wife or the boys,' recalled Joanna Pettet, who was also in Los Angeles,

> so I took my young son and went over to visit them. As Alan took me to be introduced to Victoria, we passed a bathroom and there was a tub of water filled to the brim, with clothes soaking in it – but no soap. There was a washer and dryer in the house, but Victoria wouldn't use them, either. Alan said this was her way of cleaning clothes: to leave everything in water for several days without soap, and the dirt was just supposed to settle to the bottom.

They climbed upstairs to a terrace, Joanna continued, 'and there was Victoria, sunning herself – totally naked and shockingly thin.'

With *The Rose*, Alan's compensation had leaped exponentially, to no less than $200,000. 'I've been lucky enough to earn a good deal lately,' he said, 'and I can't really say that it doesn't mean anything to me. If there's a lot to be had [as in Hollywood], I'll ask for it. But to be a millionaire does not happen to be one of my ambitions.'

That was certainly true – but it was well known to his agents and close friends that, in the words of Conrad Monk, 'Alan never believed he was successful financially. He always worried about money. If he wasn't working, he was anxious about money. This was odd, because he never had money problems, he came from a secure middle-class family – and then everything seemed to come to him so easily. I don't think he was out of work [or not receiving residual profits] for more than a week over the course of forty years, and he accumulated a great deal of money.'

It was thus to be expected that he considered remaining in Hollywood, where salaries were higher than in Britain, and where, for the rich and famous, the living is easy year-round. At first he was tempted: 'I saw Alan while I was there,' wrote Michael Linnit to Alan's London accountant, 'and he admits that his resistance to being seduced by Hollywood is at its lowest ebb.' Because there were at least five more offers on the table for Alan – all of them for films to be made in Hollywood – Michael added that Alan 'may remain for a considerable period in America . . . [and so] he asked me what the tax implications would be of him buying a house there'.

Those implications were not particularly favourable, especially since Alan was, in any case, often overextended in England. But his final decision not to relocate to Southern California, nor to accept the lucrative offers of the next two years there, had to do with his preference for London, for Derby, for being close to his roots, and for raising his sons in their native land. 'I made a conscious decision not to do some of the things I was asked to in Hollywood,' he said later. 'I didn't want to be trapped there, I didn't want to feel that I couldn't get out, or that I wasn't a free agent as an actor. I could have stayed in Hollywood after *The Rose*, but I didn't . . . and I don't think as an English actor you are ever number one [in Hollywood].'

'He found Hollywood very seductive,' Michael said in summarising that thorny year, 'but he knew it was dangerous.' To be sure, Alan's decision was also influenced by the final cut of *The Rose*: the producers simply excised most of his performance (and all his best scenes) in order to retain all of Midler's songs; the picture still ran well over two hours. As in *An Unmarried Woman*, there was little evidence of Alan's prodigious screen talent in *The Rose*: critics mentioned him only parenthetically, finding him a somewhat forlorn afterthought. Polite though he always was when speaking of the movie, and always sincere in his admiration of Bette Midler, Alan in future avoided Hollywood whenever he could. 'I wasn't happy there,' he told Gareth. Perhaps no one was surprised to hear it.

After the completion of *The Rose*, the family remained another two months in California. From there, Victoria wrote to Elizabeth Grant on 9 July.

Wonders will never cease! Here am I, in my eagle's eyrie up on the roof – with my feathered friends warbling soft melody and my leafy lovers swaying luminous green light – so their sovereign, the morning sun, shall not burn me up in his passion (no earthly lovers could compare)!

Your letter was heaven – I've just read it again. Enshrined in my green-harboured garden of demi-Paradise, amid the unclouded canyons, it brings such comfort to hear of lovely earthly life in Hampstead. I have been driving Alan to distraction with my regular deliveries on how to bring up Benedick and Tristan and conduct creative relationships – I am contemplating looking for a country cottage on our return – wish I could attend classes on how to live practically and be useful to me and the community! We shall all be back within a fortnight – oh, what riches I have to relate!

But any riches she had to relate were soon forgotten when the family returned to London. Victoria had slipped into a critical depression that haunted her through Christmastide and into early 1979.

11

Soldiers and Spies

'From the time Tristan and I were about nine,' said Benedick Bates,

> life with our mother became a constant, massive embarrassment that we kept like some kind of shameful secret. My brother and I often asked one another, 'Has Mum spoken to you this week?' It was that bad. Sometimes we found the telephone wrapped in a duvet or a carpet, because she said she didn't feel like hearing it ring. And there was no food in the fridge – we were living like feral children in an attic. At school, we had friends we could visit, and some of them found out what was going on when we started to raid their kitchens for food. When she wouldn't do our laundry, we took our clothes to Dad's house on weekends, telling him our washing machine was broken. At some point we got desperate, and we went to him and said he'd got to do something, that there was something wrong with her. Our house was in a terrible state, in complete disrepair, with no hot water, and sometimes she didn't sleep for days.

In such a Dickensian domestic setting, it was remarkable that the boys did not suffer critically from malnutrition and even worse childhood ailments, and that they had any social skills at all.

> When our school friends came round, she embarrassed us in front of them – she made fun of us and insulted them, was rude

to them. When she came to us or dropped in at Alan's when we were there, she was dressed like a homeless poor person, and she sat at the table in total silence and started writing in a note-book. If someone addressed her and said something nice, she looked at them and said nothing – or she might say, 'Oh, shut up – you are such a bore, just shut up!' That kind of thing propelled Tris and me to crave the normal things in life even more. We wanted to be clean and well dressed, and we wanted our friends to like us.

To make matters still more poignant, Victoria's irrational episodes alternated with lucid periods:

She could be extraordinarily intelligent and right about so many things. Her views on politics, for example, and on friendship, love, relationships – sometimes when she spoke about these, her ideas could be sane, lucid and commendable. But when it came to things like caring for herself, and we went to her and asked, 'Why not do something for yourself?' she threw it back at us – 'Why don't you do something about *your* lives? You and your brother need help – why don't *you* go and see a psychiatrist?' For kids struggling for identity, this was really terrible. But we never thought she was right about that, and we didn't believe we were mentally ill and needed doctors. I remember thinking, when I was about twelve, that I just didn't have the tools to deal with her.

As often with such people, Victoria could be both divisive and coherent at the same time, as some discovered. Because he often tried to clear a path through the thickets of her misery and moods, Martin's good intentions were sometimes met with rude mischief.

Once, she and I went for a walk opposite the house [in Derbyshire], and while we were talking, she quoted something – which she constantly did – and I said I had never heard it before. I thought what she said was interesting, and I asked her for the source, and to elaborate on it. But she just looked at me and said, 'It would be like casting pearls before swine, Martin.'

The dynamics of Victoria's diminished personality are not difficult to appreciate. She felt so alienated from ordinary human relations that in some way she felt her job was to alienate others – lacking any healthy self-regard, it was her task to reduce the self-esteem of others.

> On another occasion she became exasperated with me. 'Martin, just wait there,' she said. She went upstairs and came back down with an enormous armload of heavy books which she threw down in front of me, crying out, 'There, Martin – read those!'

She did not, with such tactics, endear herself to family or friends.

Nickolas was a patient and generous friend during many difficult times; he volunteered, for example, to take the boys for outings and for visits to their grandmother in Derby. 'Mary Bates liked having young men around,' he recalled. 'And because Alan was on a perpetual diet, she often said things like, "We're having very healthy food because Alan is on a regime – so I've made a rice and veggie bake," but then out came the bread and butter pudding, chocolate tarts and custard pies! She was a strong and striking woman, slightly imperious, stately as a galleon, with something of a dominating personality. But her family certainly came first in her life.'

And she certainly took pride of place in Alan's life, too. After Harold's death, he visited his mother more frequently, treating her, for example, to holidays in the Lake District, where they visited Wordsworth country and stayed in a charming cottage, surrounded by natural beauty; he also took her to Portugal. During his absences and even sometimes when he was in London, Alan asked friends like David Storey to look after Victoria 'when he couldn't take any more domestic tension', as David recalled. 'It was hard, at times, to know precisely where you were with her. Often you couldn't understand what she was saying, she was so obscure and ill-defined.'

While the twins coped with mother and school, and friends like Nickolas, Conrad and David kept vigil in his absence, Alan hopscotched across the Continent, appearing as the eminent artistic director Serge Diaghilev in Herbert Ross's film, *Nijinsky*. After working in Paris, Budapest and Taormina, the production moved back to Pinewood

Studios for interiors. For his services, which engaged him for the first half of 1979, he was paid $400,000.[*]

At this time, Alan arranged an introduction to the formidable, sometimes violent superstar dancer Rudolf Nureyev, whose sexual exploits were already legendary. During their meeting Alan wanted to discuss some details of Russian ballet history and technique, but Nureyev kept insisting that he ought to have a role in the film. Alan, of course, had no power to fulfil this demand. After the picture was released, he and Conrad visited Nureyev backstage after a performance and the dancer angrily proclaimed his resentment at being left out of *Nijinsky*. 'He was furious that Alan hadn't got a role in it for him – he had such a go at him!'

Covering the period 1912 to 1913, the movie accurately presents Diaghilev as mentor and lover to the title character, who married ballerina Romola de Pulszky and then slid into schizophrenic madness. But an awkward oversimplification mars the narrative and there is no development of character – at the end, they are mostly as they were at the outset. And, apart from some very brief ballet sequences, there was nothing much that moved.

It was, of course, essential to have real dancers playing the historic performers and perhaps they could not have been expected to be powerful actors as well. That vacuum left almost everything up to Alan, who sniffed, swirled and gambolled through his part with unctuous relish; indeed, given the limitations of the material, he gave a successful example of a one-note performance. 'I depended tremendously on Alan Bates,' said George de la Peña, cast as Nijinsky. 'I was constantly getting strength and energy from him.'

'He was the most extraordinary man,' said Alan of Diaghilev during production. In a moment of perhaps unwitting candour, he also spoke of his innate understanding of the clash between passionate love and complete commitment to one's work:

> The two men [Diaghilev and Nijinsky] had a terrific love born out of what they did. The relationship came out of their interdependence. I think Nijinsky might have been troubled about

---

[*] Thanks to Chatto & Linnit Ltd, his fees continued to rise: Alan received $130,000 for *An Unmarried Woman* and $200,000 for *The Rose*; in 1982 he was paid $500,000 for *The Wicked Lady*.

it, but Diaghilev was very secure. Whatever Diaghilev felt for anyone, the work always came first. He was a very emotional man, and he wasn't afraid of his emotions – but he wasn't afraid to be ruthless, either; it was always done in pursuit of the excellence of the work. He could be wonderful one day, then poisonous the next . . . It could be monstrous if you were on the receiving end. He had an animal quality.

For all his understanding of the role, and his immersion in it, Alan was frank about the picture's mediocrity: 'It was not, I think, a wonderful film. I think it should have really been called *Diaghilev* and been about Diaghilev, and Nijinsky should have been one of the wonderful moments in his life. Diaghilev's great – you read about him and you think, "This is one of the great visionaries of the century."'

Was it possible, enquired a journalist, that Diaghilev's 'animal quality' was the same as Alan's? 'I mustn't tell you what I've got,' he replied coyly, nor would he impart to the press 'too much knowledge'. Always wary of personal questions, he was more and more anxious during televised interviews. On Terry Wogan's popular chat show, for example, he was evidently concerned when the host's probing questions turned momentarily to his private life. Alan relied on monosyllabic answers and evident discomfort to steer the conversation elsewhere.

After *Nijinsky*, Alan went immediately into rehearsals for a television drama, made over four weeks in September of 1979. Written by John Osborne and directed by Alan Bridges, *Very Like a Whale* (taking its title from *Hamlet*) starred Alan Bates as a wealthy businessman about to be knighted. But his private life is not so successful: his marriage is empty, his friendships shallow, his health compromised; finally, he dies. Shown briefly in America as *Executive Syndrome*, *Very Like a Whale* was memorable in Alan's life only for the pleasure of working with his co-star, the estimable Gemma Jones. 'We got on so well together,' she recalled.

The picture was filmed in someone's apartment, so we had no caravans and hence spent a lot of time together. We laughed and laughed – so much that, when I was summoned back on set, I had to have my make-up reapplied. He was a very, very witty man and a terrible gossip. He spoke so proudly of his twin boys, and I said I would call in to meet them. 'No, no, no, please don't,' he said. 'The place is such a mess that your shoes will stick to the orange juice on the floor!' He painted a picture of utter chaos. The Alan I knew was a ray of sunshine, but there was another life at home, which was not as it should have been.

Alan's friendship with Gemma continued until his death and included subsequent collaborations and much sharing of confidences: he appreciated her keen theatrical sensibility, her discretion and good humour, her lack of judgement on him and her abiding confidence – to the point where he felt atypically comfortable speaking of his tangled private life.

He had an innate generosity and that, too, was, I think, part of his sexuality. Yes, he was sort of indiscriminate and readily gave himself to people, but that part of his life was never treated in the press – many people knew about it, but nobody spoke of it. Still, he was very fearful that his 'other life' would become known, and this must have taken an added toll and imposed a strain on Victoria.

As for *Very Like a Whale*, John Osborne – never easily impressed by any actor – was one of the few people to see it. 'I was completely overwhelmed by your performance,' he wrote to Alan.

Naturally, I knew you would be splendid, but I was quite un-prepared for [your] power, subtlety, depth, irony and *intelligence*. It was quite harrowing and civilised in a way that seems to me very rare indeed on the telly. You are really the most clever, *brilliant* old devil – the best do indeed get better. Many thanks and many, many congratulations. I do hope that some time we can do another.

Osborne added a postscript: 'The scenes with Gemma were quite *desolate* – oh, dear . . . !'

Alan's work in late 1979 continued apace when he went at once from the filming of the Osborne project into October rehearsals for Simon Gray's new play, *Stage Struck*, which opened at the Vaudeville,

London on 21 November, and in which Alan remained through mid March 1980. In this adroit, economical thriller, he had the role of a theatrical stage manager whose life has been spent in subordinate service to his wealthy actress wife. Suspicions of his infidelity lead her to invent an ingenious scheme to unmask and discredit him, but he simultaneously exploits his skill at stagecraft to thwart her. After devious convolutions of plot and character, the curtain on *Stage Struck* comes down with grim surprises.

Things were not so successful, nor pleasantly thrilling, in private. 'Our parents finally realised that the marriage wasn't working out,' said Ben. 'Alan was, by and large, a committed father, and he was sort of committed to Victoria, supporting her on certain levels and trying to get her to help herself. But at the same time he pursued his work and his other relationships.' The situation unavoidably affected the unhappy twins, who were referred by their teachers for an assessment with the noted psychologist, P. N. Gilchrist. In his report to the administrators of the King Alfred School in July 1980, Gilchrist noted that Tristan and Benedick appeared 'pale, rather tired-looking young men . . . lacking self-confidence . . . with an assumption that they were certain to fail'. Gilchrist, unaware of the boys' wretched diet, simply noted that Tristan's hearing, short-term memory and motor coordination were 'laboured', and both boys were 'functioning well below their capacity'.

In his summary Gilchrist accurately observed that there must be some attempt to correct the 'rather dented self-esteem' of the boys. 'With a history of much travelling and constant changes of class teacher, it is hardly surprising that their attitude to school is still somewhat anxiety-prone.' The conclusion was blunt: 'I would also attach considerable importance to the positive, warm development of father/son relationships, especially in boys of this age. If they can begin to attract their father's respect for their efforts at King Alfred's, we may well see our turning point.' To his credit and with the able assistance of a few friends, Alan took matters in hand, and in time the physical and mental health of the twins duly improved – to the point where they showed significant abilities in acting, writing and sketching during their teens.

While the boys were being psychologically evaluated that summer, Alan was on the Isle of Wight, filming a ninety-minute television drama – *The Trespasser*, based on D. H. Lawrence's second novel, itself inspired by the experience of a friend of Lawrence. Completed in only nineteen days, this was the story of a violinist, married to an unkempt shrew; he loves his children but feels trapped by circumstance and easily falls in love with his student, an able young woman. A brief romantic holiday leaves him even more deeply depressed, and finally he takes his own life. There was little Alan could do with this lugubrious material except to appear poetically troubled, which he did with an air of proper Byronic despondency.

It may seem odd that he accepted roles in *Nijinsky, Very Like a Whale* and *The Trespasser* while declining major roles offered to him – in plays and films like *The Lion in Winter, Sly Fox, Breaker Morant, Chapter Two, The Human Factor* and the musical *Kiss Me Kate*, which could have fulfilled his lifelong ambition to sing onstage. His brother Martin spoke to the point:

> There was a deep shyness in Alan, and something in him shrank from achieving the heights of fame. He reached a certain point where he pulled back from the really big time and the problems that it might bring. Another factor in not making this massive breakthrough was the guilt associated with everything at home. There he was, away on location week after week, knowing that Victoria couldn't cope. He was always eager to get back, to sort things out for the boys, but then the cycle went on. He indicated to me that he felt enormous responsibility for his neglect – but in a sense, what was he to do? He had to pursue his life, his career, he had to earn his income for them as well as himself.

There may have been another element in 'not making this massive breakthrough'. Confident though he was of his talents and conscious of his value to a production, there was an admixture of something simpler: 'I think', said Gemma, 'that Alan may have thought of himself as a simple country lad who had come down to London and somehow made good.' Nor is it unusual for anyone, actor or not, to feel a subtle suspicion that one will somehow be found out and at last considered unworthy of acclaim.

On his return from the Isle of Wight, he and the boys spent several weeks in Derbyshire, to Mary's obvious delight; Victoria remained in London, occupying herself with virtually nothing.

Continuing a ferocious schedule that autumn and winter, Alan went to Paris, where he appeared in yet another disagreeably stylish role – an amoral, sybaritic Englishman of the 1920s, in James Ivory's film of Jean Rhys's autobiographical novel *Quartet*. Alan portrayed a man who, encouraged by his complaisant wife, exploits the misfortunes of a beleaguered young woman, taking her into his home as his mistress. He gave a performance of chilling social respectability, composed of ambiguous gestures and cool, tight-lipped proprieties; it is, in short, a masterpiece of corruption at its politest – and the latest in Alan's series of shady characters.

Just as he seemed to decline (or at least not campaign for) major international roles, so he was now entering a phase in which he undertook an astonishing variety of characters who were either frankly disturbed or at least experts in the domain of off-beat sexuality. This was becoming a sort of sub-specialty for him in a résumé that began with *Butley* and continued through *The Collection*, *The Shout*, *Nijinsky*, *The Trespasser*, *Very Like a Whale* – and now *Quartet*; more such wonderfully odd roles would follow. He always underplayed them, and the counterpoint of these characters against his attractive appearance and seductive voice and manner invested the films with unexpected complexity.

This was a canny turn in Alan's career, for he seems to have understood that specifically romantic leading roles were unlikely to endure into his forties – there had been few in any case, and the most recent (in *An Unmarried Woman*) was very much a supporting character. It was prudent, therefore, for him to broaden his scope of roles, and the more eccentric the better. In this regard his choices were very probably the fruit of sound professional intuition rather than of calculated decision.

In February 1981 Alan took a call from Jerzy Skolimowski, the congenial (if somewhat enigmatic) director of *The Shout*. In 1967 Skolimowski had to shelve *Rece De Gory – Hands Up!* because of Polish censorship; now, however, the director wanted to rework the old footage, add new scenes and release it. For friendship's sake, Alan agreed to appear briefly in a non-speaking cameo, which he filmed on 16 and 17 April; his name gave the picture a certain public-relations cachet, however fleeting and insignificant his contribution.

That spring and early summer, there was far greater significance in his portrayal of a real-life writer and lawyer, John Mortimer, in a television version of Mortimer's autobiographical family drama *A Voyage Round My Father*. Alan was mostly present in the voice-over narration, but in his few scenes on screen with Laurence Olivier (as Mortimer's aged, blind father), he was the essence of restrained emotion. Nothing in the final cut gave evidence of the enormous difficulty everyone had while filming in Oxfordshire, for Olivier was frail, forgetful and cantankerous – but he rose to his on-camera moments with customary radiance and relied especially on Alan, his friend from *The Entertainer*, to be both acolyte and confidant.

Before beginning another feature film that autumn, Alan dispatched two brief tasks. First, on the evening of 24 July, he read selections from Byron's poetry at London's first international festival on the Romantic Movement in the arts, held over five days in late July. His programme was (thus the curious announcement) 'devised and refereed' by Frederic Raphael, whose biography of Byron was soon to be published; perhaps predictably, all available tickets for his recitation were sold in advance.

The second undertaking was a favour to Lindsay Anderson, who wrote to him on 27 July, while directing a new film:

Dear Alan –

It is really nice of you to want to, or be willing to play a role – make an *appearance* – in *Britannia Hospital*. There just isn't a major role that would befit your status; otherwise of course I would have asked you. But I am so glad you think it would be fun: and more than just fun – so many people, when it comes to the point, lose their humour or sense of values.

We have a 'role' which I think would be ideal, because it's not a walk-on, and it is a character on whom, in a couple of sequences, the whole focus of the picture concentrates. MACREADY is the character – unconscious in Intensive Care – whom PROFESSOR MILLAR (Graham Crowden) has chosen to supply the head to his great transplant creation. He is supposed to be dying, fails to do so, and finally is 'terminated' by Graham and Dr MACMILLAN (Jill Bennett) and has his head sawn off. Naturally it must be *a fine and distinguished head*. We are shooting this scene on THURSDAY 13TH AUGUST – my hand trembles as I write. How does MACREADY grab you?

I'm sure I don't need to say, dear Alan, what great pleasure it would give me for you to be part of this.

Love,

Lindsay

And so, on 14 and 17 August, Alan remained motionless on a hospital trolley, appearing for about a minute; as a gesture of friendship to Anderson he refused even a token fee.

Then things greatly improved. That autumn he joined two former colleagues – Julie Christie and Glenda Jackson – along with Ann-Margret and Ian Holm, in the feature film *The Return of the Soldier*, one of the finest and most underrated achievements by all concerned, based on Rebecca West's short first novel. The film's producers and distributors fell short of cash, important scenes were never filmed or half-filmed, and what remained had quickly to be edited, with uneven results. For all that, what might have been a sentimental cliché – the story of a World War One amnesiac and the wife, cousin and former lover to whom he returns – became, in the hands of such professionals, a story of complex and under-played emotions, a great haze of confused pain defining each character.

Alan's portrait of a shell-shocked captain avoided the hackneyed devices often employed to convey mental aberration; instead, he seemed to find the telling amalgam of glances, short pauses and half-concealed gestures that both revealed and concealed the sudden sting of memory. Eighty-nine-year-old Rebecca West visited the company during filming, and when she saw the finished product she was delighted. 'It was a double pleasure to see you act,' she wrote to Alan on 5 May 1982, 'and to see you acting in an invention of my own! This has been one of the most enjoyable things that has happened to me in my seventy-one years of writing, and I thank you for it.'

Glenda Jackson agreed. 'Over the years, Alan seemed to become better and better – and more generous as an actor. It was not only a pleasure to act *with* him; it was a pleasure to watch him act.' For his part, Alan felt that *The Return of the Solider* was very much Glenda Jackson's film, and in a way he was right. Ensemble piece though it was, the picture has her performance at its emotional centre: to see her derive from her character's insistent plainness and deep well of pain a kind of unselfconscious nobility is to watch a great actress at the height of her powers.

Meanwhile, the living situation of Benedick and Tristan with their mother had become intolerable to the point of physical peril. In 1982 they turned twelve and, as Ben recalled,

> We were always wearing dirty clothes, as usual, and I was doing my homework in a sleeping bag that winter – I couldn't stop from shaking, it was so cold. We were both dangerously close to hypothermia – I remember the snow blowing in through a broken window. And whenever Alan went away on a long shooting schedule, things were very rough for us. That year we knocked on his door and asked to live with him. He said we'd have to ask Mum, but that was impossible. Finally, he went into the house and he saw how bad everything was.
>
> He talked to a few of her friends and then his eyes were opened. Whether he had decided earlier to turn a blind eye to our neglect, I don't know. But that year, at last, he moved us to Hamilton Terrace and bought the house next door for us.
>
> That's when Mum's decline really accelerated – when she remained at Lavender Cottage and we were living with him. At that time, I think something in her died. Her house became more and more cluttered and, although Alan gave her an allowance, she decided to live more and more frugally. A few times he suggested that they divorce, but when the process began, she refused – why, I don't know. Alan just said, 'Well, that's that.' He wouldn't force it, wouldn't put her through it against her will.

With the handsome income he received for a film role that year Alan purchased 122A Hamilton Terrace, a coach house-cum-studio adjacent to 122, and there the twins were installed. The residences were joined by a connecting door, so that father and sons had easy access to one another but some privacy as well.

'He seemed to have a kind of guilt about the previous years,' Ben continued,

> and he began to spoil us when we moved over to him. We lived next door, but we could have access to his place all the time,

and a woman came in to cook and clean for us. So we then had a bit of a privileged life, and at last we could invite friends home from school without being embarrassed.

The house for the boys was purchased with a large portion of the salary Alan received that summer – $500,000 for a few scenes as a highwayman in *The Wicked Lady*. This may not have been the worst picture ever to engage his talents, but it certainly belongs on a short list (along with *Royal Flash*, with which it has unfortunate similarities). Faye Dunaway was the eponymous lady, a thief and killer based on a real-life seventeenth-century figure of no consequence – except that in the summer of 1982 she provided the material for this remarkably sadistic film, the sort of modish 'entertainment' luxuriating in the torture of naked women and the disembowelling of men. At least Alan could console himself that the income from this rubbish was useful.

On learning of the boys' change of address, Alan's friends were understandably relieved. 'Why did he let all that happen for so long?' asked Gemma years later, speaking for many. 'Did he just pretend it didn't exist? He certainly wasn't an unkind or uncaring man – perhaps he just swept it under the carpet and hoped the situation would resolve itself. I remember thinking that beautiful, eccentric Victoria was terribly lonely in the marriage, and there's nothing more painful than that.' Marie Malavieille, always in contact with Victoria, believed that 'she really declined mentally when the children were taken away from her', although that was unavoidable if the boys were to survive.

With Tris and Ben settled at Hamilton Terrace and busy with school duties, Alan decided that, for at least a full year, he would accept only offers that would not involve a long absence from home. By fortunate coincidence, offers to appear in two television dramas came from John Schlesinger.

First, that autumn, was a seamless transposition of Terence Rattigan's 1957 stage success *Separate Tables*, with Alan assuming roles in both its one-act plays. In the first part, he was an alcoholic journalist with a troubled, vain wife (Julie Christie, undertaking her fourth role opposite Alan); in the second (also opposite Julie, as a neurasthenic spinster), he portrayed a pretentious phoney, a retired major lacking the authentic dignity he claims. Alan completely inhabited the two roles, evoking pity for both sad, lonely men without demanding it.

The second Schlesinger production was based on an actual incident. In 1958, the actress Coral Browne had travelled with the Shakespeare Memorial Company (later the Royal Shakespeare Company) to Moscow, where she appeared as Gertrude in *Hamlet*. Into her dressing room came a man drunk to the point of sickness – the exiled spy Guy Burgess. Coral visited his apartment for a frugal lunch, spent the afternoon speaking with him about his life in Russia and, at his request, agreed to measure him for new clothes to be made in London.

Years later, Coral recounted the incident to the playwright, actor and screenwriter Alan Bennett, who wrote the scenario for what became *An Englishman Abroad*. 'The picture of the elegant actress and the seedy exile sitting in a dingy Moscow flat through a long afternoon listening again and again to Jack Buchanan singing "Who Stole My Heart Away?" seemed to me funny and sad,' he said, so the incident became the basis for a brilliant hour of television and certainly one of Alan's most deeply felt, tragicomic portrayals; Coral played herself, to great effect. Filmed in Dundee during the frigid January and February of 1983, *An Englishman Abroad* focuses more on Burgess's isolation than on his betrayal – and on the sorts of necessary accommodations one makes in forced exile.

'Burgess never tried to hide himself – quite the opposite,' Alan Bates said that year, with scarcely concealed admiration. 'He was drunk in front of everyone, he was homosexual in front of everyone and he went round telling everyone he was a spy, though no one believed him. That sort of exhibitionism may have been a defence against all sorts of things, but he certainly had an incredible mischief. He had a dreadful time in Moscow, and I'm sure he thoroughly regretted going there.'

His portrait of a lonely gay man in an inhospitable, alien culture is laced with moments of inventive brilliance: the delicacy with which he serves Coral half a tomato stuffed with raw garlic, as if it were caviar; the proud, impeccable diction, a sharp counterpoint to the prevailing drabness of his surroundings; and the refusal to indulge any of the clichés so often brought to the portrait of a slightly effete, middle-aged homosexual. Most of all, his portrait of Guy Burgess is of a man who sees no reason to beg forgiveness.

The programme received an enthusiastic critical and popular response: 'A beautifully controlled exploration of a secret life in a secret world,' according to *The Times*. 'Alan Bates's portrayal of this moral outcast of the island is as memorable a performance as one could wish.' BAFTA showered it with awards for television achievement: John Schlesinger was named best director for a single drama; Alan Bennett received the writer's award; Alan was cited as best actor and Coral best actress; and awards were presented to those responsible for the production design, music, photography, costumes and sound. When it was shown on American television, Alan received the ACE Cable Award for the best performance by an actor, as he had for *Separate Tables*.

That spring, Alan began rehearsals for a revival of *A Patriot for Me*, in which, once again, he elected to play a real-life homosexual spy – this time, the notorious Alfred Redl, an Austro-Hungarian officer blackmailed by the Russians into espionage. John Osborne's riotously muddled, controversial play about hypocrisy and betrayal, set between 1890 and 1913, had been denied a performing licence by the censors in 1965, when it had to be presented as a 'private club' entertainment. When the revival opened at Chichester in May 1983, more than three years had passed since Alan had appeared onstage; he returned as if determined to confound theatre critics and challenge the goodwill of his audiences. He was also cornering the market on a curious, theatrically irresistible kind of character – the sexually marginal figure doomed by his times not to survive them.

Furtive sexuality was not the point of *An Englishman Abroad*, but it was entirely the point in the story of Alfred Redl's terrorised, guilt-ridden officer, a Jewish homosexual who finally kills himself. 'He was a brilliant, ambitious young officer – he's unfortunate, but I don't think he can quite claim to be honourable,' Alan said that year. 'He was determined to be an officer, that was his talent. They think that one side of his family was Jewish, but everyone lied about their religion; they lied about their race; they lied about their sexuality. They lied about everything to conform, totally conform, [and] the subject of espionage and the subject of homosexuality are two things that make people bridle . . . But Redl is very proper. He is an extraordinary man who would have had a brilliant career, but he is undermined by his own nature.'

The most controversial scenes in the play, and that which had sealed its fate in 1965, were the bedroom scenes (performed mostly in half-light) and the infamous drag ball for Viennese aristocrats. But by 1983 *A Patriot for Me* seemed quite tame and even tediously protracted, not to say prolix. Alan, however, found Redl – like Burgess – impossible to reject, as did audiences in Chichester (where it played from 11 May to late July), later at the Haymarket (from 1 August to mid October) and at the Ahmanson, Los Angeles (from 5 October to 25 November 1984). The critical consensus was that his perform-ance was 'masterly', and there was considerable praise for his facial tics, his surprising inflections, the subtle twitching of the fingers, the furtive glances, the perfectly timed silences he had learned so well from Pinter. For this achievement Alan received the Laurence Olivier Award for best actor in the revival of a previously produced play.

The London run ended in October and, two weeks later, Alan was off to Switzerland with Michael Lindsay-Hogg, who directed him in a BBC teleplay based on Graham Greene's 1980 novel *Dr Fischer of Geneva*, a dark parable about a greedy and manipulative industrialist (James Mason in his last role), his benighted daughter (Greta Scacchi) and the ordinary man (Alan) she marries. 'All concerned have deliv-ered a very classy package of superb acting and thoughtful drama,' noted one critic. 'Mr Bates is extraordinarily convincing.'

The picture had a number of night shoots on the shores of gelid Lake Geneva. 'One morning at about two o'clock,' according to the director,

> we were about to return to work, shooting night scenes outside a large chateau on the lake. On my way back outside, I heard muffled sounds from inside a closet. Naughtily, I pulled the door open – and there were Alan and Barry Humphries [the actor known as 'Dame Edna'], with huge plates of chocolate cake, and they were munching away. They were always trying to be trim, and there they were in hiding, enjoying their cake.

As they approached the end of production in February 1984, Alan marked his fiftieth birthday. 'He seemed depressed,' Michael recalled,

> and I had never seen him that way. It may have had to do with his chin – he felt it was getting fuller. Was this birthday a harder one for him because he had been such a lovely-looking man in

his youth? It was the only time I ever saw him a little bit down – but of course it also could have been because we were eating cold pasta and bad ham, which was the only thing available to us that night!

In a statement that could have come straight from the dialogue of *An Englishman Abroad* or *A Patriot for Me*, Alan said that year, 'It took me an awful long time to realise that I was expected to behave in a manner that wasn't really truthful to myself.' This he uttered without elaboration – and somewhat disingenuously, for he apparently felt it necessary to continue, in some ways, 'to behave in a manner that wasn't really truthful'. More accurately, it can be said that Alan did not lie about his double life, but he dissembled. He implicitly denied the gossip by never appearing to have any serious male suitor or partner and, conversely, by appearing, when necessary, with a woman on his arm. But it must be said that his friendships with women, almost always chaste, were deeply affectionate and had their own truth.

There was no necessity, of course, for him to publicise his private life, nor to reveal what he preferred to keep quiet: being truthful does not require full disclosure, after all, and he came from a time and place that raised young men to keep their counsel. And it must be remembered that Alan was, in the words of his longtime friend Ian White, 'basically a loner. He attracted people, and they adored him – but invariably, he wanted to get away from it all.'

And therein lay a painful contest in his will, for as his friends knew, Alan hated being alone and avoided it whenever possible – while at the same time he required apartness, not only for the exigencies of preparing a role, but because essentially he did not want to share every moment of every day of his life. To the contrary, he cherished his privacy, and this inevitably caused problems in his intimate relations. 'The minute someone got too close to him,' said Arthur Laurents, speaking for many, 'he ran and the relationship ended.' Joanna Pettet used identical words. As Elizabeth Grant said, 'The real Alan was an independent soul who wasn't really interested in domestic life with a man or a woman.'

Domesticity or no, Alan was then in the midst of an intense, two-year romance with the British figure skater John Curry. Celebrated for combining ballet and modern dance with intricate athletics on ice, Curry had won the Olympic and World Championships in 1976 and had founded a touring company that thrilled audiences in Europe and America. A German newspaper caused a brief scandal by revealing Curry's homosexuality in 1976, but he ignored the publicity and pursued his career and his lovers with joyful abandon.

'It was one of Alan's most serious relationships,' recalled Conrad, 'but there was a moment when John publicly revealed that he had really fallen for Alan. With that, it was over: proclaiming yourself was the one thing you could not do with him. Alan couldn't sustain emotional bonds with lovers: he always saw them as unwelcome entanglements. People came so far and couldn't get any closer. But at the same time, he was terrified of being alone. If five o'clock approached and there were no evening arrangements, he became almost desperate.' If the deepest meaning of truthful behaviour is not to acknowledge publicly but to live out privately the implications of commitment, then of this Alan was incapable. In this regard perhaps he disappointed no one more than himself.

But there was a complication that overlapped the Curry affair – a new love Alan could neither ignore nor blithely terminate, and one that eventually endured longer than any other.

12

Champagne, Salmon and Cheesecake

A s much a successful matchmaker as a consoling physician, Patrick Woodcock had an impressive list of celebrity patients, all of whom relied on his generosity, humour and perception, if not invariably his discretion. John Gielgud was among those who came to his surgery, as did Noël Coward, Marlene Dietrich and L. P. Hartley. Abroad, his many friends included Christopher Isherwood and Don Bachardy, David Hockney, Peter Shaffer and Edward Albee. 'He was enchanting company,' according to his friend David Hughes, 'boyish and buoyant, with a gift for not letting you get away with anything, but at the same time indulging you.'

The legendary Dr Woodcock was at ease and quite open about his homosexuality; indeed, he was host for both single-sex as well as mixed parties, and he took especial pleasure in introducing lonely or unattached friends to one another. Alan Bates was among his patients, and so was a handsome young man named Gerard Hastings, who in 1982 turned twenty-two. Tall, lean and articulate, with bright eyes, a quick smile and great humour, Gerard was born in Gateshead, northeast England. He had studied art and was building a solid reputation as a gifted artist. Alan met him at one of Woodcock's parties.

During 1983, they occasionally went to the theatre together; Gerard attended a performance of *A Patriot for Me*; and Alan came to exhibitions of Gerard's art and visited his studio in Chiswick. In March 1984, Gerard went to Alan's performances in Harold Pinter's short plays *One for the Road* and *Victoria Station*, offered at lunchtime for seven weeks at the Lyric Studio, Hammersmith; Alan's fee was a nominal £100 per week. Gerard knew that Alan liked cigarillos, so he brought a gift packet, and Alan invited Gerard for a drink after the performance.

One for the Road is a powerful twenty-five-minute exposition of human rights abuses by totalitarian states. Alan had the role of a cruel interrogator in an unnamed dictatorship – a performance, as one reviewer noted, in which he was 'sleek, calm and vicious, circling his wounded victim with the casual sadism of absolute power'. Simon Gray judged Alan's acting in *One for the Road* (subsequently presented on BBC television) as 'the most restrained and consequently the most violent and hateful performance of his career' In the fifteen-minute second play on the bill, *Victoria Station*, Alan played an amnesiac taxi driver in radio communication with his dispatcher.

Meanwhile, the thirteen-year-old twins were immersed in studies at King Alfred School. Detailed reports from 1984 indicate that Tristan was 'a very pleasant pupil to teach . . . He takes a tremendous interest in games and is determined to succeed . . . He is very lively and quite talented in music and always works with interest and enthusiasm in drama – a sensitive, responsive boy.' The Head of the Middle School summarised his academic performance: 'Tristan is a very likeable boy. He is modest about his strengths such as sport, and willing to try hard to improve his written work. This report shows that this hard work is beginning to pay off in most subjects.' Ben's report was similar: 'He always involves himself with passionate energy and enthusiasm in Drama and makes a valuable contribution to the class work . . . In History Class, he has worked very hard and made great progress . . . The presentation of his work has improved.'

While Ben excelled in dramatic readings and scene study, Tristan, like his mother, tried his hand at poetry. One of his friends was a lonely boy who left school, and Tris dedicated to him a few lines he entitled 'Compassion for the Outsider'.

> I never spoke to you much at school
> Because to me you never spoke at all.
> You never seemed to have any friends –
> I remember you'd sit alone on the grass
> And watch us climbing trees,
> Swimming in the lake, or playing rough games.

You were never much good in class –
You couldn't even grasp
The easiest sum, the smallest book,
Not even a sentence on how you look.
No one missed you when you left –
Some people didn't even know you were there
But although I didn't speak to you much,
I remember you quite well.
Let's keep in touch.

At home the boys were frequently unsupervised. Alan was busy at work, or with friends, and his time with Tristan and Benedick could therefore be unexpectedly limited. When he was away, Victoria came occasionally to Hamilton Terrace; she was, as Ben recalled,

> becoming more and more unstable. She looked like a homeless bag lady; she no longer washed her hair or bathed. When she turned up at our house, she said she was just coming for a cup of tea, but she stayed for hours. Then she began to stay the night, and even, from time to time, for a couple of nights. When we told Alan that we were afraid she would do to our house what she had done to her own, he said there was only so much he could do – 'She's your mother.' Once again he told her, very gently, that she might benefit from a therapist or a counsellor, but she said she didn't need any help at all – that it was *we* who needed help. Tris and I were just beginning to have a sort of normal teenage life, with school and friends, and we didn't want Mum living with us. Some people said we should commit her to an institution. I had a friend who did that with his mother, but the woman just came out eventually, and things were still bad. We didn't want to do that with our mother.

Elizabeth Grant remained a good friend throughout difficult times. 'Victoria arrived at my home the way she went to Hamilton Terrace, virtually in rags,' Elizabeth recalled,

> and she was just unkempt and filthy, but Alan never, ever rejected her – he even took her to the theatre. He completely accepted her appearance and her conduct, which became more and more

bizarre. But this acceptance was not a good idea. We all loved Alan and stood by him, but I think there was something missing in him. He told me he wouldn't divorce Victoria because of the publicity! He didn't see the reality of it at all, or if he did, he refused to act on it. In a way, she was like Lady Caroline Lamb – obsessional, anorexic, pathetic. Alan knew she was very ill, even from the start. I asked him once why he married her, and he replied, 'I thought I could help her.' That was his way with more than one woman.

Elizabeth was on the mark in comparing Victoria to the notorious eighteenth-century aristocrat. Both Caroline and Victoria were harshly treated by tutors in childhood; both were traumatised when their mothers changed partners; both had a reputation for outrageous behaviour; and both were insistently egalitarian in their social and political views. Caroline and Victoria were both infatuated with men they insisted on marrying; both had affairs with notable men of the time; and both suffered severe mental illness that somehow did not drive their husbands to divorce them or force them into enclosure.

Another woman friend, who had known Victoria since the New York days, saw a sad truth behind her decline and wrote her feelings to Alan:

> She feels that she is some kind of awful appendage to you. You are her focus for the way she sees the world. She realises she cannot compete with all the important people around you and the work you do. In some way, she has been trying to bring you down by undermining herself and showing utter contempt for all accepted values. In order to live again in the world, she has to reaccept some of those values into her life and focus her attention elsewhere. Over the years, her conversation has often been about actors and acting, as if it were the only thing in life or the only job in the world. But she herself is not involved in this world except as your wife. She needs to be either separated properly from you or divorced, to help her recognise that the marriage is over. She obviously needs counselling, too!

Perhaps the most poignant aspect of Victoria's illness was manifest in the moments when she suddenly withdrew into her own world despite the presence of others. 'Once, Victoria and Alan came to lunch with us in London,' recalled Arthur Laurents, 'and she took out a loose-leaf pad and several coloured pencils and scribbled away. When she went to the loo, I looked at her pad – meaningless doodles.' Thus the Bates marriage continued, as if Alan and Victoria were performing some nightmarish, mad pavane in which the principals move slowly round one another, warily watching for a false step.

Alan's next theatre role was eerily close to the bone – that of the psychologically chained husband locked in a mortal battle of wills with his wife, in the two parts of Strindberg's *Dance of Death*. The play, joined as a three-and-a-half-hour marathon, opened at the Riverside Studios Theatre, Hammersmith, on 30 April 1985 and ran for eight weeks. Some critics found E. A. Whitehead's adaptation and Keith Hack's direction rather too lightweight for the depressing gravity of Strindberg – 'a buoyant, springy and often very funny production,' according to *Plays & Players*, but such a tone seemed more apt for a production of Noël Coward's *Hay Fever*. Others felt that Alan and his co-star, the admirable Frances de la Tour, rightly made the captain and his wife recognisably human – hence enabling the audience, as one critic wrote 'to see themselves in the characters, rather than sit back to observe the excesses of a schizophrenic genius', meaning Strindberg.

It is tempting to wonder if the softening of the monstrous husband in *Dance of Death* sprang as much from Alan's interpretation as from the director's choices – and equally interesting to speculate that at least part of the source of his performance was in the circumstances of his life at the time. Such may be too neat an analysis to account for the acting of so gifted an actor; but it is true that, in 1985, despite the occasional eruption of trouble from Victoria, Alan was more content than he had felt in years, and this had to do with Gerard Hastings. And private exhilaration, perhaps invariably, influences public conduct, onstage or off.

One evening that spring, Gerard drove Alan back to Hamilton Terrace after dinner at Patrick Woodcock's home. The twins were away with friends, and Gerard spent the night; he later described Alan as 'a very tender and passionate man' throughout their relationship. After that, their respective tasks enabled them to meet, at first, only on Wednesdays. 'He came to my flat and always brought a bottle of champagne and some cheesecake, which he loved. I made lunch, and we spent the afternoon together.'

But it was difficult for them to find extended private time. Gerard was still sharing quarters, and Alan would not yet invite him to stay at Hamilton Terrace, where the boys went freely to and from their rooms to their father's, and where Alan had a secretary and a housekeeper coming in each day. 'Then one of Alan's neighbours rented us a room at the top of a house, and that was where we usually met – for a while, until finally he brought me to live with him at Hamilton Terrace.' The age difference of twenty-six years was no hindrance: Gerard appreciated Alan's experience of life, while Alan loved Gerard's perceptions about the arts, his creative instincts, his energy and good humour. With great enthusiasm, Alan told Martin 'how stimulating and energetic he was – a great mate who opened up the world of art to him'.

As for the boys, Gerard remembered, 'He was never going to tell them about us, and that was really a sad thing' – perhaps sad as much for Ben and Tris, who eventually, of course, figured everything out for themselves. As the months passed, Gerard became (as Ben said) a member of the family, helping the twins with their homework, giving them his old car, which became their first; playing games and sports with them. They also joined Alan and Gerard for a visit to Patrick Woodcock's home in the south of France. 'They were such decent boys,' according to Gerard, 'kind, compassionate, fun-loving – and never flashy or arrogant. They were also keen on making their own way in the world and not depending on Alan's name or position.'

So began an intense five-year romance. 'I remember one day we were discussing cinema, and I mentioned *Whistle Down the Wind* as a favourite movie. I asked him if he knew the actor who played the fugitive in that picture, and he said, "But that was me!" I said, "Well, in that case I have been in love with you since I was six!"' Gerard learned that although Alan had dear women friends,

> they were not objects of his sexual desire. He appreciated women for companionship and men for sexual fulfilment. His erotic fantasies mainly involved men – he called attractive young men 'haunches of venison', for example. Yet sometimes, oddly, he seemed to feel very uncomfortable about his sexuality, and felt it necessary to reaffirm his masculinity, or his idea of masculinity. He actually turned to me one day and said, 'Of course, you know I'm not gay.' By this, I don't think

he meant that he was bisexual, but that he did not consider his homosexual tendencies as homosexual per se, just as sexual escapades. He hated being categorised – hated it. As a result, Alan could be very hypocritical about his sexuality, and eventually this didn't help us.

Conrad agreed: 'To me, Alan was always predominantly homosexual. Very rarely, he slept with a woman, but he was not essentially a heterosexual who only occasionally slept with men.' This was the common belief of, among others, Arthur Laurents and Ian White.

The relationship with Gerard was not a hermetically sealed affair. When Alan was onstage in London, Gerard often met him backstage after the final curtain, and they had supper at the Ivy, or Orso, or Joe Allen's – where, invariably, Alan was besieged by theatre people who stopped at their table, or by fans wanting autographs. Gerard never forgot the evening when a friend of his, a writer, approached their table, to ask if Gerard had seen his recent play; he had not, but said he had. When the man departed, Alan scolded Gerard, stressing the need always for integrity and truthfulness – and he kept up the diatribe for three days. 'But I think Alan's anger was really directed at himself. He wished he could have been truthful and open, with the kind of honesty about us that he enjoined on me.'

On Saturday evenings it was usual for them to drive directly from the theatre to Bank House in Derbyshire. 'When we arrived, we had smoked salmon and champagne. Next morning, we went shopping in the surrounding villages, and sometimes we went over to the Buxton Festival, or to visit a stately home.'

Often on weekdays and sometimes on weekends, they went to museums and art galleries; they shared exercise routines at gyms; they enjoyed opera and ballet performances, and plays in which Alan's friends worked. Over the next three years, they travelled to Bruges, Berlin, Amsterdam, Nevis – and to the coast of Northumberland, where Alan found a fisherman who rowed them out and then piggybacked them ashore to one of the secluded Farne Islands. Alan also met up with Gerard and some of his art students in Pisa, and they all went on to Florence and Arezzo, Alan driving them in a rented minibus. 'He soaked things up like blotting paper. He was astounded by the frescoes in Arezzo and by the art of Urbino. He had never really looked at paintings before, and he was surprised to discover that, like plays, they have their own inner realities to be explored and interpreted.' Nor were the twins excluded: Alan and Gerard took them to Paris, where the boys attended their first opera.

At about this time, Victoria also travelled to Paris. Alan had asked Niema to help buy his wife some clothes, which he thought Victoria might do in the context of a brief holiday. During their visit to the Louvre, a handsome young Frenchman stared at Victoria, and she returned his interested gaze before approaching him. A few days later, she returned to Niema, and the two women went back to London – minus new clothes, for Victoria's romantic interlude had allowed no time for shopping.

Gerard would not be, and was never, a kept companion. When they lived together at Hamilton Terrace, Gerard paid the food bills, did the shopping and painted the house; when they travelled, Alan picked up the hotel costs, but Gerard paid his own fare. And of course he got to know Victoria.

> Alan saw his wife as fragile and vulnerable, but she drove him absolutely mad with frustration. He felt guilty about her, and he felt very keenly that he had a responsibility towards her. He also looked after her mother, May – not only bought her a house, but cared for her, bed-bathed her, took care of her and arranged for caregivers when he was away. That was when I saw the ordinary, practical side of Alan, who didn't think that any of this was beneath the dignity of a famous man. It was one of his most lovable qualities.

It was indeed as Michael Linnit said:

> Alan was capable of being all things to all people – to men and women, children and animals, young and old. Everyone responded to his enormous warmth, spirit, sparkle and naughtiness. He was in no way arrogant – but he *was* totally vain and always aware of his success. He was grateful for it and never took it for granted.

That spirit, sparkle and naughtiness saw Alan through a difficult and disappointing play that opened at the National Theatre on 4 December 1985: he had the title role in Peter Shaffer's *Yonadab*, set during the time of the biblical King David. As the title character, 'who dominates the evening without being very plausible or inter-esting', as a senior critic wrote, Alan received a few negative notices, although the consensus was that 'the root problem is surely the writing'.

It was, Alan said, the most difficult role of his career – and no wonder, for he was onstage for virtually all of the play's two hours and forty-five minutes. 'After Shaffer's huge successes [*The Royal Hunt of the Sun*, *Equus* and *Amadeus* among others], the expecta-tions were far too high, and I wish we had been able to do it in a workshop style that wouldn't have been so easy to shoot down.' The director, Peter Hall, agreed, adding that Alan, 'like all great actors, saw the humour in drama and even in tragedy', and that sensibility he brought to *Yonadab*; Alan could not, however, lighten the proceedings.

Except once. At the beginning of the play's second act, Alan as usual addressed the prescribed line of dialogue to the audience: 'Had enough yet?' But that evening an entire claque replied with a shout that yes, they had indeed had enough. With nothing to lose, Alan ad libbed, 'Good – because it's going to get worse!' And in the perverse nature of such moments, he thus won over the audience for the rest of the performance. This unfortunate play was the excep-tion to modern works he undertook (by, for example, Simon Gray, Harold Pinter and David Storey), of which he said, 'I don't get them at first, but I get them in doing them' – by instinct more than analysis.

His schedule during the first months of 1986 would have exhausted a man half his age. He rehearsed with director Patrick Garland for an evening of Philip Larkin's poetry, *Down Cemetery Road*, presented at the Cottesloe on 16 January (and repeated at the Playhouse Theatre almost three years later). A few days after that he was being fitted for his wardrobe and had make-up tests for a feature film that engaged him from February to April – and all the while he was driving each evening to the South Bank for the play. 'I'm dominated by work,' he said that season. 'Acting consumes me, and an obsession doesn't leave a lot of time for anything else.'

Martin, among others, observed the whirlwind of his brother's life with some concern. Apart from the problems of his fluctuating weight, due to erratic diets, 'there were as yet no serious signs of ill health. But extending himself so much in his work, and worrying about

Victoria, her mother, the twins' schooling and welfare and his own elderly mother – all this must have been quietly taking a toll.'

The new picture was Andrei Konchalovsky's *Duet for One*, in which Alan played the hard-drinking, unfaithful husband of a world-famous violinist who is struck down by multiple sclerosis. Loosely based on the life of cellist Jacqueline du Pré, *Duet for One* owes its restrained poignancy and emotional power to a deeply felt performance by Julie Andrews; Alan appears infrequently in the picture, his character unsympathetic, mostly inebriated and dishevelled, and his scenes were crudely overwritten. The husband, he said, 'was not the most admirable of men – not a bad man, exactly, but weak, self-centred, totally unable to cope with his wife's condition'. Why did he accept the role? 'I needed a film just then – I had to pay some taxes.' His fee certainly helped: he was paid $250,000, which nicely offset his typically modest stipend from the National Theatre, £375 weekly.

That summer, the Buxton Opera House, Derbyshire, invited Alan to speak the title role in Purcell's *King Arthur*, with a text by John Dryden. This was neither an opera nor an oratorio but scenes with incidental music and occasional singing by a chorus of twelve. Alas, the six performances in late July and early August showcased 'a lifeless artefact', as one critic observed. Nor did Alan fare much better: 'he wandered disconsolately around the stage as though bemused at finding himself in such strange company.'

He brought the boys and Gerard to Derby for a summer visit with his mother, and there were lavish luncheons at Bank House, where Alan had installed an outdoor pool. Watching the swimmers, Mary was observed by Alan, who whispered wickedly to Gerard, 'There's the reigning monarch.' She was, as Conrad said, 'charming but formidable' – as when she turned to Gerard and asked sweetly, 'Which room in Bank House are *you* staying in this weekend, dear?' Unfazed, he replied, 'The usual room.'

In late September, still 'dominated by work', Alan rushed into an even more sinister film role, that of a bloodthirsty Irish mobster in the Mike Hodges film, *A Prayer for the Dying*. At least one of the other actors, Bob Hoskins, told the press he had agreed to appear in the picture solely for the chance to work with Alan, an experience that leavened the most demanding days of the production.

Marinated in violence, the movie in fact has two redeeming features

– the dilemma of conscience in the leading character (played by Mickey Rourke), an IRA hit man who forswears violence; and Alan's savagely cruel portrait of an undertaker who favours death and exsanguinations even for the living. This role was mostly dismissed by moviegoers at the time, but Alan completely incarnated him, oozing fatal charm even while he ordered and enjoyed the torture of others. He could have delivered a merely showy performance; instead, Alan simply modulated his voice to chilling effect and smiled icily.

Whatever their merits, *Duet for One* and *A Prayer for the Dying* (which together enriched him by $500,000) marked a major shift in his choices when he was fifty-two years old: he was a first-rate character actor who had abandoned his romantic, leading-man image. Insisting on careful make-up and convincing hairpieces, he was still fiercely protective of his looks and was ever concerned about losing his appeal. 'He hated getting old,' as Conrad recalled, 'but he also hated exercise, dieting and buying clothes with a proper fit. He had the vanity but not the discipline to achieve the looks he desired both on screen and off.' Simon felt that 'his vanity got in the way' of his becoming a great Falstaff, for example, because

> he couldn't bear to play a fat man, however nimble-tongued and quick of wit, however gorgeous in his pomp, broken in his fall – really, he still saw himself, too late in his career, as a leading man, romantic – to his inner eye lean and svelte and dashing, when in truth he was big-boned, stocky, a heavy mover . . . [H]is energy distracted the attention from his shape, as did the marvellous eyes, the handsome mouth, the line of the cheeks and the exuberant head of hair – but it grew on a round head, set on a bullish neck, and physically he was a peasant, a Derbyshire peasant, and his hands were agricultural.

Conrad vividly remembered a holiday on which he joined Alan. 'I don't want to be bothered with autograph seekers and celebrity watchers – I want to be anonymous,' he told Conrad, who followed Alan a few days later to the island of Ibiza. 'I arrived, and there in the middle of the concourse, on a blazing hot day, stood this figure in a black homburg, wrapped in a scarf. So there was this wonderful contradiction – he wanted to be inconspicuous, but he was as flamboyant as Donald Wolfit, and he could be quite disturbed if people did *not* recognise him!'

Not every aspect of the matter was amusing, as it is not for many people in a profession that places the ultimate premium on maintaining one's glamour. 'Alan found it difficult to accept that middle age was taking away some of his youthful good looks, was thickening him out,' Conrad continued. 'We always had a laugh about him dying his hair, for example. When one went to the bathroom at his house, one could see the hair dye in the basin – "You've got your Margaret Lockwood black hair back again!" we told him. He knew that we knew, but he denied it until we fell about laughing.'

'It's exhausting to keep both stage work and films going,' Alan admitted that winter, feeling unusually tired. 'Combining them takes quite a toll because the physical demands are so different. In the theatre, your effort is intense and constant. In movies, the energy drain is more deceptive, because you have to be ready to do any section of the film at any time, although you may actually do only one scene a day. Also, the effort goes on much longer. The strength that takes is very real, even if you aren't consciously aware of it.'

Before working on another television movie in February 1987, Alan participated in a poetry reading at the Prince of Wales Theatre, to benefit children suffering from leukaemia. He also narrated a television documentary (*Bridge to the East*) about Steven Runciman's historic research on the Crusades and Eastern Christendom.

That done, he hurried to Pinewood and to various locations in Greater London for eleven days of work on *Pack of Lies*, hastily but expertly directed by Anthony Page from a fact-based play by Hugh Whitemore that had enjoyed considerable Broadway success. *Pack of Lies* concerns a suburban couple (Ellen Burstyn and Ronald Hines) whose home is taken over by a British intelligence agent (Alan) for surveillance against friendly neighbours (Teri Garr and Daniel Benzali), who turn out to be KGB spies.

When Alan says, 'We need your help on a very delicate matter,' there is a tone of menace underlying the apparent nationalism; soon and sure enough, everyone lies, becomes tainted by deceit and is duly imperilled; as an obsessive agent, Alan captured the proper spirit of ruthless obsession, making patriotism almost reprehensible; seedy and silky, he was unpredictable at every turn.

He then gathered up his sons during a term holiday and sped to France, where he filmed a half-hour television episode of *The Ray*

Bradbury Theatre, in yet another version of that writer's old chestnut, *And So Died Riabouchinska*. Acting with scarcely concealed, loony glee, Alan played the role of Fabian, a mad and murderous ventriloquist given away by his own irrepressible creation, a doll 'vit a Roshin herititch'.

There was no Russian heritage in his next character – a publisher caught in a moment of crisis who wisecracks his way towards total nervous collapse in Christopher Morahan's production of Simon Gray's new play, *Melon*. Rehearsals began in early March; the company travelled during April and May to Guildford, Croydon, Brighton and Bath; and the six-month London run at the Theatre Royal, Haymarket, began on 19 June.

Simon described Mark Melon as a man

> who advocates promiscuity for his wife and himself, then has a nervous breakdown when he decides, against all available evidence, that his wife is having an affair with one of his best friends – which best friend being the conundrum that finally drives him mad . . . [*Melon*] played to good houses, thanks mainly to Alan Bates, whose performance as the brute Englishman with the chaotic soul was so dazzling that it flattered the text.

'It's crack-up time again,' Alan said of *Melon*, 'but there are some extremely funny lines on the way.' The route to the play's London version was not easy, for Simon meticulously rewrote during the pre-West End tour, once handing his leading man a new and lengthy speech just hours before curtain time. To the admiring consternation of his colleagues, Alan was nevertheless word-perfect when he stepped onstage that evening. 'I've always been able to learn at speed,' he said by way of explanation. 'Changes keep you thinking. They keep you alert. You have to understand the difference they make to the action that follows.' It was precisely this sort of unhysterical, considerate attitude towards playwrights that earned Alan Bates the profoundest respect from the likes of Osborne, Pinter, Storey, Gray and others, who were delighted to work repeatedly with him. Vain he may have been – but neither temperament nor self-absorption tarnished his working habits.

Alan's characterisation of Mark Melon was judged by one critic to be 'masterly [a word favoured repeatedly by those reviewing Alan's performances] . . . He bounces into rooms like a rubber ball . . . yet there is always something edgily over-the-top about his reactions.' Another noted Alan's 'easy, if querulous command of the stage, and [his] odd knack of being able to communicate despair and unconcern simultaneously'. But there were objections from those who found his performance 'half-manic, half-mannered and wholly familiar'.

Earlier in his career, he had thought little of disrobing during a performance, but by the age of fifty-three, as Simon recalled, Alan 'hid behind the furniture when stripping down to his underwear' in one scene, 'and pretty well stayed there, almost crouching, until the end of the scene . . . I tried once or twice, to get him out into the open, but he invariably said it was no good, wherever he went he seemed to end up behind the desk or the chair, and added that he wasn't a young man any more, there was too much of him, he was bloody well going to keep most of it to himself . . .' But Gray was not alone in considering Alan 'beautiful, in the way that no artefact can be beautiful'.

Ben and Tris, then sixteen, handsome, and now a head taller than their father, attended the London opening of *Melon* that June and were photographed backstage with him, all of them smiling broadly. When journalists asked if the boys planned acting careers, they prudently avoided a clear reply – they were busy with school, they said. They did not say that they had already been approached by a modelling agency, and negotiations were under way for them to travel near and far for advertising photo shoots.

Gerard, meanwhile, continued to be Alan's most fervent fan and constant support, which he demonstrated by frequent attendance at *Melon*. From this play, Alan turned to yet another gay character, although that aspect was not central to the amiable film comedy *We Think the World of You*, made in London over six weeks in January and February 1988. Based (almost incident for incident) on an autobiographical novel by Joseph R. Ackerley, the movie told the simple but moving story of a middle-aged civil servant named Frank (Alan) whose sometime boyfriend Johnny (Gary Oldman) is jailed for burglary. During Johnny's year-long incarceration, Frank looks after the boy's parents, copes with Johnny's shrewish wife and takes on – reluctantly at first, then with concern and devotion – the care of the boy's dog, a rambunctious Alsatian who needs nothing so much as affectionate attention and regular sprints in the park. Out of this potentially thin material, screenwriter Hugh Stoddart and director Colin Gregg fashioned a sharply amusing domestic drama on a small but splendidly human scale, infusing it with considerable but unsentimental tenderness.

Alan was direct about his attraction to the project, which he researched by interviewing some of Ackerley's surviving gay friends. 'Ackerley sought friendships with his own sex,' he said, 'but unhappily and frustratedly. What's touching about Frank and Johnny is that they like each other. Somewhere in this doomed relationship there is a genuine little spark of affection.' His performance was a delicate chain of choices, of grace notes appropriate for creating a man whose patience comes undone even as his heart expands. *We Think the World of You* is certainly one of his finest late films.

As for Alan's domestic situation, it was quietly desperate in 1988 – leavened only by Gerard and by Ian White, whom Alan invited to come over from his home in Canada. Ian was not only a trusted confidant: he was also a fund of creative ideas for the upgrading and refurnishing of Bank House and the compound at Hamilton Terrace, both of which needed work and a fresh eye for design. Ian could not have come along at a more auspicious time, for over the next several years Alan very much needed sympathetic and understanding friends.

Alan's were not the only residences in need of attention. After years of neglect, Victoria's house was uninhabitable, as Ben recalled.

> When Alan saw what her place had become, he said to Mum, 'Come live with us while I have it fixed up.' She did just that, but when it was finished she wouldn't move back. So newspapers began to pile up in our house too, and food began to rot in our fridge, and her bedroom deteriorated. 'I just don't want to rush back,' she said.

Eventually Alan told Victoria that he would be happy to sell Lavender Cottage and buy her a flat, but this offer she refused. When he said he would indeed put the cottage on the market if she was not planning on living there, she went back to it – and, as Ben remembered, 'very quickly, this really lovely, remodelled house was strewn with rubbish and looked abandoned. There was dust on the windows, no lights inside – and it came to the point that a couple of odd squatters wanted to move in, too. Then she began to get really thin. Her sister had died of breast cancer, and we were quite worried about her now, too. But Mum said she couldn't be bothered to eat. Alan was generous with her, but the more generous he was, the more she tormented him.'

And what of the boys' reaction to Gerard? 'At first we never thought much about Alan's intimate life,' said Ben, summarising the feelings of himself and his brother.

> When I was very young, I denied it – it was too much for me to absorb. But then, one of my first girlfriends asked me how long my Dad had been with this one man. I replied that I had never talked to anyone about it before. It was a big relief to speak with her, and to laugh off my anxiety and realise that of course my father could do whatever he wanted. Later, when I discussed Gerard with Alan, he spoke of him as a friend, but not as a boyfriend or lover – and he never defined or described his sexual orientation. But when he was in this serious relationship, we knew what it was. The fact is that Gerard was a good friend to Tris and me.

That same year, Gerard spoke of an artistic collaboration with Alan, but first he had to complete another television drama. *The Dog It Was That Died*, based on a radio play by Tom Stoppard and made in May and June 1988 in Manchester, reunited him with Peter Wood, who had staged *Poor Richard* on Broadway in 1964. Simultaneously a satire on espionage and an exploration of moral crisis, the script featured a spy knowingly recruited by opposing sides. His suicide attempt fails, his fall broken by a dog that dies instead. Alan, as the head of MI5, conveyed the humour, the honour and the ultimate tragedy of the situation.

During the spring and summer, he and Gerard were immersed in artistic and literary research. The theme of the Salisbury Festival that year was fire – a four-year elemental cycle was planned – and, from 3 through 17 September artistic director Mark Eynon was bringing together opera singers, musicians, actors and artists to present a variety of programmes in Salisbury Cathedral, at the Playhouse and at the Arts Centre. Stravinsky's *Firebird* suite was heard, for example, as were Handel's *Fireworks* music, Haydn's *Fire* symphony, de Falla's *Ritual Fire Dance* and soprano Gwyneth Jones, who sang Brünnhilde's Immolation Scene.

On the evening of Friday, 16 September, a multimedia event called

A Muse of Fire was presented at the cathedral. Devised by Gerard, who was painter-in-residence at Salisbury that season and executed the impressive backdrop for the event, this imaginative, candlelit offering synthesised poetry, drama, music, painting and lighting effects, while Alan read appropriate texts from Michelangelo, Dickens, Lawrence, Milton, Shakespeare, Donne, Blake, the Scriptures, Hardy and Frost among others. Their programme was so successful that it was later repeated for a charity event at the Playhouse, London, and was exported to the Edinburgh Festival in 1989.

Between performance dates Alan rushed to France for twelve days, to appear in Pierre Jolivet's film, *Force Majeure*, in which he played a human rights lawyer trying to persuade two young men to accept their responsibility for the imprisonment of a friend on drug charges. Alan's French was heavily accented but acceptable; his supporting performance was merely straightforward, as the indifferent role required. It was no loss that *Force Majeure* was never distributed in Britain or America, for the rights to it were, for reasons that defy rational explanation, snapped up for a Hollywood remake. Alan was glad to be home for Christmas, weary but optimistic for a new year.

13

'Sorrows . . . in battalions'

Alan dedicated the first half of 1989 to a pair of plays that gave him and audiences enormous pleasure: Chekhov's *Ivanov* and Shakespeare's *Much Ado About Nothing*, which opened in Guildford before moving on to Richmond, Bath and London. His co-star in both productions was Felicity Kendal, much admired for her skill in both comic and tragic roles, and destined to be Alan's close friend as well as a valued colleague. When she won the *Evening Standard* Award as best actress of the year for these two plays, Felicity told the crowd, 'Six months with Chekhov, Shakespeare and Alan Bates – what more could anyone ask?'

'Sometimes during rehearsals, Alan was quite angry with himself when he was trying to get something right and didn't think he had done,' she recalled years later.

> But when you were onstage with him, your own nerves vanished and you were completely relaxed, because he was absolutely focused, he had total concentration. Alan was always the star, and he behaved as if he led the company – not with any arrogance, but with enormous generosity that came from his self-confidence about who he was and what he was about. That sense of who he was spread throughout the company.

Felicity's friendship with Alan was rooted in their shared under-standing of the dramatic material and their remarkable ability to listen to one another onstage – a talent not always found among actors. To watch them was to observe two players giving and receiving from one another a rare energy, to the delight of spectators. Like Gemma and Georgina, she became one of the few colleagues admitted to the precincts of Alan's private life.

'Victoria was very, very strange and very, very sick. I recognised just what Alan was doing by his attentiveness to her. By looking after her and giving her what she wanted, he behaved as if the illness made no difference and that everything could somehow be all right. If she went into a corner or made conversation impossible, he said, "Oh, she's having a quiet moment, let's have coffee," and he carried on as if her behaviour were quite normal.'

In early autumn, Alan appeared as a devoutly religious police inspector in *Mister Frost*, a movie set in England but made entirely in and around Paris, under French director Philip Setbon. (In some countries it was released as *Mr Frost*; in all his other pictures the director was identified as Philippe Setbon.) The title character, played with polite menace by Jeff Goldblum, is not only a sadistic serial killer but, as it emerges, the devil incarnate, which explains his name: in Dante's *Commedia*, Satan is frozen in ice at the bottom of hell.

At first, only Alan's character believes the truth about Frost, but eventually even a coolly rationalist psychiatrist (Kathy Baker) comes to accept the notion. On the page, the screenplay tackled some provocative ideas: the nature of evil; the popular but misperceived conflict between faith and reason; and the venerable Gallic idea of the transfer of guilt – themes that may have encouraged Alan to sign on. But during production everything became subordinate to the standard exigencies of the horror genre and an improbable, wildly disordered continuity. The movie advanced no one's career, and Alan's appearance was reduced to a series of wise, knowing glances.

By the end of October *Mr Frost* was complete and Alan proceeded to Munich, where he met up with Gerard. They went on to Berlin, where another French director, Claude Chabrol, had invited Alan to play a corrupt media genius in perhaps the only movie ever released simultaneously with two titles, as the opening credits oddly state:

CLUB EXTINCTION

A Film by Claude Chabrol

Alan Bates

Jennifer Beals

Jan Niklas

in

DR M

By whatever name it is discussed, the film, set just before the year 2000, is a fascinating failure – a kind of updated version of Fritz Lang's silent 1922 classic *Dr Mabuse der Spieler*. Even more grisly than *Mr Frost*, the picture has Chabrol's grave social-moral concerns – in this case the potentially lethal effects of mind control by television, which here leads legions of people to suicide. In the role of the mogul Dr Heinrich Marsfeldt, Alan created a slick madman whose mechanical heart works best when he views people suffering and dying. *Club Extinction/Dr M* has the kind of chaotic untidiness that often leads fans to hail merely obscure movies as profound. Alan took no special pleasure in either the Setbon or the Chabrol film, except that he came home with a total of more than $300,000 for his efforts.

But the nonsense of *Club Extinction* was overwhelmed by real-life drama in Berlin. On 9 November – first on television in their hotel suite, then in the crowded streets – Alan and Gerard saw the Berlin Wall come down. 'We went along and joined the throng,' Gerard recalled, adding that they chipped away at the wall and got a piece of it for a keepsake. Home for Christmas, they then sped off for a four-day holiday in the Canary Islands, returning to Hamilton Terrace on the evening of 12 January 1990.

On precisely that date, thousands of miles distant, an appalling tragedy was unfolding.

When they finished their studies at King Alfred School, Benedick and Tristan were engaged by a London modelling agency, where their good looks and poise made them suitable candidates for work in the fashion industry. At the same time, Tristan became a wild partygoer, drinking to excess and falling in with a crowd that routinely indulged in hard drugs; Ben, on the other hand, had nothing to do with dangerous habits, preferring instead a few drinks in the evening with friends.

During the end of summer 1989, the agency sent the twins to Tokyo for some lucrative fashion work. There, they were comfortably set up in furnished flats, and they made new friends easily among an international group of models. On the morning of Friday, 12 January, Tristan went to a physician for inoculations against malaria, cholera and other tropical diseases, as he was to depart for some different modelling work in South-east Asia. That evening he and Ben met others at a bar, where word went round that heroin was available. Tristan slipped away to a bathroom with some people who offered the drug, while Ben returned to his apartment.

'Tristan's room-mate rang me on Saturday morning, the thirteenth, to say he had not come home on Friday night,' Ben recalled. 'That was very unusual for him, but we told ourselves that Tris was probably with a new girlfriend. By Sunday morning there was still no word, and we knew something was definitely wrong. We began to ring other friends, but no one had heard from him. Then it occurred to us that maybe he had been arrested for something, so we went to the police and reported him missing.'

The Tokyo police then informed Ben that they had found the body of a young Caucasian male – 'in the public lavatory of Ajiro Park, in Minato Ward, Tokyo', as the report stated. A representative of the modelling agency first went down to the morgue and he reported to Ben that the body was indeed Tristan's. Ben had to make the official identification. 'It was horrendous. I thought, "This can't be true, they've made a mistake." At first I thought the body didn't really look like Tristan's – but no, it was.'

At Hamilton Terrace, Alan and Gerard were watching videotapes of *The Mayor of Casterbridge* when the telephone rang. Gerard answered and handed the receiver to Alan. 'A moment later,' Gerard recalled, 'Alan just seemed to go mad – he became completely hysterical.' ('I could hear him going to pieces,' Ben said.) Gerard tried to calm Alan and then said they had to inform Victoria at once. They rang her, saying she had to come immediately to Hamilton Terrace. When she arrived and learned the news, 'she was calm and practical and started to prepare for the journey with Alan to Tokyo.'

Gerard also rang Ros and Michael, and they ran interference against an intrusive press. Felicity Kendal lived not far from Alan, and after Ros rang her she raced to his side. 'The dignity with which he conducted himself was extraordinary,' Felicity recalled. 'It was something I can never forget.' Gerard drove Alan and Victoria to Heathrow the next day and they departed for Japan. 'Gerard was a tremendous support to Alan, Victoria and Ben,' according to Martin.

Ten days later, Alan, Victoria and Ben returned with the body, and Ros and Martin met them at Heathrow. 'They appeared from the passenger exit looking desperately sad and exhausted,' Martin remembered. 'Alan's words were simple and unforgettable: "We've brought Tristan home."'

Autopsies conducted in Tokyo and London confirmed traces of the anti-cholera and anti-malarial medication he had received, as well as alcohol and heroin or opium. According to the Tokyo police investigation, Tristan had left the bar and was on his way home when he fell ill in Ajiro Park. He entered a lavatory, where he collapsed, unconscious; his lungs quickly filled with fluid, and within moments he was dead.

'My brother and I were just nineteen,' Ben said. 'I felt lost in the world – a real focus had gone out of my life. He was not centred, but I thought we were good for one another, and suddenly I was completely vulnerable and off-balance.'

'It was generally known at the time', said Michael Linnit, 'that Tristan's death was caused by drug abuse. Alan never verbalised it and his way of coping was to block it. We wanted only to bring him comfort – and if silence on the cause of death helped him, then that was fine with the rest of us. During those early months of 1990 he was like a pendulum – breaking out in heart-wrenching sobs, then offering strength and comfort to others, then swinging back into great depths of misery.'

'When he came back,' according to Felicity, 'he seemed to have aged twenty years. He saw the absurdity of the situation, but somehow – and it was breathtaking – he was able to be in that terrible moment without blaming fate or other people. He didn't want to shut away Tristan's death or ignore it. He wanted to discuss it, he wanted it recognised.' For months, sleep was difficult, for Alan constantly found Tristan in his dreams and then he awoke, disconsolate.

Victoria, who at first had seemed so composed, took a great step further back from reality. As preparations went forward for Tristan's memorial service she said to Alan, 'Everything's going to be all right. All we have to do is get him home, keep his body warm, and he'll eventually come round – he'll come right back to life.' Alan could find no response to this chillingly heartbreaking statement.

'Tristan's death was the most hideous form of shell-shock I can imagine,' Alan said. 'I suppose I was lucky – I had him for twenty years. He was my gift . . . The pain of his loss will never leave me – you see, we got on so well as father and son, and I loved him. He was a boy who left a great mark on anyone he met, and his friends always speak of him. But he is with me – he is always with me. I can't say any more, I have to leave it at that. One has to go on . . .'

It is no exaggeration to state that something died forever in Alan Bates that January of 1990. 'It would be a betrayal of my son,' he said to Gerard, 'if I don't feel the pain of his loss for the rest of my life.' Then and later, when he discussed the matter with friends, Alan often concluded, with a heart-rending murmur, 'It's unacceptable . . . just unacceptable.'

Years later, he spoke at length to journalists.

> It's a very shocking thing to lose a child. It made me think a great deal about what I believe or don't believe – about life and the afterlife. Not that I've come to any great decisions, of course – but I do know that he hasn't gone. People don't disappear from your mind when they leave you physically . . .
>
> It's tempting to go all wacko and say, 'He spoke to me yesterday.' Wacko or not, I believe in his presence – the mysteries of going are the same as the mysteries of coming . . . I wasn't mad with grief, of course – but I was consumed, just consumed utterly. You have to go to the extremes, or you won't come out the other side. You stand a chance if you let yourself be wrecked. Suppress it and you're in big trouble. And you have, in the end, to find a way to come to terms with it. So you go on . . . I don't expect to get over it. I don't even want to . . . People ask, 'How do you cope?' All I can say is that you do.

But he could never 'get over' it, and he always had to cope with an enormous burden of guilt for the fate of his son, which Alan felt was the result of his failed marriage, his devotion to his career as if acting was the most rewarding lover, and his refusal to acknowledge the long period of the boys' wretched existence with their mother. Complicating this was his need to insist publicly that Tristan's death was due to an allergic reaction to an anti-cholera injection: any other explanation, he believed, would harm his favourable publicity. It would also open up the entire issue of his family life and history, so he encouraged the benign fiction of a happy home with his wife and sons. 'Three handsome men and a beautiful woman,' he had said proudly, indicating a photograph of himself with Victoria and the boys. 'There we are, all together – the family!'

There were several memorials for Tristan during 1990: a private funeral at Christ Church, Hampstead, on 24 January, completely and efficiently organised by Gerard; a burial service two days later, at All Saints Church, Bradbourne; and on 16 September, again at Christ Church, Hampstead, for a larger public that included Tristan's schoolmates.

David Storey recalled the January funeral:

> Alan stepped up to the coffin, stood with his hand on it for a moment and then turned to those assembled and began to speak in very moving terms. But then the noise of a vacuum cleaner started up somewhere in the vestry. He continued to speak, but it got louder and louder. And then there was a very Alan moment. He said, 'Just a moment, please,' and he disappeared into the vestry. When he returned, the noise had stopped and he continued speaking with the same emotion. That was a genuine actor. His grief was authentic, and the noise of the vacuum had been an intrusion on the performance he was giving. It somehow had the kind of irony he was fond of in moments of great feeling.

At Bradbourne, as Martin remembered, 'Alan had to call on all his skill and experience to get through the visible emotional faltering as he delivered his heartbreaking remarks.' At the September memorial, Alan again spoke eloquently:

> Tristan's family are overwhelmed by the affection so many people have shown by being here today, and by the way that the King Alfred School have honoured Tristan's life this week.
>
> Victoria, Benedick and I know that our lives will never be the same again, but we are glad that Tristan stayed with us for nineteen years. His life was a gift for which we are eternally grateful. We are grieving at his loss, but our grief must become positive, just as his life was positive – a happy childhood with happy and successful school years. He was charming, humorous and wise, a young man who, as his drama teacher Tony [Grounds]

has just described, often looked after those younger than himself; he was also healthily ambitious and, in the last three months, quite clearly on the brink of considerable success. His latest portfolio of photographs showed him suddenly aware of his own potential: stylish, graceful, dramatic, outrageous and imaginative. His brother Benedick had for one and a half seasons been doing considerably better than Tristan, but it was Ben who described to me with pride his brother's sudden surge forward to a point where only two weeks ago he had achieved the offer of a job in America with a renowned art photographer. His ability as an actor had begun to show through in his modelling work.

In his private life and as someone about to realise himself through his work, Tristan had a rival and an equal – his brother Benedick, and for all of us who love them, please give your thoughts and energies to him. In their nineteen years, Tristan and Benedick have touched a great deal of life – travel, adventure, close and loving relationships with colleagues at school and at work, young men and women, some of whom have travelled from Los Angeles and Tokyo to be with them today; and a bond known to few people. They are twins and they greatly valued this extra dimension.

Tristan is with us – he has not gone, so let us slowly turn our tears to joy at having known him.

Alan concluded by borrowing lines from *King Henry IV, Part Two*, to which he made appropriate emendations:

> Yet weep that Tristan's dead; and so will I;
> But Tristan lives, that shall convert those tears
> By number into hours of happiness.

As for Victoria, she looked even more desperate and shabby with each passing week. Alan was unable to persuade her to come into the church at Bradbourne, so he asked Marie Malavieille, who had arrived from Paris, to encourage her. 'I walked outside with her for a while,' Marie recalled, 'and she finally did go in – but only to the vestibule of the church.' It was as if something in Victoria still denied the reality of her son's death: if she saw nothing that confirmed a funeral and interment, then no one had died.

*   *   *

'One has to go on,' Alan had said, and in 1990 he did just that – with a ferocious, undiluted and relentless energy that was also something of an escape mechanism. 'After Tristan died,' recalled Martin, 'Alan became obsessed with working constantly, taking role after part after role. He tried to lose himself in work as a way of coping with the tragedy, and it eventually exhausted him.' Conrad felt that 'Alan was never the same after Tristan died. He worked, but the light went out. I think he felt guilty that he hadn't seen more of the boys, and now it was too late for him to do anything for Tristan, although he was certainly completely supportive of Ben. Alan began to put on weight, and there was a cloud over his life.'

To come to terms with the tragedy, one of the means he took was to hire a private detective in Tokyo, charged with finding the source of the drugs Tristan had taken. But as Alan later told David Storey, he soon had a message from the girl who had actually supplied the heroin. 'She said that if Alan explored the situation further, she would be killed and an entire international can of worms would be opened. Alan was racked by this and felt very frustrated. In the end he took the inspector off the case.'

His punishing, self-imposed schedule began on 2 April, when he started rehearsals as Claudius in Franco Zeffirelli's film of *Hamlet*, produced over the next three months in London, West Lothian, Aberdeenshire, Kent, Surrey and Thionville, France; his colleagues included Mel Gibson (Hamlet), Glenn Close (Gertrude) and Helena Bonham Carter (Ophelia). Alan's performance was magnificently subtle, as he conveyed both the perfidious passion and the timorous eccentricity of Claudius. One of his finest moments occurred during the sequence at Ophelia's graveside: 'Another nineteen-year-old,' he said after shooting the scene. 'At least I knew how to behave. Actually, I suddenly saw death everywhere – everything was connected to death, everything was sharpened, heightened.' But he was displeased with the final version of the film, which he thought cut far too much of the text and many of the actors' finest scenes.

From Shakespeare he went into another Alan Bennett teleplay – and as another gay man, this time Marcel Proust, in *102 Boulevard Haussmann*. The seventy-minute drama was based on a time in the novelist's life when his maid and his physician tried to sever his relationship with an attractive young male musician he repeatedly brought to his apartment late at night. The director, Udayan Prasad, was greatly impressed with Alan's brilliance at conveying the subtlest shadings of feelings for the television camera close-ups. 'Alan had never read Proust,' according to Bennett, 'but he was completely absorbed in the role. And he was not only going through his own difficult time – he was also looking after [his mother-in-law] May in her senility.'

Ben, meanwhile, was making every effort to put his life in order. He auditioned for drama schools that spring, then went to Canada for a holiday with his girlfriend. While there, he learned that he had won a place at LAMDA (the London Academy of Music and Dramatic Art), and on his return he began a regular course of studies to be an actor.

But all was not well between Gerard and Alan. 'By the spring of 1990, Alan was not the same person, and we began to bicker and argue – over small things at first. Neither of us was an angel at the time. On the one hand he was trapped by his celebrity and on the other I felt unable to cope with it. There were enormous pressures living with someone so powerful and well-known.' More to the point, Gerard (then thirty) began to feel the serious imbalances in the relationship with Alan (then fifty-six), who always belonged first to his public and was perpetually concerned about the public's reactions. 'Finally I told him I felt like I was just his bit on the side.' Conrad remembered that Alan 'never acknowledged Gerard in public. Gerard always had to walk two paces behind, or come earlier or later to a party if they were both invited – but they mustn't be seen together.'

A deciding factor in the separation occurred when Alan arrived home with a stranger and proceeded to open a bottle of champagne for them. With that, Gerard left. 'We continued to speak on the phone for a while, but there was a lot of anger and resentment, and Alan often asked, "What do you want me to do?"' Gerard replied that some honesty would go a long way, but by 1991 they were essentially no longer a couple. 'All his life', as Gareth Wigan said, 'Alan both wanted and feared a lasting union with someone, but it eluded him.'

For six weeks in November and December 1990 Alan was in Lisbon, filming ('in highly unorganised chaos', as producer Graham Leader later said) an ill-fated movie called *Shuttlecock*. This was a strangely incomprehensible project about the difficulties of a young Englishman

(Lambert Wilson) in relating both to his son (Gregory Chisolm) and his father (Alan), a Resistance hero during World War Two who suffers a mental breakdown years later.

'I had read the script,' said Alan, 'and I liked it at once. The two things it is about, I've experienced and thought about a lot – the first is the parent-child business, three generations trying to understand each other; the other is the theme of heroism and cowardice, how people can be brave at moments and do appalling things as well.' Apparently these things seemed clear to him on the page, but during filming and editing, much of that clarity became muddied.

The final product, directed by Andrew Piddington, was never released theatrically; it turned up once on London's Channel 4 and then vanished. Darryl MacDonald, a film festival director who saw *Shuttlecock* twice and briefly but seriously considered backing a public screening, summarised the opinion of many: 'It's difficult to follow any thread of the story, difficult to engage any of the characters, and three-quarters of the time it's impossible for the audience to tell what the hell is going on.' As a critic, MacDonald was on the mark.

Seen years later, *Shuttlecock* is remarkable only for Alan's performance as a man traumatised by his own memories, his guilt and his confrontation with his son, played with admirable restraint by Lambert Wilson. Alan succumbed to none of the clichés so often attached to the role of a mute, withdrawn psychotic; instead, the man's frightened and frightening situation was communicated by blankness in his eyes and a shuffling gait.

Home in London, there was a letter from Gerard. In his reply, Alan addressed the objection that he was unwilling to accept the consequences of his sexual inclinations and therefore incapable of commitment to another man:

> . . . I think because I'm separated from V, I think of myself as unmarried, but of course, legally I am. Because Tristan and Ben were independent, travelling and earning their own money, I thought of myself as free to live my own life again. But of course I'm still a father to Ben and even still to Tris. And as for coming out, as Simon G said, 'You can't; it's not even true. That's not the whole story with you' (as of course Ben and Tris are evidence of) . . .

Six weeks apart have given me some perspective. I had feelings of loss, loneliness, bewilderment and anger. I found also to my relief that I can live without you if I have to. Life will not be without meaning or empty. But you are the best and most rewarding relationship I've known.

So *where are we*? Once a parent, your children are always your prime moving force. That is the nature of parenthood. In life with Ben and in death with Tristan, my spirit has to be with them. But if you find a *companion* on the way who can give, like you can, then one is lucky. You must not be restricted or feel *blackmailed* emotionally by me. We must both be FREE. But we must agree on rules of living or just be friends. We must obviously TALK as well as write letters. I found, in these six weeks, that many another relationship could begin for me – with girls and with boys (or should I say, with *women* and with *men*) and one of them was very much in the air and still is – so life would not be devastatingly over, but I suspect that the most rewarding friendship would be. I don't know – anything can happen – you can't really promise anyone the rest of your life, much as one romantically wants to . . .

We both want to have our cake and eat it – but we have both nevertheless felt hurt, misunderstood and slightly used (especially me, he cried!).

Perhaps I hide behind my family – feel safe behind them – I don't know. Perhaps I don't want the commitment I say I do . . .

Early in 1991 Alan's poor eating habits and caloric indiscretion began to take a toll: he was diagnosed with Type II diabetes, and his doctors warned that if he did not make major changes in his life he might soon have to inject insulin and could perhaps suffer the same fate as his maternal grandfather, who died of the illness. 'He loved food,' as Martin said, 'and his schedule was full of lunches, dinners and supper parties. His diet really played havoc with his body, for he lost weight for one role and put it on for another – he was really in the trap of fame, with all its pressures.'

Alan had good intentions about his diet, but his resolution faded when confronted with a splendid dessert. 'I'll just straighten the edge of this cake,' he liked to say, slicing a second or third piece. He often said, 'But these biscuits really have no sugar at all!' and he frequently asked a restaurant waiter, 'Which dessert has the least sugar?' If the reply was that they were all, alas, rich in sugar, he said that then it did not matter which he chose, and his fancy went this time to an éclair. And so it went.

As the pressures accumulated, so did the crush of distracting work, which was as deliberate as the indulgences at table. For nine weeks that spring, Alan portrayed another mentally disturbed patient – an illustrator whose sexual fantasies may or may not have correspondences in real life, who may or may not have committed murder, and who may or may not have a complete emotional collapse in a railway car. *Secret Friends*, directed by Dennis Potter from his novel *Ticket to Ride*, preferred arty obscurity and narrative ambiguity to any kind of clarity, so that viewers could be sure of nothing. The result was 'mired in complexity', one critic complained, while another dismissed it as 'tortuous and repetitive'. Perhaps because of the role and his own manifold confusions, Alan looked little more than distraught during the entire thing, but without his customary nuance.

In July, he had no better luck with a television drama called *Losing Track*, the story of an emotionally arid man who travels from India to England for the funeral of his estranged wife and has to sort out his troubled relationship with his young son. Again he played a gloomy man who had to explore for the first time his deepest emotions – precisely the sort of role that always attracted him. As for his income, Alan's accountants noted that in the previous eighteen months he had earned more than £200,000.

These two assignments did not require lengthy journeys, as both were made in England. But the third required Alan to work that summer not only in London, but also in Los Angeles, Dallas and New York. An ambitious, two-part television miniseries to which he brought great humour and subtle empathy, *Unnatural Pursuits* was written by Simon Gray. Alan's character, Hamish Partt, was indeed 'Gray's most openly confessional portrait to date', noted the *Observer*'s Michael Coveney, 'reflecting his own experience of alcoholic alienation in the American theatre'.

Alan elaborated. 'Partt watches his life crumbling and even relishes it [like other leading characters in the Gray catalogue]. However much of a wreck he is himself, he sees everyone around him incredibly sanely and with affection. He understands ego, paranoia, the

With Julie Christie
in *The Go-Between*
(1969)

With Dominic
Guard in *The Go-
Between* (1969)

With director
Joseph Losey and
screenwriter
Harold Pinter
filming *The Go-
Between*

With Laurence Olivier in *Three Sisters* (1970)

In *Butley* (1971)

Nickolas Grace, 1972

Alan, Victoria and twin sons Benedick and Tristan (1975)

In *Celebration* (1975)

With Bette Midler
in *The Rose* (1979)

With Gerard Hastings
(1986)

With Julie Andrews in
Duet for One (1986)

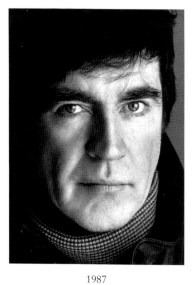

1987

With Felicity Kendal in *Ivanov* (1989)

Tristan Bates

Alan Bates, CBE: At Buckingham Palace, with Ben, Mary and Martin (1995)

With Angharad Rees, 1999

At Bank House

Investiture of Sir Alan Bates at Buckingham Palace, with Ben (March 2003)

With Joanna Pettet (May 2003)

At home, October 2003

Benedick and Claudia
Bates with their
daughters (2006)

nonsense of everything. He's constantly coming up against other people's obsessions and, at the same time, he's smoking and drinking himself into a rather bad condition. It's loosely based on Simon Gray himself.'

Not quite so loosely, according to Simon: 'Alan Bates played me right down to my chain-smoking, my pigeon-toed gait and my wheezy laugh, as I followed the fortunes of one of my plays from London to New York by way of Los Angeles and Dallas.' (To Simon Gray's lasting credit, however – and much to the relief of his many friends and admirers – he soon overcame his dependence on alcohol and continued his extraordinarily prolific and successful career.)

The calendar was even more crowded in the years to come, and whatever Alan thought of the projects when they were complete, he had always perceived redeeming features at the outset. In fact, his jobs that year towered over the big, noisy adventure comic-strip movies coming from Hollywood. 'I despair of some of today's hugely successful films,' he said. 'Look at movies like *Terminator* and *Lethal Weapon*. They're pretty awful. I suppose it's a wild, excessive escape that people want. But you watch something like *Basic Instinct* and you wonder, "Who are these people?" No one lives like that – or if they did, it wouldn't be for very long. It's slick film-making, but it's also voyeurism and cheap entertainment that doesn't engage any serious element.' He could have been a first-rate critic.

Alan went to Greece the following autumn for the country's première of the Zeffirelli *Hamlet* and to receive an award from the University of Athens, in recognition of his contributions to world cinema. 'I am not at all sure that I am qualified,' he told the audience.

> I feel as if at some point I shall be asked to give a lecture or take an exam, and I will be found out. But if the work of an actor is to enlighten himself and his audience to a greater awareness of everything we live with, and if some of the work I have done has had this effect, then that is the only reason I can imagine that remotely justifies this gesture. I particularly said *some* of my work because there is also some of it that does not remotely come into this category.
>
> The chance connection between me and your lovely country has been made possible by Nikos Kazantzakis and Michael Cacoyannis, and I think it is to that legendary book, and

happily legendary film, *Zorba the Greek*, that I owe my presence here.

It is very special for me to receive this compliment from the University of Athens – Athens, the capital of Greece, which is the foundation of our civilisation. In your historic country I have only met with generosity and affection, which I reciprocate. I hope you enjoy this unusual film, which I'm very proud to represent, and I hope Mel Gibson is suitably envious of the tribute you have paid me tonight.

In November he appeared with a few colleagues at a benefit for the reopening of the Richmond Theatre; the programme, entitled *Saki*, consisted of amusing and sometimes chilling excerpts from H. H. Munro. Alan also offered a one-man poetry reading in December to benefit the Almeida Theatre. At the end of the year, Ben told his father that he found 122A Hamilton Terrace empty and forlorn; it was, after all, the place he had shared with Tristan. Alan volunteered to exchange residences, so he turned over number 122 to his son and moved into 122A; eventually Alan bought a house in London for Ben.

Ben, meanwhile, was doing quite well at LAMDA – except for the occasional, intrusive embarrassment caused by Victoria. 'There was a major production at the end of my first year,' he recalled,

and I had a good part in it. Dad came and was most enthusiastic, and he told Mum. She then came along to see it. She didn't sit in the auditorium but crouched in a corner against a wall and scribbled in her notebook, never watching the production. Her behaviour during the performance was troubling and disturbing – and distracting for everyone onstage. Word got round that she was my mother, and I realised that I had to keep her out of things. I felt that I had at last begun to have an independent life, and I didn't want to be burdened with problems I couldn't resolve. Growing up had been so problematic – her illness, Alan's complex relationships and his comings and goings as an actor, Tristan's death and then trying to put my life together – it was all a very tall order.

And it was a dilemma without a term. One early winter day Ben went to Lavender Cottage with some food for Victoria, and she looked so dreadful that he said he was going to summon a doctor. Despite her refusal to see one, Ben brought a physician to the house; Victoria agreed to see him only outside, in the garden. The doctor advised high-calorie, liquid-protein drinks and foods easy to digest, which Ben immediately bought. 'But when I returned a week later, the drinks and food were still in the fridge and not a single item had been consumed.' In early 1992 Ben had a telephone call from one of Victoria's friends, that his mother looked worse than ever. 'I went round,' he recalled, 'and she was so thin that she seemed wasted away.'

In March, Alan was in New Mexico, filming Sam Shepard's *Silent Tongue*, with the twenty-one-year-old actor River Phoenix. A curious combination of revisionist Western, Greek tragedy and old-fashioned ghost story, the picture certainly had nobly uncompromising themes: the destructive power of blind adherence to the self-glorifying American myth of the Old West, an indictment of the white man's treatment of the Native American, and a savage critique of atavistic materialism. Playing a boozy Irish showman and vendor who sells his own daughters for a profit (shades of *The Mayor of Casterbridge*), Alan came perilously close to slicing ham, but there were depths of remorse in his watery glances, and his scenes with Richard Harris and River Phoenix gave unusual poignancy to the often bewildering narrative.

Ben came out to New Mexico in April, and father and son took a brief holiday in Los Angeles after filming was completed. When they returned to London on the last day of the month, a telephone call informed them that Victoria's mother was gravely ill. Alan was at her side when she expired, aged eighty-six; the death certificate gave pneumonia and senile dementia as causes of death. He took charge of all the final details.

Victoria, meanwhile, went further into almost autistic withdrawal, even when she arrived unannounced at the homes of neighbours like Niema or Elizabeth. 'She wouldn't come in if I had other guests,' recalled the former, 'but only if I was alone, and even then, she just sat sadly, without saying a word.'

Victoria knew about the deaths of her mother and sister, but the events blurred into a kind of dream and seemed not to impress her. She then telephoned Marie Malavieille in Paris, asking if she might come over to visit; Marie sympathetically explained that her apartment could accommodate only one guest, and her mother was there at the time. Victoria then rang Elizabeth in Halesworth, Suffolk, who said she was welcome to come.

On Friday, 29 May, Victoria arrived. Elizabeth kept detailed notes of those days, hoping they would help Alan to make some difficult but necessary decisions. 'I was not surprised at her filthy, greasy hair, her dirty clothes and her huge, thick brown toenails – for some years she had looked like that. But I was alarmed because she was very emaciated – she weighed no more than perhaps six stone [less than eighty-five pounds] and looked like a photo of a starving African child.' Elizabeth also noticed that Victoria's feet were swollen, a sign of fluid accumulation and perhaps heart failure. She prepared a meal of carrot soup, a ham omelette and yogurt, which Victoria ate before retiring.

For a week Elizabeth had her hands full. Victoria developed severe, round-the-clock diarrhoea, 'and she slept all day or lay in a chair in the garden or sat, staring into space in the living room. She had lost all her previous interests – poetry, alternative medicine, everything.' When Elizabeth suggested that Victoria see a doctor, 'she said imperiously, "There's nothing wrong with me! I'm as strong as a horse!"' Shouldn't they tell Alan where she was? No reply. Did she know where *he* was? Silence.

A friend of Elizabeth came for a visit and, after several attempts to draw Victoria into their conversation, Elizabeth said, 'Well, we'll get out of your way, Vicky.' With that, Victoria snapped, 'Yes – get out!' – which evoked Elizabeth's rejoinder, 'Now, Vicky, you are not going to be rude to me in my own house. You've got to behave yourself.'

After dinner Elizabeth expressed her concerns to Victoria about her illness, her need of medical attention, and the anxiety she must have been causing Alan and Ben by her unexplained absence. 'Oh, do you think so? I never get the feeling they think about me at all.' In the ensuing days Elizabeth had to perform nursing duties for Victoria. Then, on Thursday, 4 June, Victoria could not be found when Elizabeth returned from the village.

'The point of these notes', Elizabeth concluded on 5 June, 'is to show that Victoria is seriously mentally and physically ill. It is very doubtful that she will agree to see a doctor, as she has never seen one as long as I have known her (seventeen years). She has got steadily worse and, in my opinion, is now dying from malnutrition. She has acute mental problems, certainly she is psychotic, and I think it is cruel to withhold treatment for her just because she won't accept it voluntarily.'

Because Elizabeth intended her pages for Alan to take to doctors, she continued:

> There is no doubt in my mind that she should be hospitalised, and there is no alternative to doing it forcibly. She will have to be in a secure place initially, otherwise she will just leave. Whether her physical state can be cured, I don't know – but I think it very likely her mental state could be greatly improved by drugs. She will never agree to take pills, so she would have to have an implant of some kind.
>
> I think it is a disgrace that her husband has met with so little help from the medical profession, and I hope these notes will help the right decisions to be made.
>
> The suffering she inflicts on people near to her because of her psychotic behaviour has led to her suffering from great isolation. She behaves impossibly. She is pushed away. And she suffers.

Later, Elizabeth added a coda for Alan about that week.

> When she first arrived, she talked about how she couldn't live with Alan – his style of life was too busy, there were always builders, secretaries, and people coming in and out. I think she was regretful about this, though accepting it . . . She told me that what she really wanted was a domestic life with Alan and Ben, sitting down to meals, etc. I thought to myself, uncharitably, it's a bit late for that, but I didn't say anything. But the domestic life was definitely uppermost in her mind – food, the preparing of it, the eating of it, the criticising of my cooking were really her major interests. And the home.
>
> One evening, she started to talk about Alan. She said, 'Oh, how good he is! I can't begin to describe it!' Later, she said, a bit defensively, 'I love Alan and he loves me!'
>
> I am quite sure that all she wanted was to get better, and she couldn't understand why her body was letting her down. She had never been to doctors, and it was an article of faith that she could cure herself.

Meanwhile, there was no sign of Victoria in London. Ben and Alan rang one friend after another, but no information was forthcoming except from David Storey, who had encountered her a few days earlier, on Hampstead Heath. 'She was talking to a tree – some time before, she had told me she spoke to certain trees on the Heath at certain times of the day.' She did not see him, and he thought it best not to interrupt her mystical reverie, for that usually evoked an unpleasant reaction.

Ben and Alan then reported her missing. On their second search-and-rescue mission to her house, they found a diary indicating that she intended to go away to regain her health and strength. There was also a travel agent's telephone number and an airline booking code. With inexplicable energy, Victoria had somehow managed to travel to the Club Med, a holiday resort at Isola Caprera, just off the north-east tip of the island of Sardinia, where the family had once gone on holiday.

On Sunday morning, 21 June, just as he learned these details, Alan received a telephone call from the hotel. When Victoria arrived, she was very ill, had refused to eat, and now she could no longer walk. Alan and Ben could not obtain seats on a flight to Sardinia until Monday morning. By Sunday evening the hotel management had to summon an ambulance from the local clinic. 'She refused any examination,' according to the medical report issued later. 'Due to a lack of cooperation, it has been impossible to obtain details of her medical history, either personal or family. Mrs Bates also refused a blood test. The patient does not speak Italian and does not want to cooperate either verbally or by allowing any examination. Tomorrow, 22 June, she will be sent home to England via European Assistance [air-ambulance]. Her skin and nails are in a very bad condition, and the whole of her body is in a chronic state of deterioration.'

At nine o'clock on the morning of Monday, 22 June, as Ben and Alan were preparing to depart for the journey, the telephone rang again. As hospital officials later wrote succinctly, 'The cause of death, in the absence of a thorough medical examination, was apparently loss of weight and massive bodily deterioration due to the chronic disease, cachexia' – a general term for advanced wasting syndrome.

Valerie June Ward Bates, who preferred to be styled Victoria, was dead at the age of fifty-two.

14

Keeping in Touch

'Neither Alan nor I thought she was going to die,' said Ben, 'and following so soon after the tragedy of my brother, her death was another tremendous shock for us. We knew she was ill, and we knew desperate measures were called for if she was to survive. But she would have had to cooperate, to want to live. Alan felt terrible guilt over her death, and his grief was deep and evident – but somehow it wasn't as profound as the experience of Tristan's death. In some way, of course, Mum's passing was a big relief for both of us: her life was just miserable, and it had become intolerable to her.'

On 4 July 1992, Victoria was buried beside Tristan in the church-yard at Bradbourne, Derbyshire. Marie Malavieille arrived from Paris and drove up from London with Alan, who turned to her in the car and asked, 'Wouldn't it be wonderful if she were here with us now, on the way to a country holiday? Wouldn't it be wonderful if . . .' Like Ben, Marie had the impression of a terrible cloud of guilt through which Alan would have to make his way.

'Victoria walked alone in life,' Alan said in his eulogy at All Saints.

> She was a solitary, poised and often dignified figure. Family and friends have tried to walk with her, to engage in her life, and to draw her into theirs.
>
> But she did not see her role in life in that way. She was provocative, uncomfortable, challenging, curious, intelligent, and often, suddenly, utterly childlike and sweet. She was a mixture of Ophelia and Kate. Various adjectives and comments have been

made about her to me very recently, and they are a fascinating kaleidoscope – 'a magic lady . . . a demon . . . a rascal . . . London will not be the same for me without her . . . generous . . . pure . . . a free spirit . . . swimming against the tide . . . an understanding of the outsider' – and, most interestingly, 'a reluctant incarnation'. Her need to needle and upset people was often disturbing, but not without value. She forced those who knew her to question their values, their priorities, even if it was only to reaffirm them; she made you *think* about them.

Two small examples of the more charming type: Once with friends, our host told an anecdote which I could see was funny, but it did not make me want to laugh. But I was a guest and I did laugh, and Victoria turned to me and said – publicly – 'Is that laughter genuine, or is it just polite?' The desire to strangle [her] became almost a reality. Another time, when giving a Question-and-Answer Session on the theatre in America, I answered a particular question from the audience. A voice I recognised suddenly called out, 'You are not answering that gentleman's question.' Controlled and furious, I said, 'It's all right, ladies and gentlemen – that's my wife.' Of course, I then had to stagger through an attempt to re-answer the question.

Victoria had certainly got being impossible down to a very fine art. All the 'Victoria stories' are funny in retrospect, but were very disturbing to live through at the time. She was on a burning quest throughout her life – she searched poetry, literature, nature and the philosophies of East and West voraciously: *The Long Search* [by Ninian Smart] and *In Search of the Miraculous* [by P. D. Ouspensky] are just two titles of books that stay in my mind. She has left us a treasure trove of books – a library. She has awakened our curiosities by very alarming and uncomfortable methods. She loved jazz – I often thought that it was a symbol of her personality, its unpredictability, and its often discordant notes. She was like an abstract painting – you think you're being fooled; it maddens you because you cannot understand it, and yet it's very attractive and hypnotic. You are *not* being fooled (well, maybe sometimes) – you are being asked to look beyond the obvious, to extend your horizons. She asked that of herself and us.

Sadly, she did not or could not create a structure of everyday life to support her on her quest. She did not realise, until too late, that the chores of life are the comforts of life and on them you can build your higher aims and they will support you. But there was never a situation in the development of the children when I did not listen to her, her contradictions and perversity, and there was always at least one shining perception, even vision, of their needs and of their state of mind.

I think she suffered a frustrating childhood, and this could have been the source of her difficulties. She shared this with, and was helped through it, by her late, lovely sister, Tricia.

Victoria was not remotely interested in the material things of this life, she needed to feel secure – who doesn't? – but beyond that, she asked for nothing material and did not want it even when it was given. She shared this quality with her late, dear mother, May. She could see the world for what it was, and people for who they were – she did not judge them, she just knew them. She was often sweet and kind to strangers and people whose distress touched her. And she shared all this with her late, beloved son, Tristan.

Victoria was a beautiful woman and a highly intelligent one, with great unrealised gifts for writing and poetry. Upon leaving school her headmistress said to her mother, 'We have only had one other student as gifted as your daughter – no door will be closed to this girl.' Indeed, no door was closed to her; mysteriously, Victoria closed the doors herself. She attracted wonderful friends who, without exception, over the years, and especially in the last few weeks, tried to help her and stop her from falling. But she was proud and would not see doctors. She would either keep herself alive according to her philosophies, or she would die. There is nothing more courageous than her last journey alone, where she must have known of the possibility that she would not return. That courage was matched only by the dignity with which she met the news of Tristan's death.

It was a strange and profound love we had for her – she maddened us, she seemed often hopeless and helpless. She would not let anyone help her, she drove us away – but we all keep looking back at her because we knew that there was a unique and wonderful woman trying to escape from problems, the source of which are a mystery. Shortly before he died, Tristan was talking about his family to a friend, and he said, 'I can describe my brother to you, and I can describe my father – it is not possible for me to describe my mother. She is a mystery. You will just have to meet her.'

In many ways, she was ahead of us – *ahead of us* – reaching for something which I pray she has found.

I thank her for our wonderful sons, for her challenge – and for her infinite courage.

Victoria Valerie June – rest, rest, perturbed spirit.

'You either collapse or you carry on,' Alan said later, reflecting on the deaths of his son and wife. 'You go through a trough of bewilderment. It's a physical as well as emotional loss. For a year or two you think they are going to come through the door. You could come to the edge of, well, madness.'

His feelings were often deeply troubling: 'I wasn't mad with grief,' he admitted to a journalist in 2000, 'but I was consumed – just consumed utterly . . . I was filled with a sense of utter insecurity. Life comes right into your face – it was bleak. Now, after all this time, I can deal with my life alone. I'd like to have a companion, but I can be alone. And I find that I can be sort of happy. Sort of.'

As before, he took refuge in work. In August Alan received the text of David Storey's new play, *Stages*, to be directed by Lindsay Anderson and presented in the Cottesloe auditorium of the National Theatre; he agreed to do the play at once, for the typically modest theatrical compensation (£572.46 weekly, plus £64.41 for each performance). Rehearsals began on 5 October, the première was on 18 November and the play ran to 20 February 1993. At his request, the theatre programme informed patrons that 'Alan Bates wishes to dedicate his work in this play to his late wife, Victoria Valerie June'.

Stages was the third collaboration for Alan, David and Lindsay, following the successes of *In Celebration* and *Life Class*. It was also the play with the most allusive and demanding style of language – and it was certainly the most difficult enterprise. 'By the time of *Stages*,' recalled David,

Lindsay had become almost unmanageable. His later years were characterised by a great deal of disappointment over the reception of his work and the fact that he could never raise money for the scripts he had prepared. He became increasingly bitter and venomous. During rehearsals, Alan quietly told me more than once that he was close to leaving the play because he found Lindsay so impossible to work with. It was tragic, because it became clear that Lindsay had no feeling for the play. He sat through lighting rehearsals without saying anything at all. But Alan didn't want to punish him by leaving the play because he simply couldn't work with him.

There was another reason for Lindsay's bitterness and Alan's resentment of him. 'Lindsay had a great battle with his homosexuality throughout his life,' recalled David Storey. 'He just couldn't come to terms with it. That conflict was central to his life, and out of it came a terrible cynicism and an attitude that was more and more sour and embittered.' As David further recalled, Alan found Lindsay's homophobic remarks offensive and intolerable, and this put further distance between director and actor. 'I don't think that Alan's sexual life induced in him any cynicism or bitterness at all,' David added. 'He was often lonely, and I thought there was a great sadness in his life for the lack of a permanent partner. But he had such enormous charm, vitality and sensitivity, and people were always drawn to him.'

In *Stages*, Alan played the central character, Richard Fenchurch, an artist on the verge of madness, trying to consider his past career and his idealised love life with something like equanimity. As with so many of his roles, Alan had now developed a solid penchant for characters 'out of step with the world', as a critic wrote that season – in other words characters similar to himself. 'It's fun to play difficult characters, people who are on the edge, not quite coping because they can't be bothered' he said. 'I find that interesting.'

In light of the past two years, it was remarkable (and perhaps therapeutic) that he could perform in *Stages* for its three-month run. Each night he portrayed a man at the end of his emotional tether – a painter and writer who is losing his mind but finds, in this tragic descent, that it has been precisely the pain, guilt and lack of confidence that have provided a lifetime of creative energy. Critics agreed that Alan gave 'one of the great performances of this or any other year . . . The intrinsic beauty of the performance, the writing, the whole production, is that [Alan] takes us step-by-step with him on this slow descent among the ghosts of his own past . . . He effortlessly holds the stage and our attention, with a quiet tenderness of which I, for one, had not hitherto thought him capable . . . I did not know he had such passion in him.' At this distressing time of his life, many of his friends and colleagues saw the deep reservoirs of pain and guilt that haunted him daily; nevertheless, as another critic observed, 'with his powerful stage presence, skill and conviction, he was a poetic "one-man show" in himself.'

But it was a triumph painfully achieved. 'I remember going behind the scenes one evening before a performance of *Stages*,' recalled David, 'and Alan was sitting at a little card table, eating supper alone, with tears streaming down his face. I said, "Alan, you know you don't have to go on tonight . . ." and he replied, "David, it's the only thing that will save me."' Despite his low spirits – of which very few people were aware – Alan once again provided a unique bond of friendly collaboration for the cast. 'I was so impressed with his companionship with the other actors,' David said, 'and that companionship, once again, nourished all their performances and gave the production extraordinary quality.'

Although there was a cast of seven in Thomas Bernhard's *The Showman* – for which Alan began rehearsals after *Stages* closed in February 1993 – it was once again essentially a one-man show. But the play, about a raging, dyspeptic actor-manager trapped in the provinces, was not so highly praised as Storey's. After seven weeks at the Almeida Theatre it closed on 26 June. As he had dedicated *Stages* to Victoria, so Alan insisted that the programme for *The Showman* bear the statement: 'Alan Bates wishes to dedicate his work in this play to his late son, Tristan Bates, a young actor.'

With little time or inclination for relaxation, Alan prepared for a television adaptation of Charles Dickens's difficult and gloomy novel *Hard Times*, in which he appeared that autumn; to achieve a hundred-minute version, the cast and crew required seven weeks of arduous production. Made for the BBC TV's educational branch, BBC Schools, the tightly compressed and impressionistic interpretation of the book, written and directed by Peter Barnes, was broadcast during school hours. Alan's performance as Josiah Bounderby was of a wily and bullying banker with a broad comic streak – not unlike his Michael Henchard, the formidable mayor of Casterbridge. Filming was completed in early November.

Amid the haze of pain that enshrouded him from 1991 through 1993, Alan spontaneously reached out to those in similar emotional turmoil. While filming *Hard Times*, he was informed that twenty-three-year-old River Phoenix (his co-star in *Silent Tongue*), after taking cocaine, heroin and marijuana, had dropped down dead outside a Los Angeles nightclub. To the young man's family Alan at once wrote:

My son Benedick and I were deeply upset to hear of River's death, especially having worked with him so soon after my other son's death, Ben's twin, Tristan.

River and Ben developed an immediate rapport, and River was enormously sensitive about what had happened to us, so I am able to understand your grief very fully, and know exactly what you are going through.

Your son was unusual, extremely gifted, compassionate, and Benedick and I just felt very fortunate to have known him.

I know from your statement to the press how proud you are of what he achieved in so short a life. He had a real burst of glory and seemed to be a shining light for many people. I find now that nearly four years have passed since Tristan's death, [and] however often the actual loss and grief may strike, my pride in his lovely nature and potential, and the influence he spread among his contemporaries, give me a huge strength, and I know that you will also be able to feel that.

I met your daughter, Summer, very briefly during the filming of *Silent Tongue*. I hope I see her again and meet all of you some time.

God bless you all.

In February 1994, Alan marked his sixtieth birthday. Simultaneously there was a cascade of offers to work in film, television, theatre and spoken recordings. That same winter he learned that his old flame, John Curry, was suffering the ravages of AIDS, and so Alan visited frequently, even offering to share nursing duties with Curry's mother who was in constant attendance. At that time any contact with AIDS patients was still widely and wrongly considered to put one at risk of contagion, but, as with May Catchpole, Alan thought only of the patient's suffering and loneliness. On 15 April forty-four-year-old John Curry suffered a heart attack and died in his mother's arms.

Three days later, he began four months of work, playing the title character in *Oliver's Travels*, a romantic detective story that aimed for both suspense and whimsy but failed to achieve either. Directed by Giles Foster from a script by Alan Plater, the project might have succeeded as a one-or two-hour teleplay; instead the BBC wanted a format that ran four hours, and *Oliver's Travels* was finally little more than a protracted travelogue of Wales, the Scottish Highlands and the Orkney Islands. For Alan, the compensations were working with Sinéad Cusack and a fee of £300,000. As one senior critic wrote admiringly, 'Mr Bates simply pays no attention to the script's shortcomings.'

An avid player of crossword puzzles and anagrams, detective Oliver loses his position as a professor of comparative religion and wanders about in search of life, love and the perpetrator of a crime. Asked how he played many such characters – witty but troubled, clever but forlorn, apparently direct but actually enigmatic, unlucky in love and emotionally uncommitted – Alan could only reply, 'I'm not really sure, because I don't know how one acts in the first place.'

Such a modest approach to his craft did not prevent him from taking it with absolute seriousness, nor from supporting others who had the will and talent for achievement. In this regard, that year Alan became the third Patron (after Laurence Olivier and Alec Guinness) of the Actors Centre, which had recently relocated to Tower Street, London. Founded in 1979 by a consortium of performers, the Centre's aim was to provide classes and workshops as well as a meeting place for actors to exchange ideas, experiences, information and mutual support. Through masterclasses and study groups offered at nominal fees, the Actors Centre became the pre-eminent London venue where actors could collaborate to increase both their knowledge and their skills.

As members, staff and the Board of Directors recalled, Alan was not merely a nominal Patron: he took an active interest in the Centre and was a frequent visitor to its workshops and performances; he also donated £50,000 for a small auditorium in Tristan's name. 'He embraced the Actors Centre and treated the whole place as a special part of all that he stood for,' recalled Board member Mark Stephens. 'He dropped in constantly, minded about our progress, came to many of our plays in his son's theatre, hosted countless events [and] put together several shows for our benefit . . .

Alan often said, "Ultimately acting is about compassion," and it was this insight that informed all the work he did on behalf of the Actors Centre.'

At a reception honouring him as Patron, Paul Taylor came to offer good wishes. 'He had been completely undermined by the deaths of Tristan and Victoria,' recalled Paul, who at once sensed Alan's melancholy and extended the hand of reconciliation. Very soon their former romance, long cooled by time and distance, was ardently rekindled.

In fact, the revived alliance went so far that the couple decided to look for a flat they might share. 'Well, this might do nicely,' Alan said as they inspected one available residence. 'This room could be mine – and that, over there, could be yours . . .' This struck Paul as odd and he said so, but there was no reply. Later Alan said he did not want another deep connection to anyone after Victoria's death. During this second chapter of their relationship, he and Paul never did share a home. They did, however, take weekend holidays in countryside hotels and on the Continent, and they returned to Derby for visits with Mary.

In 1995 the Prince of Wales sponsored the recording of selections from Shakespeare, to be read by more than two dozen actors. This was not mere titular patronage by Charles, who was closely involved in every aspect of the production, drew up a personal list of preferred readers (John Gielgud, Nickolas Grace, Juliet Stevenson, Alec McCowen and Alan among them) and even read, quite expertly, a selection from *Henry V*. Alan's contributions were selections from *Antony and Cleopatra* and *As You Like It*.*

His day of audio recording was far more rewarding than the movie he made that year – an uncompromisingly dreadful and repellent thing called *The Grotesque* (released in America as *Gentlemen Don't*

---

* A few months earlier he had recorded thirty-eight poems from A. E. Housman's collection *A Shropshire Lad*. During his career Alan made more than two dozen recordings of plays, poems, short stories and novels, some of them abridged versions of projects in which he had starred. In each case his richly nuanced baritone, never exploited for mere virtuosity, brought listeners deeper into the texts. He was well paid for his efforts: for a few hours' recording of some poems by William Blake, for example, he was paid £1,000.

Eat Poets, which in this picture they do indeed). As a loony aristocrat obsessed with dinosaur bones and medieval alchemy, Alan huffed and puffed his way through Patrick McGrath's screenplay, which served up poisoning, murder and cannibalism. Neither Alan's insolent take on madness nor the sleek chill of a performance by Sting could redeem the movie, in which the only attractive element was the setting – Sting's own baronial Lake House, located on a sixty-acre estate in Wiltshire.

Although decently compensated for this regrettable endeavour (£50,000 plus a share of any profits), Alan fared much better that autumn for a day's work on behalf of the Union Bank of Switzerland, for which he filmed an unusual commercial and was paid 300,000 Swiss francs, calculated at £163,666. The spot had not a single verbal or visual reference to money or banking, as Alan – drenched in a haze of blue light – intoned W. E. Henley's poem 'Invictus'.

> Out of the night that covers me,
> Black as the Pit from pole to pole,
> I thank whatever gods may be
> For my unconquerable soul.
>
> In the fell clutch of circumstance
> I have not winced nor cried aloud:
> Under the bludgeonings of chance
> My head is bloody but unbowed.
>
> Beyond this place of wrath and tears
> Looms but the Horror of the shade,
> And yet the menace of the years
> Finds and shall fine me unafraid.
>
> It matters not how strait the gate,
> How charged with punishments the scroll,
> I am the master of my fate:
> I am the captain of my soul.

John Gielgud and Ben Kingsley, who recited excerpts from Shakespeare and Shelley, filmed other commercials for the same company. The connection to banking may well be sought, although a spokesman for UBS rather grandly stated that the readings called attention to commitment, honesty, sincerity and timelessness – hallmarks, he said, of the Bank itself.

Things became more serious in late summer when Alan agreed to return to the stage in Peter Hall's production of Ibsen's *The Master Builder*. After performances in Oxford, Brighton, Plymouth – and at a festival in Greece – the cast came to the Haymarket on 13 October. 'It was a terribly difficult play to do,' recalled Alan's co-star and friend Gemma Jones, who played his wife, 'and I'm not certain it was entirely successful. Alan has wonderful instincts about a role, but if his instinct fails him he can flounder somewhat. He gave a fine performance, but I don't think he would have put it down as one of his happiest times.'

That season, after attempts to control his diabetes with oral medication, Alan had to begin routine and regular testings of his blood sugar levels and to inject himself with timely doses of insulin. But more and more often he thought of the insulin as a passport to indulge in forbidden sweets: the medicine, he wrongly reasoned, could simply be increased to counteract his indiscretions. When he had an evening theatre performance, he generally consumed a bowl of pasta an hour before curtain. With all of this medical self-monitoring, as Gemma Jones added,

> he retained his amazing humour and professional generosity, and he alternated one fad diet with another, and with alternative therapies. And all the while he was wonderfully vain, the very definition of an actor. While we were doing *The Master Builder*, he was having dental implants that he thought would much improve his appearance. Well, the palaver about those teeth, that had to be bathed and swished and flossed – what a saga!

(And what a cost: Alan paid £10,500 for the implants.)

'He had such a full life as an actor,' Gemma continued. 'He just loved the work, he loved the professional socialising, he loved the eminent position he held among his colleagues. He was really happy in his métier – and most happy when he was working.'

As the master builder Solness, Alan continued his variation on the theme of representing, onstage and screen, an album of ego-driven, psychotic or at least profoundly disturbed men. His most recent, wholly congenial movie or television role had been Chris Baldry, in *The Return of the Soldier*, fifteen years earlier; and it can be argued that his last really sympathetic characters had been created almost forty years before – Cliff Lewis in *Look Back in Anger* and Edmund Tyrone in *Long Day's Journey into Night*.

In a way this shift was both prudent and courageous. On the one hand, Alan knew that romantic leading roles were now out of the question for him; on the other hand parts for sixty-two-year-old stage actors who could easily please audiences were mostly to be found in facile comedies for tourists. Instead, he chose the more difficult, less attractive and yet more incandescent parts on film and in the theatre. Hamish Partt (in *Unnatural Pursuits*), Richard Fenchurch (in *Stages*), Bruscon (in *The Showman*) and McCree (in *Silent Tongue*) were, at the least, unpleasant creatures and, at the worst, terrifying. But they were also enormously challenging characters unlikely to be forgotten by audiences – virtuoso roles he could tailor to his own original, unpredictable talents.

One element in his decision had to do with his commitment to serious projects. 'I sometimes wonder about this huge swing to stage musicals,' he complained at the time.

> Are people so easily satisfied with something that is so light? With so many of the musicals today, you go through the exit door and you can't even remember you've been there. It's quite pleasant when you're there, but it doesn't stay with you at all. It's rather like [the American television soap opera] *Dynasty*. It doesn't do anything for you. It doesn't feed you. It's as if you went into a trance, and when you come out of it, you've forgotten it. And that's why theatre is relevant. People don't stay in that trance-like state; they strive to get out of it. They seek a spiritual solution or some kind of help – it may not be the orthodox one, but people seek more than they're getting. Theatre isn't religion, but it can feed people.

In that spirit he felt ready to undertake Solness, a man of merciless ambition, afraid of losing his primacy to a new generation of architects. 'I knew this was a hard play,' Alan told a journalist at the time of the London opening, 'but I didn't realise it was quite so tough. It's a dark, dark play, and I enjoy these monstrous parts because they are a side of me that's not [usually] expressed . . . Solness and I are both at the point where we have achieved a great deal, but we are wondering about our lives and accomplishments.'

Difficult though his Solness was, the critics approved his achievement: 'Alan Bates enters like a lion at twilight,' according to a typical report. 'Like all actors of the very first rank, he stakes out his emotional territory within minutes but without seeming to do so: he knows he is in command, and you can tell at once that this is going to be a great performance . . . If modern tragedy itself has any moral value, this is it.'

Peter Hall, who had known Alan since the time of *Look Back in Anger* and had directed him in *Yonadab*, recalled that Alan as Solness used his mature sexiness with a kind of offbeat and unexpected carnality. 'Like all great actors, Alan saw the humour in drama and even in tragedy. The only disappointment, for me, was that he did not do more of the classics.' Such was the lament of many who were disappointed that Alan did not undertake the great roles of the past – Lear, for example, or Prospero, or James Tyrone or Willy Loman. 'I like doing things that are not often done' was his defence and it was difficult to counter. There would, however, be one great Shakespearean role late in his career.

The production moved to Toronto in January 1996, for a six-week run at the Royal Alexandra Theatre. Before leaving London, Alan and his family attended a December investiture ceremony at Buckingham Palace, where he was honoured with the designation and insignia of a Commander of the Order of the British Empire – which made him Alan Bates CBE, but not a knight with the title 'Sir'. Once again word quietly circulated that Alan's knighthood, so long expected in theatrical circles, had again been denied by pressure from the Queen's sister.

'On the flight out to Canada,' recalled Gemma, 'he had me laughing so hard that I almost choked, and this set the flight attendants worrying. It was doubtless something hilariously libellous that he had said about someone. He loved that – to be the one to shock and to tell you something you didn't know. As I remember, we both laughed for almost the entire journey.' The Toronto press received the production most enthusiastically, and the play ran until the end of February.

Chilly, damp London seemed almost tropical after the weeks in frigid Toronto. There was a new Simon Gray script waiting for Alan's consideration – *Simply Disconnected*, which revisited Simon Hench, whose efforts to enjoy a recording of *Parsifal* were constantly interrupted during *Otherwise Engaged* in 1975. Twenty-one years later, in this serio-comic sequel, Hench is no longer a publisher, his wife is deceased, and the intrusive telephone and answer machine have been – well, simply disconnected. On 8 April rehearsals began under Richard Wilson's direction; the play opened at the Minerva Studio Theatre at the Chichester Festival on 10 May and ran to 1 June, and the production then moved to Richmond, Bath and Malvern for an additional four weeks.

For those onstage and in the audience, *Simply Disconnected* was a demanding but rewarding play, leavened with Gray's trademark humour. 'He is someone who has gone into a state of recluse,' said Alan. 'He lost his wife and a child that may or may not be his. Highly dramatic characters appear – a brother, an old friend from his wild youth, his wife and someone who may or may not be his son.' Alan expertly played Hench as quick-witted, emotionally inert but endlessly intriguing. 'He was quite wonderful in *Simply Disconnected*,' said Simon years later. 'He was very mysterious and moving, and it touched on so much of his own life. The play didn't come into the West End, unfortunately.'

The play's crisis occurs when Hench is suddenly confronted with a drug-addicted young man frantic to know if he is Simon's son; he enters, threatening to shoot him for the seduction and abandonment of his mother. That role, Julian Wood, was assumed by none other than Benedick Bates, who had graduated from LAMDA in 1993 and had accumulated impressive credits – among them the title role in *Don Carlos* and the enamoured sailor in *The Rose Tattoo*. His participation in *Simply Disconnected*, at the age of twenty-five, was due solely to his expertly offered audition and not at all to preferential treatment; in the event, critics judged his performance a 'beautifully executed' portrait of 'harrowing anguish'.

'We come to each other as two actors, not as father and son at all,' Alan told a journalist. 'The only way our relationship might show is in the ease of playing together. We can advise each other and ask advice of one another in ways that wouldn't go down at all well with other actors.'

With the play's run completed at the end of June, Alan and Paul took a three-week holiday and, for some of that time, Ben joined them. Gemma asked Alan if Ben knew about his private life, 'and Alan said he didn't think so, but not long after that, Ben said, "Oh, I know all about it!"' After some reasonable adolescent confusion about his father's unconventional excursions, Ben had come to accept Alan's life without ruckus or resentment.

On 22 July father and son began rehearsals for another Chichester production. *Fortune's Fool* was Mike Poulton's adaptation of a play by Ivan Turgenev that dated from 1848. Set on the country estate of a young couple (Rachel Pickup and Benedick Bates), the action focuses on an ageing nobleman named Kuzovkin (Alan), once cheated of his fortune and now fearing eviction from the house. Family secrets and class struggles interlace the plot, and the major revelation occurs when Kuzovkin reveals that he is the father of the young bride. 'It was a tough and tricky play, flawed and hard to pull off,' Ben recalled, 'and we had to struggle with cuts and revisions all during rehearsals that summer.' Part of the difficulty was caused by the chaotic action of minor characters, choreographed by director Gale Edwards to dash hither and thither on and off the stage.

As it lurched towards its première on 21 August, the production became ever more problematic – a situation, Alan believed, that had to do with inappropriate choices made by Edwards. In a rare foray into open criticism, he wrote to her during the run at Chichester:

Dear Gale,

This is difficult to say, but I must say it.

I feel that you, consciously or unconsciously, have not trusted me in this play, nor have you trusted the play. I'm having to *fight* to play the part, because in Act I there is just too much going on. The first section, I know, presented you with a problem; it is now clear that it should have been realistically played or/and drastically cut. I had great doubts about your approach but your energy, intelligence and apparent love of the play (not to mention lack of rehearsal time) stopped me from questioning you too much.

I know the actors involved don't enjoy having to play 'forced comedy' with lines that aren't basically that funny. I find all the broken furniture, the musical interludes and revue gags almost impossible to play through or alongside. I just sort of *stop* till it's all over. The dinner table [scene] also is full of gags and interruptions that would frankly make Kuzovkin stop talking, knowing that he was being ridiculed. Act II is marvellous – it is wonderful to play with Rachel [Pickup] and Ben, who are direct and emotionally truthful and play the scenes with me and not with the audience. I feel all this should be addressed seriously before the tour begins in Richmond. I'm sorry I feel this way.

Alan

But his critique had little effect on the director's subsequent discussions with the cast or on the pace of performances in Richmond, Edinburgh, Malvern and Bath. Still, Alan played his role with a poignant, damaged dignity – an absurd but moving figure trapped by time and circumstance. 'In Chichester, it really hadn't been much good,' as Simon Gray recalled. 'It was a plodding and ponderous fable, badly lit and erratically acted by the supporting cast – although he himself, at the ebullient centre, had been Alan enough to give the evening a charge – but really, it had floundered along, and he'd been depressed by the impoverished lighting, the helter-skelter staging – but on the other hand, his son Ben had been in it, for Alan a great thing, perhaps the greatest thing, to be onstage with his son, it justified the enterprise.' *Fortune's Fool* completed its post-Chichester tour on 12 October.

For the remainder of the year, Alan and Paul tried in vain to salvage a sadly deteriorating second act of their relationship. 'I began to lose my sense of self by trying to be so completely involved in the theatre world,' Paul said years later. 'I understood that Alan's priorities were his son, his work and his mother. I loved him, but I needed to care for myself, too, and I was developing other professional interests. We both realised that our life together could not go forward.' The personal incongruities accumulated and, by Christmas 1996, Paul and Alan separated, without rancour or bitterness.

'When intimate relationships happened, Alan committed to them completely,' said Felicity Kendal, 'but he also knew when a chapter was closing, and when his feelings had changed.' Michael Linnit agreed:

He fell in love very often and thought it was for life, and so did the partner. But when it got to a certain point, it was cut-off time and wonderful, soft, romantic, loving Alan showed real steel. One could go so far and then one got to the steel and could not get past it. He had just a tiny speck of ruthlessness at that point. People got so lost in the wild romanticism of the international, handsome movie star who was so funny and charming. They thought their prayers had been answered, that it was Christmas and one's birthday all in one day. They went along on this cloud of love until suddenly it rained very heavily. This was sometimes amusing to his friends, but never to those involved in a love affair with him. Those he had chosen were starry-eyed, but there was no way it could last forever. He needed to be loved by everybody, just everybody.

Michael was on the mark: Alan Bates was indeed far more suited to lifelong friendship, and to warm and enduring professional relations, than he was to a durable private life with anyone. Despite his occasional naughtiness and preference for a bit of intrigue, he was a man of unassailable goodwill who essentially did not have a single enemy, and he certainly never intended to wound or offend, as even his most dejected, rejected lovers attested. The sting of parting was acute for those left behind; that it was so indicated the delight, the pleasure, the stimulation and the sheer fun that intimacy with Alan had provided for each of them. It was perhaps ironic that the eventful year 1996 concluded with Alan's single West End performance of a pastiche of theatre material called *Let's Keep In Touch*, the final words in one of Tristan's poems.

The new year 1997 began with a prestigious honour: in January, Derbyshire University bestowed on him an honorary Doctor of Letters degree at a joyous academic celebration. 'Alan Bates is one of England's most distinguished actors,' said J. H. Powers in his speech.

> His career has been studded with awards. He received an Oscar nomination for his performance in the film *The Fixer* in 1968. He gained the *Evening Standard* Best Actor Award in 1972, followed by the Antoinette Perry Best Actor Award in 1973. The Variety Club of Great Britain presented him with its Best Stage Actor Award in both 1975 and 1983, and he then won the BAFTA Best TV Actor Award in 1984. His long record of outstanding achievements as an actor was recognised in 1995, when he was appointed a Commander of the Order of the British Empire.

He was educated at the Herbert Strutt Grammar School in Belper, Derbyshire, and became fascinated by acting when his mother began taking him to the Derby Little Theatre Club, where one of the leading actors was a certain John Osborne, subsequently better known as a playwright. With his interest fired at an early age, and driven by a determination to succeed, he gained entry to the Royal Academy of Dramatic Art, along with a galaxy of other actors who are now also household names, such as Rosemary Leach, Roy Kinnear, Albert Finney, Peter O'Toole and Richard Briers.

After finishing at RADA, he joined the Midland Theatre Company, but six months later left to become a founder member of the new English Stage Company, and thus shortly afterwards to play in the first performance of John Osborne's *Look Back in Anger*. His notable film career has included *The Entertainer, Whistle Down the Wind, The Running Man, Zorba the Greek, Georgy Girl, Far From the Madding Crowd, Women in Love, A Day in the Death of Joe Egg, The Go-Between, Nijinsky, The Wicked Lady, Duet for One, Hamlet, Silent Tongue* and *The Grotesque*. Far more numerous are the offers he turned down because he felt that scripts were not very good. On television, his appearances have included *The Mayor of Casterbridge, A Voyage Round My Father, Separate Tables, An Englishman Abroad, Pack of Lies, The Dog It Was That Died, Unnatural Pursuits, Hard Times* and *Oliver's Travels*.

Throughout all of this, which has brought his work before a wide audience, he has maintained a nearly continuous presence as an actor onstage. Surprisingly, he has done relatively little work as a Shakespearean actor, focusing instead on contemporary drama with memorable performances in plays by Simon Gray, David Storey, Alan Bennett and Harold Pinter. He appears to be attracted by the challenge of the new and untried role, and thus is one of those actors whose dedication to his art provides inspiration and support to new writers.

This season sees the twenty-first anniversary of the new Derby Playhouse, on whose boards Alan Bates's appearances have been a warmly welcomed homecoming. He is one of the Patrons of the Playhouse's Anniversary Appeal, which is seeking to develop facilities worthy of one of the country's most successful regional theatres. This is therefore a particularly appropriate year to celebrate the achievements of one of Derbyshire's most famous sons. The University wishes to recognise his contribution to the realisation and interpretation of contemporary drama, and thus to contemporary writing for the theatre, film, and television, by its first-ever award of the Degree of Doctor of Letters *honoris causa*.

Alan's acceptance speech was remarkably personal:

I want to thank Derby University for this honour they have given me. A feeling of not really being qualified has, at this moment, rather overwhelmed me, but I am also overwhelmed at the compliment you have paid me.

To be honoured in my own city, where I was born, and where my family go back for generations, is for me very moving. Derby was not a city when I was born, nor was there a university, nor a playhouse. There have been many changes, amongst which is a much greater awareness and promotion of the arts, much of which is due to this modern University and various individuals here. The University is particularly important in the fields of Social Work, Arts Therapy and Adult Education.

. . . Whenever young people ask me what they should do with their lives, I always ask them, 'What do you do best and what do you like best? If it is possible for you to do one of those things, then your contribution to life will be as full as it can be . . .'

My mother and father were wonderful examples of people with very fine musical gifts that completely enhanced their lives and gave them resources which they otherwise would not have had. Neither of them sought fame or money, although both could certainly have made a living from it, and to me they proved the point that the doing is all. They taught music, they played for themselves and each other, and for the local community. The conductor Sir John Pritchard, who began his career with the Derby String Orchestra, thought highly of their abilities . . .

There is a marvellous quotation from the great Nelson Mandela's inauguration speech: it applies to everyone, whatever they have been inspired by – adventure, sport, philosophy, religion, science, the arts, whatever:

'Our deepest fear is not that we are inadequate, our deepest fear is that we are powerful beyond measure. It is our light, not our darkness, that most frightens us. We ask ourselves: Who am I to be brilliant, gorgeous, talented, fabulous? Actually, who are you *not* to be? You are a child of God. Your playing small doesn't serve the world. There's nothing enlightening about shrinking so that other people won't feel insecure around you. We are all meant to shine as children do. We were born to make manifest the glory of God that is within us. It's not in *some* of us, it's in *everyone*. As we let our light shine, we unconsciously give others permission to do the same. As we're liberated from our own fear, our presence automatically liberates others.'

Alan then cited a letter from George Bernard Shaw to Janet Achurch, whom Shaw considered a genius of an actress and whom he had chosen to play in his *Candida*. After advising her against a blond wig for the role, he continued:

What you have to do is to play the part. You have not to make a success. New York must notice nothing: it must say 'Of course', and go home quietly. If it says 'Hooray', then you will be a mere popular actress, a sort of person whom I utterly decline to know. You must confine yourself strictly to your business, and do that punctually and faithfully, undisturbed by any coveting of success for yourself, or me, or the play.

I urge you to go to church – once a day at least, to tranquillise your nerves. Read the Gospel of St John and the Lives of the Saints; they will do everything for you that morphia only pretends to do.

Remember: the religious life; no ambition; and no golden hair. I know that you will understand my advice and take it – for ten minutes or so.

Alan concluded with a pointed and personal observation: 'I think the arts must be about broadening people's vision and, above all, to be compassionate, to understand the person who does not, or cannot, conform, who is "different" in some way or other – to make those who are comfortable with life understand those who are not. We are challenged by these outsiders, and they are also our teachers.'

As he wrote and delivered those words, Alan may well have thought of characters like Ben Butley, Simon Hench, Alfred Redl, Richard Fenchurch and Kuzovkin; and the roles he had played in *Whistle Down the Wind*, *King of Hearts*, *The Fixer*, *The Collection*, *The Shout*, *The Mayor of Casterbridge*, *Nijinsky*, *The Return of the Soldier*, *An Englishman Abroad*, *Separate Tables* and *102 Boulevard Haussmann*. He may also have thought of himself.

And then, still haunted by the memory of Tristan's poem, which had given him the title for his recent theatre piece, Alan quietly said to his audience, 'Let's keep in touch', and sat down.

Late that winter he began rehearsals for Simon Gray's new play *Life Support* – the twelfth collaboration between actor and playwright in thirty years and the sixth time Alan was directed by Harold Pinter. 'He's given me so much wonderful work over the years,' Alan said of Simon, 'and we see each other socially – we're good friends and meet regularly. I feel a great affinity with his sense of fun . . . and with the substance that lies beneath.' Of Pinter, Alan appreciated that the director was 'disciplined but also flexible. He has a very good understanding of each individual actor, what pressures they might be under, and [he] takes time to deal with that. After all, he's an actor himself. These people are part of my life. We have an understanding that makes it all so much easier. We know each other's strengths and vulnerabilities.'

The play was set in the private room of a London hospital, where Jeff Golding (Alan) attends his wife (Georgina Hale) – a patient reduced to a persistent vegetative state by anaphylactic shock following a bee sting. He talks to her and encourages others to do the same, and there are visits from Jeff's brother (played with wily, wary humour by Nickolas Grace), from Jeff's agent and a young doctor. But at the core of the one-hundred-minute play is an exploration of Jeff's desolate guilt: precisely what happened to his wife, and does he bear some responsibility for her condition?

'This play has been a catharsis for me,' said Alan. 'I do know from my own experience that with people you love, when they have died or virtually died and you feel you have lost them, you still seek communication with them when they are no longer there. I still speak with my wife and son, and with my father, who died some while before them. I take enormous comfort from it and don't find it morbid at all. They don't go away completely. Everything that was most powerful about them stays. Knowing that helps you to go on.'

Performances began in Guildford on 10 June and continued in Oxford, Bath and Richmond before coming in for a twelve-week run at the Aldwych, London, in late July. The critical consensus was that Alan was 'magnificent'. Nickolas Grace, recalling his friendly reunion with Alan in the play, said that he was 'the master of understatement and always had a fine sense of repose. In rehearsals, you just couldn't see how he worked. There were the usual Batesian mannerisms – touching his left ear with his right hand, for example, and clearing his throat, and tousling his hair – but these never became annoying clichés.' On the personal level Nickolas took advantage of a few moments alone with Alan one day to discuss something they had both avoided over the years. 'I told him how much he had hurt me in 1973, and that I needed him to say he knew that and was sorry. He did, and it was easy for us to remain good friends.'

Among the several meanings of its title, *Life Support* considered the ethical complexities and terrible grief surrounding a patient without detectable neurological function. The play also asked precisely what it means for people to support one another in life. As Alan said, playing the role had been a catharsis for him. It also directly influenced his next decision – to appear in a television movie made that autumn in Italy, a true story of someone whose mechanical life support was removed.

15

The Climates of Love

On 13 November 1997, Alan arrived in Rome, where he worked for six weeks on *Nicholas' Gift*, a television drama based on a true story.

In 1994 Reg and Maggie Green, their seven-year-old son Nicholas and their four-year-old daughter Eleanor travelled from their home in Northern California for a holiday in Italy. As Reg drove his family south from Rome along the autostrada, they were attacked by highway bandits who mistook the Greens' rental car for that of a notorious diamond merchant. The masked crooks fired shots, and Nicholas took a bullet in his head.

When told by doctors that their son had no brain activity and no chance of recovery from what is called a persistent vegetative state, the Greens decided to remove their son from the mechanical life support system and donated Nicholas's organs – his heart, liver, pancreas and corneas – to people in dire need. The media at once took up the story and soon Italy rallied to what became known as the Nicholas Effect: within a year, organ donations, previously very rare in Italy, more than doubled. At the same time the family founded an international charity to see some good emerge from their tragedy.

During the filming in Rome that autumn and early winter, the Greens arrived, to provide important facts and details for the cast and crew. Jamie Lee Curtis, who played Maggie Green, befriended her and gave an admirably restrained performance, while Alan created a portrait that drew on his own experience of loss. Speaking of young Nicholas and of Tristan, he told a journalist: 'You don't want your grief for the person you love to go away – but you have to live ou your own span, too. And this film is a lesson to us all – that a ver good thing came out of a very violent moment.'

He admitted that, like *Life Support*, this project was also 'a catharsi – I suppose that revisiting the major moments of life can't help bu be cathartic. Nicholas made sense of his own life by having lived i but his parents made sense of the life he didn't get to lead by doin what they did. They weren't vengeful, they saw what had happene for what it was – a horrible mistake – and they cut right through t the positive. They have kept a steady line on that ever since. Ther are too few of those people around, people who can get above it.'

Alan's performance was singular in his career. In the scenes befor the boy's death he is a loving, attentive father, neither overprotectiv nor condescending. When the tragedy occurs he is at first almo narcotised by incredulity and terror, then his grief – evident in th subtle twisting of his mouth and the haze of pain in his eyes – sufficiently muted so that he can be strong for his wife and daughte His avoidance of bathos meant greater dramatic effectiveness withou overplaying for the television cameras.

'The memory of the loss of his own son clearly added an ext dimension,' recalled Reg Green. 'The scene [in which] Nicholas ha just been shot and is taken away in an ambulance, he told me, wa one of the bleakest moments of his [professional] life – though h was fully aware, of course, that [the ambulance] was just a stage pro with a boy actor inside. It was the ability to sink himself into th character he was playing, and yet remain detached enough to cop with all the fussy complications of film-making, that helped mak him such a compelling performer.'

On 4 April, after a two-week visit with his mother, Alan travelled t Sofia, Bulgaria, for work on the film of Chekhov's *The Cherry Orchar* directed by Michael Cacoyannis and produced in and around th abandoned summer palace of the deposed king. 'It's a strange an exciting place,' Alan said of Bulgaria, 'like a country in limbo tryin to decide what its future should be.'

As the brother of the aristocratic Madame Ranevsky (exquisitel rendered by Charlotte Rampling), Alan played the fussy Gayev as th embodiment of touching ineptitude, his grand designs fading int words and, finally, stunned silence. Bearded and clad in layers of heav clothing, he relied on the subtlest glances, the smallest gestures and finely tuned shifts of intonation – the entire apparatus of movie acting that he had completely mastered and that never seemed calculated.

On his return to London, he submitted to surgery on his left knee, to remove torn cartilage and to correct a long history of painful calcium deposits that had accumulated in the joint. 'It took me nine months to learn to stop limping after that,' he said, but he was never idle. During his recuperation he recorded Ian McEwan's novel *Amsterdam*, one of four recordings he made that year. Soon he was back on form and jettisoned his walking stick, but he declined several film offers to spend more time with Mary, indomitable and in-dependent as ever at ninety-four. 'He had a very profound relation-ship with his mother,' as David said – an impression shared by everyone who knew mother and son. 'But at times I felt that this held him up in some respects – in his personal life, for example. His bond with her was the dominant one of his life.'

That relationship was not without shadow. Among others, Elizabeth recalled that Alan frequently became furious with Mary: 'She has seduced us all,' he said more than once, and when Elizabeth asked what he meant, he indicated that there was a 'terrible hold, a control she had exerted over all of the family'. That may have been but a response to a specific moment, but some close friends sensed that a polite veneer covered over a hostility that co-existed with deep devo-tion. Conrad, for one, recalled that Mary was 'very proper, but a bit of a dragon – charming but formidable'.

Between December 1998 and February 1999, Alan read the voice-over narration of a six-part television documentary on real-life spies, their backgrounds and techniques. The producers rightly considered him the logical choice in light of his portraits of (among others) Guy Burgess and Alfred Redl, and readily agreed to pay him £6,000 for six days of work on *The Spying Game*.

Amid this recording schedule there were interruptions both profes-sional and personal. On 6 January, he went to Turkey for a week to film his role as 'The Storyteller' in a lavish, two-part television produc-tion of *Arabian Nights*. 'People need stories more than bread itself,' he tells Scheherazade, whose mentor and marriage consultant he becomes. Draped in heavy robes, with a long, thick beard and turban, he keeps her and the audience on course for half a dozen tales, because, as he says, 'stories tell us how to live and why.' *Arabian Nights* was magnificently photographed and remains an astonishingly entertaining epic, both eye-catching and whimsical, brightly written by Peter Barnes and cleverly directed by Steve Barron. To the surprise of critics and viewers, it delighted children even as it amused adults.

'Who are you?' asks Aladdin (Jason Scott Lee) when the ring genie arrives.

'Omar Khayyam. Who do you think?' replies the genie (John Leguizamo).

Aladdin soon has his chance to make a wish. 'Everybody asks for money,' says the genie with a bored sigh. 'Why don't you ask for something new and exciting?'

'How about some kind of flying machine?' Aladdin suggests, wanting something better than a mere magic carpet.

'Flying machine? So you can fly all over the world? Hah! Maybe we could have drinks and someone would serve us peanuts! A flying machine? Maybe we should stick to the money.'

By mid January he was back at home, considering the possibility of a winter holiday – an option discarded when his mother died, apparently of a heart attack, on the twenty-sixth.

His eulogy was vivid, loving and necessarily etiolated. 'Although we are here today in grief,' he began,

> we are principally here to celebrate a triumphant life. Mary was triumphant in her philosophy of life, her certainty in her own values, her absolute faith in the structure of family life, her loyalty and devotion to her husband, Harold, and her wonderful manners. She was also a great travelling companion – a holiday with my mother was a real pleasure. She was great fun. She would store memories of happy times and quite consciously bring them out and relive them when she was lonely and sad, to make herself feel better. There was a style to her: whenever she knew anyone was coming to see her, she would take great pains to present herself and dress herself to her best.
>
> I am not talking about a saint, and there were areas where she did not quite meet her own standards from time to time. She could be very touchy, although it did not last. She would fuss in a very annoying motherly manner, right up to a week last Sunday and, like many devoted mothers of sons, she sometimes made it

difficult for the wives and partners of her sons to pass the 'critical test'. But she was quick to praise and admire when she saw something well done. Her compassion and understanding of human nature extended to everyone, however frail.

For Mary's grandchildren and her nieces, she became almost a Pied Piper – she had a genius for children. She did not expect them to meet her on her own level or do as she did, but she had the wisdom to enter into their worlds and their minds. Not only family, but her lifelong friendships were faithfully sustained and never forgotten. A recent friend described her as 'a wonderful and timeless lady', and this was one of her secrets. She did not simply belong to her own generation: Mary belonged to the three or four generations that followed hers, and she was equally at ease with them all.

On the very last day of her life, Mary was discussing current events and life in general with her grandson and his girlfriend, enjoying a candlelit dinner with us, for which she had provided various dishes and suggesting, as the meal ended, that we would all be wise if we had an early night, and then borrowing a video from me just before she left, on the life of Jacquelin du Pré. A pretty spectacular last day for a lady aged ninety-four.

Mary has left us a powerful legacy: she has given us a huge awareness of each other as a family.

Three of her greatest passions were music, poetry and tennis. She played tennis into her sixties and the piano into her eighties. She never, never hungered for wealth or the trappings of life – just life itself. Mary is a tough act to follow, but follow we must.

His own following act occurred in Ireland that March, where he assumed the role of Calpornius, the father of the eponymous *Saint Patrick: The Irish Legend*, of which, as Alan rightly muttered, the less said the better. Drenched in saccharine piety and utterly lacking in historical accuracy, the television movie presented Patrick mostly as a sideshow miracle worker. The production was typically summarised by critics as 'completely absurd', but Alan's £30,000 salary for two days of work subsidised the cost of the new car he coveted, the most expensive model manufactured by Renault.

His princely emoluments for movie and television work once again offset the modest income from stage work that year. On 12 April

1999, he began rehearsals for a new production of *Antony and Cleopatra* which marked his return to the Royal Shakespeare Company Stratford for the first time in twenty-six years. The production, which opened on 23 June, transferred to the Barbican, London in January of 2000, then toured before closing on 29 April. (His knee surgery the previous year had forced him to withdraw from an earlier production with Helen Mirren.)

Steven Pimlott's Stratford production was, for the most part, severely judged by critics – not least of all for the ages of the title characters: Alan was sixty-five, Frances de la Tour fifty-five. But that was perhaps a myopic assessment – Godfrey Tearle had been an impressive Antony at sixty-two and Edith Evans a radiant Cleopatra at fifty-eight. The loudest objection against this production, however, concerned the opening scene, in which Antony is seen earnestly pleasing Cleopatra his head in her crotch. That bit of stage business was deleted when the production went to the Barbican, as Alan recorded in a message left on Alan Bennett's answer machine: 'I'm sure you will be relieved to learn that for our London debut, the director has elbowed the offending cunnilingus and replaced it with a walk-down in kingly garb. While this might seem a radical change, it is, I suppose, only the difference between coming down and going down, though there's no doubt which one the audience prefers.'

The leading couple were praised for conveying a rueful nostalgia appropriate to lovers aware that they are vainly attempting to recapture a half-forgotten youthful passion – smouldering embers rather than fierce fires. 'Bates is gloriously reinstated as a major classical actor,' wrote one critic, 'and Miss de la Tour is on blistering form. His quicksilver speech and darting thought sets the tempo. He starts with his head in Cleopatra's lap and ends lost in her arms. He has kissed away kingdoms and provinces – and triumphed all the same.'

For another reviewer, 'Even his jealous rages and furious disappointments have an elegiac feel. [The character's] charisma and magnanimity are still there, along with a sensitivity and reflectiveness missing in almost every Antony – but a wry wistfulness predominates.' As a lusty but weary hero, he was Cleopatra's king but also her slave, alternately melancholy and playful, and he infused the character with both palpable self-loathing and wrenching tenderness.

Performances continued at Stratford that summer, although Alan was sidelined with a nagging respiratory infection and could not go on for a week. It was then announced that his health forced his withdrawal from the imminent production of *Timon of Athens*, for which he had already begun rehearsals and which had been scheduled to join *Antony and Cleopatra* in repertory from midsummer until early autumn. He did, however, resume his full schedule of performances as Antony in mid July.

Still living and working in Stratford that September, Alan learned of a terrible accident. From the time of *Royal Flash*, he had known the actor Christopher Cazenove, who had been married to (but was now divorced from) the popular television actress Angharad Rees from 1973 to 1994. Their son Linford had recently completed a graduate degree at Cambridge when he was killed in an auto accident on 10 September at the age of twenty-five. Ros, who also represented Christopher and Angharad, rang Alan with the news and asked if he would accompany her to the memorial at St Paul's, Knightsbridge. At the service, Ros recalled, Alan was touched by the dignity and restraint of Linford's parents and by Angharad's bravery and beauty.

'Alan wanted to reach out and help,' Ros said, 'and when he got together with her soon after, he was able, with his immense kindness, to help her get through this dreadful time.' As Angharad remembered, 'We didn't really know each other well, although our paths had crossed. But he was very concerned about me and understood my agony, because he, too, had lost a young son.'

She and Alan met several times during the autumn of 1999: in November she accompanied him to the gala première of *The Cherry Orchard* and in December to the Savoy Theatre, where he read two poems at a centenary celebration of Noël Coward's birth. Their rendezvous continued into the new year, when *Antony and Cleopatra* came to London. 'Has friendship touchingly turned to love for actors Alan Bates and Angharad Rees?' asked one columnist in February, after they were seen arm-in-arm at the Royal Opera House and after his reading of Thomas Hardy poems for a National Trust benefit at the South Bank Centre. Another was less coy, calling Alan 'her new love'.

Angharad Rees was born in Wales in 1949 and by 2000 – after appearing in more than forty movies and television programmes – she had begun a highly successful second career as a jewellery designer. Petite and strikingly attractive, with bright blue eyes, a warm smile

and an engaging manner, she found an instant rapport with Alan. 'H
was very, very kind to me,' she said,

> and very supportive. We talked and talked, especially during ou
> many times at his house in Derbyshire, and I learned a grea
> deal about his parents, his upbringing, and all those delicate
> secret things that he said he shared with very few people . . . H
> often couldn't get out of situations that were bad for him. H
> had meandered into them and would give people the wron;
> impression, and then he had to enlist help to extricate himsel
> It was more complicated than it need have been, most of al
> because he never learned to say no . . .
>
> There was a very great joy in being with Alan, and this I wil
> always treasure. But he had a very strange life. For one thing
> he grew up with a mother who apparently had a negative atti
> tude to sex. Then came his marriage, which he tried to cop
> with but didn't know how, and evidently Victoria felt completely
> left behind and desperate. I was surprised to see that he kept ;
> lot of her belongings. He had photos from her modelling day
> on the walls in Derbyshire. I asked him why there were nc
> natural, casual photos instead of those highly posed shots – they
> weren't real, they were of a model on assignments.

In many ways, as Alan's friends recognised, Angharad was a benevolent influence on him. His blithe lack of concern for his diet alarmed
her and – gently but firmly – she tried to keep him on course, but
this was for the most part a futile enterprise, like her encouragement
that he join her in mild exercise. 'He wasn't a physical countryman
at all. When we went out for a picnic in Bradbourne, I used to say,
"Come along, we'll walk" – but he said no, he would drive. He hated
exercise, although he could do a very physical performance, like his
remarkable Antony. Otherwise, he was usually lying down with the
papers or watching television. He leaped into action on the stage, but
not in daily life.'

Alan found enormous comfort in his deepening intimacy with
Angharad, who, for her part (as she said), 'absolutely adored him'. She
also appreciated his sense of humour and, at first, his 'quite naughty'
love of gossip. 'Nobody was spared, and sometimes I had to tell him
to stop certain comments about people – and then I began to wonder

what he said about me in *my* absence!' His love of tittle-tattle and scandal was never mean-spirited or cruel, but it was certainly indiscreet: Alan routinely asked friends for the latest 'dirt', and there were moments of slightly guilty hilarity in every social situation.

That year he took Angharad on a tour of Harley Street and introduced her to his various doctors. 'He was amazing: he liked to wind people around his finger and get the advice he wanted to hear. But he did not look after himself – in fact, he was quite cavalier about his illness.' In this, as in other areas of his private life, 'he was not about to alter his habits and needs, and certain of his choices were difficult for me to accept'. For almost two years she tried to do just that.

The London run of *Antony and Cleopatra* ended on 6 April. A week later Alan and Angharad were in New York, for Ben's wedding to Claudia Santorelli, an American he had met in London several years earlier. At the rehearsal dinner at the Café Luxembourg, on the fourteenth, Alan was expansive.

> Welcome, everyone, to the opening ceremony of the wedding of these two exceptional, graceful and much loved young people – Claudia Marie and Benedick Arthur. We so appreciate your coming here from Germany, France, the UK, Australia and all over the US. It says a lot about Benedick and Claudia that you've all found your way here.
>
> New York is where I met Ben's mother, Victoria . . . and where Ben met his dark-haired, brown-eyed beauty, a lovely, intelligent, funny and gifted person. You are a lucky boy, Ben, and I am lucky to have such a daughter. Claudia: my mother spent her last day with you and Benedick – she really loved and admired you. Nothing could have made her happier, and she was overjoyed that Ben had found such a special woman to share his life. Ben: you are a strong, wise, kind, compassionate, innately good, loyal and loving young man. You are non-judgemental and can be totally relied upon. You are a true friend to me, and now [i.e., at this stage of their lives] I turn to you for advice. You are also wonderfully funny, lively company. You are a fine actor, loved by all who work with you, and I am so proud of all that. I am even prouder of the courage, wisdom and fortitude you've shown

since the loss of your mother and your beloved brother Tristan
both of whom, I know, would be so proud of you and Claud
today . . .

Raise your glasses, please, and wish good luck, long life and
the happiest marriage to Claudia and Benedick!

As Ben recalled, the happy occasion was marred only by Alan
uncertain health. 'He was perspiring a lot, and although he was appar
ently in a lovely relationship with Angharad, he seemed unhappy an
unwell. He was injecting more and more insulin so that he could ea
what he liked. He was not a heavy drinker and drinking was neve
a problem for him. He had a glass or two of wine or a vodka an
tonic, but no more – but even that, of course, is bad for a diabeti
And he had a pudding, and an ice cream . . .'

In May, Alan and Angharad travelled to Morocco, where he appeare
in another television miniseries – the biblical story *In the Beginnin*
for his brief appearance as Jethro (the father-in-law of Moses), Ala
received $160,000. The weary couple returned home and soon,
Angharad remembered, 'I just curled up and sobbed. We were ver
close, but it was difficult because I had not yet given way to my gri
over the loss of my son, and I didn't realise this. More than onc
Alan said, "Let's get married," but I told him that he didn't have t
say that.' However, there was, perhaps predictably, another complexit
for Alan did not surrender his independence, or his predilection fo
male companionship.

Martin spoke for many when he said that 'deep down, Alan di
not want to marry again. He couldn't commit fully of himself. Perhap
"old age" and his romantic streak had impaired his judgement, so th
he was tempted. But I think he was too involved with work, an
maybe it was a touch naïve to think he would go down the marriag
road.'

That summer Alan was at Batsford Park, the 250-year-old Cotswo
estate once owned by the Mitford family. There, and subsequently
London studios, he worked on the literate and witty two-part Britis
television drama, *Love In A Cold Climate*, based on a pair of auto
biographical novels by Nancy Mitford. As the petulant and grump
head of the Radlett family (a character based on Mitford's famou
father, Lord Redesdale), Alan played a xenophobic aristocrat wit

great comic bluster. 'You cannot help but have fun with a script like this [by Deborah Moggach],' Alan said. 'Uncle Matthew is so outrageous and so politically incorrect . . . He despises foreigners and says the most awful things about them. But underneath the mock rage and the fiery temper, he's a lovable old softie, really.' Perhaps not quite so lovable: in book and movie, the man's blustery pride terrorises just about everyone.

But Alan humanised the man in a poignant scene, when Matthew is reunited with one of his daughters, presumed to have been killed during the wartime bombing of London. Trying mightily to withhold his tears of joyful relief, he turned beet-red, embraced the girl, choked back his emotion, then recovered his composure, shook his head and mumbled something like 'Br-r-r-r-r'. This was pure Alan – a concisely realised moment in which conflicting emotions are imaginatively and splendidly poised.

Kate Harwood, the show's producer, recalled 'the support and encouragement he gave the young director [Tom Hooper] and the younger members of the cast, and the friendship he gave to all of us. It was also a crackingly funny performance that he clearly relished giving.'

'I read the books on which it was based and did a little research,' he said later. 'Research is strange because you have to know as much as you need to know, but no more – because you have to let your own imagination go, to create a character. You can't be absolutely rigid; you have to have a little flexibility – to respond to the character.' Because he did just that, audiences and critics were able to react with the appropriately complex feelings. His Matthew Radlett was infuriatingly irresistible.

That project completed, Alan went immediately to Budapest, where he worked for a week in August on a television movie based on Mark Twain's classic, *The Prince and the Pauper* – in which his appearance as Henry VIII provides the only endurable moments. Heavily padded in royal brocades and sporting a red wig and beard, Alan was all but unrecognisable until he spoke, and his rich voice lifted the script several notches.

In early September he was back in London, rehearsing for the American production of a two-character play by Yasmina Reza that would mark his return to the New York theatre after an absence of twenty-seven years. *The Unexpected Man* was a seventy-five-minute

play about two strangers sharing a train compartment as they trav
from Paris to Frankfurt – he an ageing writer, she an admirer of h
work. They speak monologues of their inner thoughts and do n
directly exchange a word until the final moments. But what mig
have been merely a facile conceit was indeed acutely written ar
exquisitely performed – a duet about life and loneliness, needs ar
fantasies.

The play opened at the Promenade Theater, an off-Broadway hous
on 24 October 2000 and ran until 28 January 2001; Alan earned prai
for his 'delicious acidity' that 'made the character's pride, melancho
and insecurity appealing . . . Bates makes the torment amusing ar
touching, as it should be.' Angharad accompanied him to New Yo
and came to the play 'at least thirty times', by her own count. 'I was
obsessed with him, but I appreciated him, and when he was aw
from me I watched his films.'

His New York circle turned out for the play and, during the seaso
he enjoyed several visits with old friends like Arthur Laurents ar
Tom Hatchard. 'Earlier, he had been rather stingy [when we din
out],' Arthur recalled, 'but in the last few years of his life, Alan beg
to pick up the bill. He became more outgoing, more generous, ar
more comfortable with himself – and he had not been so earlier.'

That season Alan also indulged his love of opera and dance, invitir
this or that friend or colleague to join him for performances at th
Metropolitan and the New York City Ballet, where people oft
recognised him and approached with words of admiration or reque
for autographs. Regarding Alan's generosity and patience, frien
recalled that, when a handicapped beggar approached him, he at on
poured out the contents of his wallet. Nor was he angry when th
fellow suddenly revealed himself as hale and healthy, and happily leap
into a taxi with his ill-gotten gains.

That deception did not deter him from such repeated genero
gestures. Another time Alan dined with a family visiting from Engla
and, on leaving a restaurant, they saw a homeless man curled up
a doorway. 'Alan went over to the guy and spoke to him for seve
minutes before giving him some money for food,' recalled Mil
Palmer. 'It wasn't just the money he gave but the time he spent talkir
to him that made Alan the person he was.'

There were pleasant evenings that season with Claudia and Be
who observed that Alan was more and more careless about his di

hence, as Ben recalled, 'he was becoming more sluggish. Also, his relationship with Angharad obviously had its ups and downs. She was a good companion for him in many ways, but he really didn't like her well-intentioned supervision of his diet. And, of course, Alan was his own man, set in his ways. I think the demands of that relationship asked of him a lot of things he wasn't prepared for.'

When the play closed, Angharad returned to her work in London while Alan went to Pittsburgh in late January for three days of work – a small role in *The Mothman Prophecies*, a psychological horror thriller starring Richard Gere. As usual, Alan made his brief appearance memorable – in this case as a retired university scientist who believes that the dead can send cryptic messages to the living about impending tragedies.

Two more feature films were on his schedule in quick succession that first half of 2001. In late February he worked another few days, this time on *The Sum of All Fears*, based on a Tom Clancy novel from 1991. Again, his role was small, but he set a mood of unnerving nastiness as a neo-fascist European businessman intent on detonating an atomic bomb in an American football stadium. 'It's a part like any other, except it's shorter,' Alan said puckishly to a journalist, 'and it was fun to play a really awful guy. I'm really not making a specialty of these things – they just come along. It's the old actors' saying: when you're in something, you think, "When is this going to end?" And the minute it's over, you think, "I'm out of work – what's wrong?" I never know what I'm going to do next. Some people know [their plans] for the next two or three years, but I don't. I enjoy the moment.' As Ros Chatto recalled, 'He loved doing those wicked characters and the more he did them, the more offers he got. He thought they were deliciously amusing to perform.'

The subsequent 'moment' to be enjoyed lasted nine weeks that spring and, indeed, provided delicious amusement for him, for the large, stellar cast and for audiences worldwide. Robert Altman's production of *Gosford Park* was a wittily cynical riff on the Agatha Christie tradition. 'The script [by Julian Fellowes, who won the Academy Award for best original screenplay] was first-rate,' Alan said, 'and we had a big hit on our hands. I had no qualms about signing on straight away.'

In the picture he created a character as memorably eccentric as Uncle Matthew in *Love In A Cold Climate* – this time the head servant of a large English country house. As the imperiously stuffy Jennings, Alan struts about in white tie and tails, mutters to himself, nips at whisky and is even more autocratic than his master, whose murder occurs during a weekend shooting party – an event of far less significance than the movie's exploration of class distinctions. 'I liked playing a locked-up man with a lot of turbulence underneath,' Alan added.

In addition to filming the complicated interiors at Shepperton Studios, Alan travelled for location filming to Syon House, Brentford and Wrotham Park, Hertfordshire. His performance had a remarkable inevitability, as if he knew first-hand the social terrain and its mostly tedious denizens. But, in fact, the atmosphere of a vast country estate in 1932, with its numerous workforce and colourful array of patrician owners and visitors, comprised a world largely unfamiliar to him, so Alan again turned to research – but not to books. Instead, he relied on a man named Arthur Inch, a retired professional servant who had been employed in just such a setting decades earlier.

'Alan clung to him like a life raft,' according to Altman, who added that Alan worked longer and harder than anyone else in the picture. 'He stood in the background and was tertiary, but he was there every day, very attentive, working with [Arthur Inch] on the finer points of being a butler. I can't think of an American actor who can do that.' The result was a performance of which one wanted much more on screen.

The production that springtime had been a pleasant experience, but the 'sluggishness' Ben had observed was worse and Alan had a nagging headache. On 7 June tests at the London Clinic revealed a benign tumour in his pituitary gland – a microprolactinoma, which is neither a brain mass nor a sign of cancer, and was not something for immediate alarm. Instead of adding yet another medication to his regime, he and his doctors preferred simply to monitor the situation – a wise option, for six months later he was symptom-free and the tiny growth remained unchanged and unremarkable.

By late June he was on an aeroplane again, heading for two weeks in Toronto, to work on *The Salem Witch Trials*, a four-hour television miniseries for the CBS network. As Sir William Phipps, a governor in seventeenth-century Massachusetts Bay Colony, Alan countered a gaggle of hysterical performances with refreshing gravitas, as if he had briefly wandered in from another era. The climate in Canada was pleasant and the working conditions agreeable; so was his fee of

$250,000. His gross income for movie and television work in 2001 exceeded $685,000 – certainly enough for a comfortable life even after paying taxes and the expenses of a high lifestyle. But it was not the kind of money commanded by a small platoon of Hollywood stars who were routinely paid five, ten or even twenty million dollars per picture.

Even more enjoyable was his midsummer engagement at the Theatre Royal, Windsor, where he appeared with Ben in *Dorian Gray*, an adaptation of the Oscar Wilde novel. 'Benedick Bates is made for the title role,' ran a typical review. 'Not only does he have beauty, he also has his father's magnetism [and] the same power.' Alan was the corrupting Lord Henry, 'an evil influence [as Alan said] but a man of seductive arguments. He corrupts a young man on the cusp of his adulthood at a vital moment. It's a gothic tale of survival based on choices.' As for his own decisions over the years: 'I've wondered whether they have always been the right ones – but doesn't everybody, whatever we do?'

Looking back, he wondered that year whether he had ever really wanted huge stardom. That would certainly have meant more publicity and greater wealth but also, inevitably, more encounters with the dreaded media and a deeper probe into his private life. In addition, Alan may have known that he had sometimes selected difficult or even so-called art house films (*The Fixer*, *The Three Sisters*, *In Celebration*, *Quartet* and *The Cherry Orchard*, for example). Related to this was his suspicion that fame was not only a fickle mistress but also a potentially destructive one. He avoided the heights of stardom, then, not only because he feared losing his privacy, but also because he would not allow anything or anyone to be so close as to threaten his independence and hunger for work.

As for a common problem – whether professional ambition should be allowed to diminish or threaten personal relationships – Alan told Martin, 'It's one's duty to develop one's talent to the full, and in the end your children will respect you all the more for doing so.' As he said so often, so he advised others – to be 'driven' by success towards success.

The sinister atmosphere of *Dorian Gray* was completely absent from Alan's next task. *Bertie and Elizabeth* was a conventionally polite and sweetly deferential treatment of King George VI ('Bertie', christened

Albert, who died in 1952) and his queen consort, who was still livin[g] in 2001. Alan played Bertie's father, George V, with a crusty benev[o]lence, but he could not compensate for the arch sentimentality of t[he] production.

Within days of completing that, he travelled to Ireland, where [he] easily went from playing an English sovereign to portraying a boo[zy] Irish lawyer, in Bruce Beresford's film of *Evelyn*, starring its produce[r] Pierce Brosnan. Based on true events, the story told of a single fathe[r's] battle against the Irish Church and state to win custody of his chi[l]dren. Alan's was not the central role, but it provided the structur[al] fulcrum. Lured from retirement to help in an apparently hopeless cas[e,] the lawyer feels deeply the plight of (as Alan said) 'a husband wh[o] brings up his children alone' – a situation all too familiar to him.

Brosnan, who from the start had no other actor in mind for Ala[n's] role, was deeply impressed with 'the little details of his acting, t[he] tempo of his character's life, of keeping the inner life going' througho[ut] the filming that autumn. Few people in the company knew that Ala[n] was in acute pain from an arthritic hip, or that the walking stick [he] used as a prop for the tippling lawyer was a necessity.

'Life with Alan was difficult because of the distances between us whe[n] he worked,' said Angharad, summarising her relationship with him [at] the end of 2001. 'I don't think I expected a normal life with him [–] that's quite rare if you're with an extraordinary person.' However, t[he] breakdown of their intimacy had to do with more than just [his] frequent trips away from London. 'He could be quite a handfu[l,]' Angharad continued, 'and I just didn't have the resources to deal wi[th] it. I loved life with him when it was good, but when it wasn't [I] couldn't cope. Finally, I realised it would be better if I left – I realise[d] I had to get out. I never stopped loving him, but he changed [his] mind a lot, about all sorts of things. He was a very complicated ma[n.]'

'Complicated' was the word most often used by those who love[d] and admired Alan, and much of that complication and complexi[ty] concerned his relations with women. As Ian, Conrad, Simon an[d] others knew from his confidences with them, he liked to appe[ar] publicly with women and to cuddle with them privately. Howeve[r,] his serious romances and his most passionate sexual life occurred wi[th] men; and whereas the termination of a male relationship was usual[ly] quiet and dignified, he could easily launch into a spasm of irration[al] resentment against a woman. Joanna, Yardena, Angharad and a few actresses with whom he worked found themselves in a kind of black comedy with him, for Alan, as Ben said, 'led them on to expect more than he was willing to give'. He had no malice, but misery ensued.

'I think Alan's attractiveness and charm often led him – unwittingly? – to give out wrong signals,' said Martin perceptively. 'I've even wondered if, over the years, he mischievously enjoyed the challenge of sorting our relationships – the drama of it – much as he relished the challenge of work. All this made the man something of a mystery: he was always somewhat out of reach and this made him fascinating – but however much of a tease he could be, people loved him for it.'

In many ways within and outside these relations Alan was – as he was in most aspects of his life – a deeply tender-hearted man, as Simon put it. But it must be acknowledged that he could also display an astonishing lack of feeling towards women. It was clear why he terminated these relationships: among other reasons, as Elizabeth said, 'he was an independent soul who really wasn't interested in domestic life with anyone.' At the same time, as David recalled, 'He spoke more and more frequently of his loneliness, and I think there was a kind of desperation [in his romantic choices] to appease that loneliness.'

If it was clear why he terminated intimacies, it remains somewhat problematic as to why – especially in his mature years – he began relationships with women in the first place. Each of them took him and the possibility of marriage or cohabitation with absolute gravity; he, always otherwise engaged with work and flirtations or affairs with men, did not. In the case of Victoria, the attraction certainly had to do with her fragility and dependence: she evoked his deepest caregiving instincts. And with Angharad he sincerely condoled in her time of profound grief. Others, like Joanna and Yardena, had various strengths to which he was attracted. In each case he eventually resisted and resented these relationships – but perhaps what he really regretted was a situation he himself had set in motion.

One close friend compared him with a shoplifter who could not help himself; he was a kind of foolish romantic, madly in love – but briefly, and after a time he asked himself (and said aloud to a few friends), 'What have I done? How do I get out of this?' At the same time, and almost invariably, Alan found himself involved with people who sometimes forced the issue. 'People often wrote scripts for him that he refused to play,' as Ian said.

The synthesis of this motif in his life occurred at the time he and Angharad separated. His first impulse had been to propose marriage, which she rightly suspected was ill-advised, and which she declined, to his relief. An analogous pattern described his reactions to men: he proclaimed undying devotion, but after a time he was desperate to extricate himself when he realised that he was not, indeed, in love at all, or that the rush of passion had faded and could not be transmuted into something enduring. Perhaps it was no surprise that he had chosen to recite, at Noël Coward's centenary, 'I am No Good at Love'. So much was true of romantic love for him – but there was never any doubt of his love for his family, his sons, his friends, his work and for those who struggled in life.

On 26 January 2002 Angharad replied to press enquiries about herself and Alan, but with her usual dignified discretion: 'We are very good friends, but this is not something I want to comment on.' Through his agents, Alan said only that this was 'absolutely not a spiteful situation'.

16

After All, Bliss

Just before Christmas 2001, Alan submitted to a routine physical examination prior to departing for New York. The results were, in medical language, unremarkable, and there was no cause for alarm – if he remained faithful to the diabetic's regime. His doctor's report showed that, at ninety kilograms (one hundred ninety-eight pounds), he was slightly overweight; that he was still self-injecting insulin ('but you have not been giving yourself enough'); he took aspirin preventively; he did not smoke and drank alcohol only in moderation; and he was taking medication to control his blood pressure. The benign growth in his pituitary gland was stable, and 'full examination . . . did not reveal any significant abnormalities'.

His diabetes, however, could have been better monitored: 'Alan, the levels of your sugar are not satisfactory,' Dr Paul Ettlinger wrote, 'and I MUST ask you to keep better control of this. I would urge you to do a bit more testing of your sugar levels and give yourself more insulin as appropriate.'

The journey to New York was for a Broadway production of *Fortune's Fool*, which had been rethought and improved since the Chichester staging. With Arthur Penn directing, Ben repeating his role and Frank Langella co-starring, Alan began rehearsals on 21 January 2002; after performances in Stamford, Connecticut the play opened in previews at the Music Box Theater in Manhattan on 8 March and began a regular schedule there on 2 April.

'It is a play that is both extraordinarily amusing and yet also – and this is Turgenev's and also Alan Bates's genius – eventually extraordinarily

259

moving,' according to the *New York Post*. 'Alan Bates, from humble start
humiliating finish, doesn't put a foolish step, futile gesture or insinuati
tone wrong. This is a performance to cherish: always the exemplary tec
nician, he reveals a sad heart and shabby passion you'll remember all yo
life.' The critic for the *Times*, agreed: 'Mr Bates brings out the Rom
candles, and it is a spectacle no lover of acting should miss. Playing
shabby, self-effacing Russian aristocrat, Mr Bates turns one sad fellov
humiliating moment of drunken grandstanding into a triumph of timin
technique and continuously startling insights.' In addition, *New York* mag
zine praised Alan's 'masterly performance, brimming with controlled gus
larger than life-size yet microscopically detailed'.

The long, drunken monologue in which Kuzovkin reveals his secr
also revealed Alan at his most triumphant – comically precise, dr
and tender, but with a dignified desolation. 'Bates is still an actor
the top of his form,' wrote the visiting critic from the London *Tim*
'He was brilliant,' recalled Arthur Laurents, 'and I don't use that wo
casually.' When the season for prizes came, the prestigious Tony Awar
went to *Fortune's Fool* as best play; to Alan as best actor; to Fra
Langella as best featured (supporting) actor; and Drama Desk awar
were given to Alan (who received several other theatre awards) a
to Frank.

'I'm astonished,' Alan said on receiving the Antoinette (Tony) Per
Award from the American Theater Wing on 3 June.

> For various reasons, I haven't been here on Broadway for twent
> eight years, and this is like a hallucination. I really do have
> thank a wonderful, wonderful company, which happens to inclu
> my son, [and] my part would be nothing without the great Fra
> Langella as my counterpart. Thank you, thank you, all – I ca
> believe it!

As always, he was at his happiest during the run of a play, when l
colleagues became his extended family. 'It was then he felt m
complete,' as Conrad said. 'That's what he lived for.'

The season of glory concluded with a magnificent performance
21 July. 'The producers wanted to extend the show,' Ben recalled, 'b
Alan was exhausted and began to suffer various ailments. He h
gastric distress, acid reflux, lower back pain and difficulty walkin

Acupuncture briefly alleviated the joint pain. 'He had done huge roles before without any trouble,' Ben continued, 'but now he was often sick.' As Simon remembered, 'The things that were wrong with him got worse – the knee, the stomach, the fatigue.'

Still, he was not one to slow down, much less stop – and that turned out to be an imprudent decision. He returned to London for more medical tests, which showed, first, that he would benefit from a replacement of his arthritic hip.

This was scheduled to follow his month-long stay in Canada, where he arrived on 11 August, having signed to appear in *Hollywood North*, whose title refers to Toronto. This occasionally amusing movie was intended as a satire on just about everything that can go wrong from script through production; for the most part, however, everything did, even in the making of *Hollywood North* itself. As a paranoid, gun-toting, cocaine-snorting, faded Hollywood star, Alan tore through the role of Michael Baytes, joining the swagger of Rod Steiger to the dark menace of Robert Mitchum (both of whom are mentioned in the script). Despite hip, back and leg pain, he served up a satiric stew of a character unlike any in his prior repertoire.

On 9 October he entered King Edward VII Hospital in London, where doctors performed a total left hip replacement. Discharged on the seventeenth, he then suffered severe pain and had to return to hospital, where the surgery was repeated. 'I had the Queen Mother's own doctor and it's gone wrong!' he cried.

More than anything, Alan hated the necessity of declining several roles that autumn. For once in his life he was the one requiring some attentive care and, at this point, he began to ring up his old flames – primary among them Joanna and Yardena.

Both women came to London. 'I never had a friend like Alan,' Joanna said later. 'Over the years, he was the first person I called when anything bad happened, or when I got a movie role, or when there was some difficulty or some happiness in life. He was always there for me. Now it was my time to help him.' And so she did, moving to London and staying with Alan at Hamilton Terrace. Yardena, meanwhile, tried to offer assistance too, but for a series of complex reasons due to no one's fault, the atmosphere seemed not well suited to accommodate two women in one house. Joanna moved in, while Yardena waited patiently on the fringes, ready to be of help if she could.

As late autumn turned to a cold winter, Alan came to depend very much on Joanna. He spoke with her about the future, anticipating a complete recovery from his hip surgery and (as he hoped) total control of his diabetes and hypertension: they would live together, he said, travel together, perhaps take a second home in Palm Springs, the social heart of the California desert. They drove in his enormous touring automobile – 'a ridiculous car built for cross-country driving', as Simon described it – and went back and forth to Derbyshire for shopping expeditions; at one stop Alan paid two thousand pounds for a stone table for his garden. He very much wanted a lifetime companion, and his choice seemed to fall on Joanna.

In January 2003 Alan was informed that, should he choose to accept, he would be knighted in an investiture at Buckingham Palace, set for 19 March. There was not a person in his circle, nor in the theatre world, who did not believe the honour was long past due. Letters and cards jammed his post box and messages accumulated on his answer machine. Flowers arrived in abundant profusion – and with all of this Alan was supremely delighted.

However, he was disappointed that he was unable to travel to New York for the birth of Claudia's and Ben's first child, on 17 January he felt more and more unwell, though at first there was no indication of grave illness – merely a deep lassitude and waves of what seemed like indigestion. Then, to the astonishment of friends with whom he dined, he lost his taste for rich foods and elaborate desserts. Finally, the results of additional medical tests came in on the twenty-seventh: 'There are multiple liver metastases and a tumour in the body of the pancreas which is inoperable. Of course surgery is completely out of the question for any form of curative intervention.' Consulting with the doctors and specialists, Alan chose chemotherapy and radiation in an attempt to shrink the tumour.

He rang Ben at once and Martin soon after. 'I've got cancer, but don't panic, I'll be fine. I'll beat this. It's not a good kind to have, but I'll beat it.' When Alan told his secretary, Rosemary Geddes, he was equally calm: 'Don't worry, love – I'm determined to get through this.' But when he enquired further of his doctors, he was told quite bluntly that few patients in his condition lived longer than four to six months after diagnosis.

The first round of chemotherapy was administered after Alan entered the London Clinic, Devonshire Place, on 4 March – a date fixed so that, should he have adverse reactions, they could be countered in time for his knighthood. For the once-weekly infusions he was to remain overnight to be monitored, and the staff moved a bed into his room so that Joanna could remain with him. 'But when he learned he would have to pay a large fee for the extra bed,' she recalled, 'he decided he could remain alone overnight. Alan was, to say the least, always thrifty.'

On the morning after one of these hospital sessions, Joanna arrived to find Alan in the bathroom, trying to cut his hair very short. 'Look at my pillow,' he told her, pointing to tufts and fistfuls of his hair, which had fallen out because of the medicine. So she helped him to style what remained, making a mere fringe of white hair, no longer dyed, seem very much the high style.

Such was his appearance when he appeared on camera in late March, discussing *In Celebration*, *Butley* and *The Cherry Orchard*. These commentaries reveal at once what a brilliant drama coach or teacher Alan Bates might have been, or even a director. Perceptive but not cloying, serious but not academic, Alan addressed each work in fascinating detail and was not self-referential, like so many stars of lesser lights. He was, indeed, one of the most articulate and best-informed actors of his or any generation and here, as always, he never used notes, never read from a prepared script. To hear his reflections and observations is to realise how totally he was a man of the theatre, and how intelligently he approached his craft.

The chemotherapy treatments continued throughout March and April, but usually with side effects he could endure – hence his investiture as Sir Alan Bates on 19 March at Buckingham Palace proceeded. For the event Ben came from New York, joining Alan's relatives from Derbyshire and a legion of friends in London. Elizabeth gave a party, and Alan was in high spirits. All during that spring and summer Alan rarely referred to the illness, which, as he knew, very few people survived. 'His doctor told me it was terminal,' said Joanna, 'and I asked if Alan knew, because he hadn't said anything. The doctor said that Alan knew the truth very clearly.' Intimate and affectionate conversations with Martin continued through the year. 'It was all desperately poignant,' Martin said, 'for Alan knew he was to die – we all knew it, too, and it sometimes made conversation difficult.'

Nevertheless his attitude was optimistic, and being with him was never awkward for anyone. 'When I get over this,' he told Joanna, 'we'll go on a long holiday to the Greek Isles . . . we'll visit Michael Cacoyannis . . . we'll go to the south of France . .' He was looking with great hope at the time he had left, 'and he wanted a good and comfortable life,' Joanna added. 'He wanted to make up for the past – to travel more, to be with his family and friends.' He said he could do just one film a year from then on, that he had enough money to live well without doing any more than that. 'I never thought I'd hear you say *that*!' said Joanna with a laugh, and Alan had to laugh too.

Ros gave a party while Alan was receiving his treatments and, because by this time more people knew the situation, he spoke of it – but only, as Felicity recalled, to make amusing comments. 'He must have been frightened,' she said, 'but he didn't allow fear to change the person he was.'

'With the chemo,' Joanna added, 'he had a kind of "high" the day after treatment. Several times I found him on a ladder at three or four o'clock in the morning, sorting through cupboards or bookshelves and rearranging things in beautiful pieces of luggage or cases.' As Arthur Laurents recalled, Alan had enjoyed shopping for suitcases in New York: 'During the run of *Fortune's Fool*, he'd come down to Greenwich Village and make Tom go out to shop with him for suitcases – why, nobody knew. Not even Alan, I suspect.' But when he returned to London, Alan indeed found a use for the various pieces: to contain memorabilia.

With a sudden surge of energy and in good humour, Alan departed for Paris on 30 April, where he worked for two days in a pair of brief sequences in *The Statement*, directed by Norman Jewison and starring Michael Caine. Elegantly outfitted and carefully made up for his few moments before the camera, he played the role of a French government minister, a morally ambiguous character involved in the protection of former Nazi collaborators. Doubtless aware of the irony, he also replied, that season, with positive interest in the idea for a script based on Jim Crace's novel *Being Dead*; the project never went forward.

During his week-long stay at the Hotel Raphael in Paris, Alan had several free days and he took advantage of Paris in May. After receiving a letter from a fan eager to meet him, Alan agreed to an introduction.

Before he returned to London on 7 May, he had spent at least two days and one night with this handsome young man who became the latest (and, he of course said, the greatest) love of his life.

'He decided to have an affair,' as Felicity recalled. 'Now what sort of person, knowing that he's dying of cancer, sets up a situation like this? One sort does it – the Alan type, who loved loving people and who loved people loving him, and somehow he had a magical way of organising it. He was also shameless in his desires, and his attitude to romantic entanglements was just like his attitude to desserts – "I really shouldn't, but I'll just have one more" – and he did!'

'He was an incorrigible romantic,' as Alan Bennett said. 'He was always in love or on the edge of love, and it was always with the one who was going to be the love of his life – no matter he had told you exactly the same thing about somebody else six months earlier and six months before that. Status, gender or familiarity didn't matter – always, this was going to be the real thing.'

From the filming in Paris, Alan said he had learned a valuable lesson. 'It's taken me all these years to realise that I don't have to take on the entire responsibility of a major role in a picture,' he said to Conrad Monk. 'I can go to a film for a week, do my job, finish it, get paid and leave!' With that in mind, Alan worked for a day in Derbyshire that June, providing a brief off-screen narration of a funeral eulogy for a film called *Meanwhile*. Frequent visits to Bank House and the surrounding countryside brought him considerable serenity that year. He loved the landscape and wildlife more than ever, and was delighted to see pheasants feeding in his garden.

With a sudden rush of energy Alan agreed to appear in a three-hour-long Roman epic made for television – *Spartacus*, produced in Bulgaria from mid July to early August. He worked – word–perfect as usual in every one of his scenes, an altogether astonishing achievement since he was unwell from the time he arrived in Sofia. As the consul and later senator Agrippa, Alan spoke as the conscience of ancient Rome. For a few scenes, the editor had to cut away from him and focus elsewhere because he was so ill, but his voice was strong, assured and reassuring.

Opposing the bloodthirsty tactics of the most feral senators, his Agrippa was a briefly seen but significant character, and Alan played him with a weariness that derived from his illness but was simultaneously suitable for the character's high ideals. 'Now tell me some dirt – all the gossip' he bids Flavius near the conclusion. It was a pure Alan moment, full of mischief and fun, intended to distract from cruelties one was powerless to prevent.

During production, few in the film company knew of his condition, for his manner and attitude were, as usual, warm, collegial and droll. His presence in the film was the only reason for viewers to tune in when *Spartacus* was broadcast the following year; otherwise this was the sort of witless television fare that required talented actors to say remarkably silly lines: 'These are the Thracian slaves – pretty good, huh?' and 'I give you food, housing and a good time, and this is the thanks I get?' In at least one scene an actor blithely chews gum as another speaks further inanities. And in the absence of a compelling narrative and reasonably intelligent discourse, the producers simply chose to offer an escalating assortment of bloody, brutal and sadistic sequences that appealed to viewers' worst instincts.

Alan was relieved to be home in London on 4 August, for he was despite his cheerful attitude, evidently very ill indeed. Perhaps to his astonishment – or perhaps not, as the event may have been carefully planned – his young Frenchman arrived from Paris, moved into a flat and presented himself with every intention of being taken for Alan's permanent partner. If not a surprise to him, the fellow's arrival certainly was to Alan's family, and to Joanna, Conrad, Nickolas, Paul, Yardena, Gerard and Simon – all of whom were in devoted attendance as the situation became more critical. But no one wished to deny Alan whatever comfort derived from his latest *amour de rencontre*; Paul, for example, offered his home as a rendezvous point for the couple. Still, the sudden appearance of someone new on the scene caused some intrigue; mischievous to the end, Alan seemed to enjoy watching people negotiate delicate manoeuvres.

Martin travelled frequently to visit Alan, as did Ben from New York – until he received an offer that greatly pleased his father, who insisted he accept: the part of Joey in a Boston production of *Butley* with Nathan Lane in the title role, which ran from 24 October to 30 November. One evening Alan visited Conrad and spoke proudly of Ben; then, when he talked of the past and of the twins, he broke down, weeping.

On Monday, 12 October a memorial service was held at the Royal

Court for the renowned stage designer Jocelyn Herbert. At the conclusion David Storey was leaving the theatre: 'I was approached by a very swollen, unrecognisable figure who seemed to know me. He put his arms around me, noticed my consternation and said quietly, "It's the chemo, you know." To my horror, I then realised it was Alan. We just stood there and clung to each other.' Not long afterwards, Alan and Joanna dined at the Ivy, where even the staff, who knew him so well over many years, failed to recognise him.

The following weekend, with typical good grace and humour, Alan gamely fulfilled a promise he had made to Elizabeth Grant, who had invited him to celebrate the opening of a new arts centre in Halesworth, Suffolk. Walking was difficult, but his voice was robust and full: 'I couldn't decide on a suitable reading for this occasion,' he said, taking the stage to enthusiastic applause, 'and so I chose an unsuitable one.' When the laughter subsided he read – in a strong Scottish accent – a long narrative poem by William McGonagall, universally acknowledged as one of the worst poets in the history of the English language. He intended his selection – all sixteen quatrains of 'The Burning of the Exeter Theatre' – to amuse and entertain with its horrifically bad verse:

'Twas in the year of 1887, which many people will long remember,
The burning of the Theatre at Exeter on the fifth of September,
Alas! that ever-to-be remembered and unlucky night,
When one hundred and fifty lost their lives, a most agonising
    sight . . .

. . . I am very glad to see Henry Irving has sent a hundred
    pounds,
And I hope his brother actors will subscribe their mite all round;
And if they do it will add honour to their name,
Because whatever is given towards a good cause they will it
    regain.

As Alan stepped down painfully from the platform, he waved and smiled. It was his last appearance before an audience.

He did, however, go with Martin to the Royal Academy of Arts, to see an exhibit of pre-Raphaelite art, for which Alan had a special predilection and Martin, as artist and art teacher, unique knowledge.

'It was a touching experience, because he was so weak and slow in moving around the gallery and had to take frequent rests. But it was an important experience for us – sad, but also enjoyable.' Back home, he endured the unpleasant effects of radiation treatments, which had replaced chemotherapy.

One day in late November, when Alan's secretary Rosemary was at Hamilton Terrace, she went to the kitchen to prepare tea. Suddenly he turned to Joanna: 'Could you please straighten the pictures on the wall, Jo? They're all crooked!' But the pictures were perfectly aligned; she then saw that one side of his face had slumped. When the doctor arrived, he examined Alan and asked what he could see. 'Jo,' Alan replied, 'sitting on the edge of the bed – and another Jo, standing behind her.' He had suffered a stroke and was immediately taken to hospital. His humour, however, was unaffected: 'One of you had better adjust your make-up,' Alan said to Joanna as they bundled him into a car.

The ravages of diabetes, pancreatic cancer and a stroke took a fearful toll during the early weeks of December. Joanna spoke at length with the doctor, who confirmed what Alan already knew – that his time was now very limited indeed. Ben arrived from New York and left the hospital room only infrequently, sitting quietly, holding his father's hand, encouraging him to take a bit of food, sharing all the news for which Alan was eager. How was Ben's and Claudia's baby girl, his first grand-child? What news of the Rialto, what was the theatre gossip in New York?

Until the middle of the month Alan was able to telephone to friends, but he did not always say he was in the London Clinic. 'He rang me twice,' said David, 'but he made no mention of the fact that he was in hospital – he just wanted to chat, and he didn't speak at all of his illness.' Eventually Alan said he wanted to see his friends, and he did not have to wait long. 'Word had got out by this time,' Joanna recalled, 'and now there was a constant stream of callers to his bedside.' The hospital room then became the locus for a collective series of reconciliation scenes, of final poignant encounters, affectionate gestures, expressions of forgive-ness for mutual misunderstandings. Nothing was forced, melodramatic or artificial.

Simon was, like Martin, Nickolas, Conrad and Joanna, among the most frequent visitors. If he was going to die soon, Alan said, it was all right. 'I've had a good life. I've done everything I want, really. Yes, it would be all right.' To Conrad he spoke similarly: 'I've really had a marvellous life, I've played marvellous parts – and it's really all been terrific.'

He had been the golden boy to virtually everyone who knew him. 'He was one of those people everyone wanted to do things for,' Conrad said, 'and they did, and he let them. He never had to make much of an effort, nor did he have to plead for attention or affection. It all came to him, for everyone wanted to be near, to help him – in his illness just as they had done in the good times.'

'The nurses adored him,' recalled Felicity.

> He made it easy to be cared for, and he took away everyone's embarrassment about being sick and dying – the kind of embarrassment that is such an English thing, but he had none of it. Even if he was afraid, and he must have been, he dealt with it by holding your hand, by ordering a quiche for you, by making a joke so you could laugh with him and not be sorry for him. Alan had an extraordinary need to love people. His manner wasn't, 'Come to see me and tell me you love me,' it was, 'Come to my bedside so I can tell you that I love you.' His generosity to friends and his dignity in those last weeks and days is unforgettable. He sat there, and the lights were on – and *he* was on. His attitude was, 'Well, this is happening to me and that is happening to me, but let's talk about something else . . .'

It was the best example of which Yardena had rightly spoken: Alan was letting the deeds arrange his life, and he accommodated himself to life even at its close. As she had written to him not long before the end, 'We said it all, didn't we – and what we didn't do says it all.' They had a rare understanding and there was, finally, mutual forgiveness for whatever there had been of misconstruction and confusion.

He looked back in anger at nothing and at no one, not even himself: 'I can't use that word, "anger". What happened was what happened, and what is, is now.' That was no glib observation, for he went deeper: 'When you're young, you may say, "I don't believe in God, so I won't go to church." But later you reach a stage when at least you start to wonder why others *do* believe. You find out because you *want* to.'

'He was never a burden to anyone,' said Alan Bennett. 'He held court as long as he could, and when he tired, he made it easy for his friends to be with him.' Angharad arrived: 'There was something extraordinarily beautiful about him, even then,' she said. 'He was like a splendid emperor. He lay there still and silent, and he seemed the soul of serenity and wisdom.' Paul agreed: 'He lay there, listening to music. His beard had grown white, some of his hair had grown back, and it was snow-white. He looked noble and full of wisdom. He'd had enough; he was tired and ready to go.'

'I saw him in hospital a few days before the end,' recalled Gemma, 'and he still wanted the gossip, he was still able to laugh at the latest scandals and follies of life. I wondered then whether he would come to some final, great revelation about himself, but I think he had always lived in that mad bubble of the actor's life. I never had the impression then, or earlier, that he was inclined to seek counselling for his private struggles, or that he was steeped in guilt for anything. How he loved life!' Georgina Hale came, too: 'He wore an eye patch, because of the stroke, but he was in a playful mood and asked what part he thought would be right for him now. I suggested the phantom of the opera and he laughed uproariously.'

The last days in the life of Alan Bates had a kind of remarkable inevitability in tone and content. Everyone with any substantial link wanted to visit, to be with him, to allow the healing of memories, and he welcomed everyone without exception. 'He received his friends until nearly the end,' Simon recalled, 'sitting in a chair by the bed, a rug over his lap, full of delight and above all attention. He wanted to hear everything that was going on in our lives, gave sympathy and advice where things were bad, and shared in any pleasures and successes. He was Alan as I'd always known him, the very best of best friends.'

He much enjoyed this concluding act of social life. 'It's amazing,' he said to Joanna. 'Everyone wants to be the last one to see me alive – everyone wants to have my last words! Well, I try to give them something good to take away.' Ros and Michael were there, and Gareth, who was visiting London from Los Angeles, came for a visit, too. 'Alan was out of bed, sitting in a chair,' Gareth recalled. 'We chatted for a half-hour about the old times and then I left. I felt very privileged to have that chance to say goodbye, although neither of us said goodbye.'

During the intervals between his callers, Alan listened to opera recordings. 'Bliss . . . bliss . . . bliss,' he whispered, and for a while he was able to hum along gently. Ben was present constantly, and one afternoon, during a peaceful interlude, Alan turned to him.

'The real people who take care of you are the people who love you,' he said knowingly, looking directly at his son. 'And that is because only the people who love you understand.' He paused before continuing, 'You're the only person who can do it right, Ben.'

'But that's because I love you,' Ben replied.

On about 20 December the doctors withdrew all medications and prescribed morphine, but Alan wanted only enough to dull the keenest suffering. He wanted, after all, to be as alert as possible for as long as possible.

The entire cast of surviving characters seemed to come to the London Clinic at Christmastide, even those whose relations with Alan had been complicated or unhappy. Terence Stamp arrived; there had been some jealous tension between them during the production of *Far From the Madding Crowd*, but now there was only kindness and laughter about the silliness of any mutual misunderstanding. Peter Wyngarde visited too, and neither of them alluded to any past unpleasantness.

Gerard arrived, and they sat quietly, holding hands. 'He looked radiant. His face was very pale, and his hair, beard, bed gown, the sheets, his socks, were all white – he was like a gleaming tomb effigy. We talked and laughed for a while, then he said, "You know, Gerardio, I think I treated you very badly when we split up."' Gerard said that had been true, and it had been very difficult for him at the time. 'And then, without hesitation and with some solemnity, he said that he was sorry for it all, adding with a grin, "But didn't we have some great times and great laughs?"'

The morphine, Alan said, had the same effect as a strong vodka and pineapple juice on an empty stomach, and he became a little slow of speech, occasionally losing the thread of the conversation. At one confused point he stopped, looked at Gerard and said, 'I can't remember what the hell I was talking about! It's good I'm not doing King Lear tonight!' A few days later Gerard returned with his partner, Davie Evans, 'and Alan could not have been more gracious. Before we left, he said he was amazed how gentle and easy everything was: "If this is it, I want you to know that it's not so bad after all – really, it isn't."'

Of his nearly seventy years, it can only be said that Alan Bates indeed achieved what seemed right for him to achieve and what he wanted to achieve. 'He never really had a choice about being an actor,' said Michael. 'He was one of those rare beings, a conduit to a gift, a talent that he gave others – like Rembrandt or Pavarotti. They did not learn what they did; they honed a gift they received. So it was with Alan.'

He also had a magnificent balance about his profession and his contributions to it. 'Yes, he loved his work and was entirely committed to it,' said Felicity, 'but he didn't think that acting was a matter of life and death.' That attitude saved him from the crassest kind of ambition and a cruel exploitation of his status, and it enabled him to be the most congenial colleague. As David emphasised, other actors seemed to give their best performances when they were working with Alan.

One of the few actors of his time to cross easily from theatre to film and back again for almost half a century, he conquered both stage and screen in equal measure – not always as a leading man, but as a valuable, even an indispensable constituent. He often made a good play or film seem excellent, or an ordinary one memorable. He made audiences aware of enormous depths in a character and this he accomplished without, it seemed, an atom of calculation – and that, of course, was itself the height of a supremely graceful artifice.

He enjoyed his Shakespearean roles – perhaps Antony most of all – and the wistful and dark figures of Chekhov, Ibsen and Strindberg intrigued him and were clearly remembered by audiences too. But it was the plays of his own time for which he had a unique affinity – hence he enlivened the disarticulate anguish of Harold Pinter's characters, the incisive searching of David Storey's and the bitter, ironic bemusement of Simon Gray's. On the screen, it was his tender, marginal or confused men who most appealed to audiences, perhaps because the close-up revealed so much that was tender and confused in himself: the mysterious fugitive of *Whistle Down the Wind*; the calm repression of the arid poet in *Zorba the Greek*; the amnesiac hero of *The Return of the Soldier*; the disaffected spy in *An Englishman Abroad*, almost noble in his isolation. For the most part he played flawed or incomplete men, and even the most awful of them were recognisable as authentically human, as cautionary characters in a fable to which he gave astonishing life.

Instead of diminishing him, the tragedies that attended Alan's life enabled him somehow to grow and never turned him into a tragic figure. He could sometimes be frugal to the point of parsimony, but in important ways he repaid the world and his friends with the kind of undiluted generosity that comes from comprehension and compassion. And at the finale, as Simon memorably wrote, he was 'imperial in his dying, deeply happy with what had come to him at the end, his Tony Award on Broadway, his knighthood, all that was due had come at last'. Professionally, nothing was lacking.

In his private life, he wanted most of all to have one true and enduring relationship, to love and to be loved by one faithful man. This eluded him – although perhaps he was not, as many sympathetically observed, cut out for such a bond. Despite that, Alan's most memorable characteristic, as Ian said after more than a half-century of friendship, 'was the enormous love he engendered, that he drew from people, and that he gave them in return'. Gemma, Felicity and many others agreed: even after one acknowledged his indiscretions and his apparent callousness, no one could ever stop loving him. His predominant characteristic was a generous heart.

By Christmas he had slipped into a coma. During the evening of 26 December, because the Clinic's cafeteria was closed for the holiday, Simon and his wife Victoria brought food for Ben, who had not left his father's side for days. The Grays remained until he had eaten, then kissed Alan's forehead and withdrew. Joanna and Martin were nearby, vigilant to the end.

On Saturday evening, 27 December, Ben was alone in the room with his father. He awoke to hear Alan's breathing, which had throughout the day become more laboured. In the quiet darkness, Ben listened for several moments, and then there was only stillness and silence.

Notes

For economy's sake, details of interviews conducted for this book are supplied only at the first citation; unless otherwise stated, subsequent quotations from the same source derive from the identical interview with that source.

Epigraph Page

Tell the truth: Quoted in Zucker, p. 26.

Chapter One

Though he didn't exactly: Martin Bates, in written notes to DS, June and July 2006; and in interview, 10 May 2006.

You always knew: From the draft of an unpublished article on AB for *Woman's Weekly* by Julia Beasley.

I think he could have been: Georgina Brown, 'Master of disguise', *Evening Standard* (London), 13 October 1995.

She said she didn't: Benedick Bates to DS, 25 April 2006.

We sent Alan out: Ashley Franklin, 'A Tribute to Sir Alan Bates', *Derbyshire Life and Countryside*, May 2004, p. 73.

She shuddered: Ibid.

I remember the strictness: Zucker, p. 18.

very quiet: Franklin, art.cit., p. 74

I wasn't academic: Ibid.

It was not an unhappy childhood: Frank Rasky, 'He's a real gasser',

Toronto Star, 3 June 1967; see also Angus McGill, 'Alan Bates', *Woman's Own*, 14 January 1967, p. 8.

became infatuated: Zucker, p. 18.

I can do what we've seen: Recalled by Martin Bates.

I'd found: 'Bates – at the crossroads', *Showtime*, March 1967, p. 16; see also Scavullo.

they took it to be: 'Alan Bates Talking to Sheridan Morley', *Flair*, January 1970, p. 34.

He really knew: Franklin, art.cit., p. 75.

His mother and father: Ibid.

I was smashing: From the unpublished article by Beasley.

but Alan was obviously: Derby *Evening Telegraph*, 17 February 1967.

Arthur, the boy prince: 'King John Spectacle: Two Outstanding Characters', Derby *Evening Telegraph*, 15 February 1949 (review by 'S.D.').

I was attracted: *Honey* magazine (UK), January 1962, p. 27.

with considerable lyric understanding: Claude W. Gibson, report on Alan Bates: Speech and Drama, Grade V (Examiner's Ref. No. 17, dated 2 December 1950).

Alan told me: Letter from Claude W. Gibson to Mary Bates: 10 September 1950.

He shows great: Claude W. Gibson, report on Alan Bates: Speech and Drama, Grade VI (Examiner's Ref. No. T55, dated 7 April 1951).

We seem to be the youngest: Ian White to DS, 21 October 2006.

When Barnes packed in: 'The Changing Face of RADA', the centenary book published by the Royal Academy of Dramatic Art, London, 2004.

It was concerned: Zucker, p. 18.

It's nice to be able: From the unpublished article by Beasley.

Chapter Two

One of the first things: Conrad Monk to DS, 15 May 2006.

melodious language: L. H. Meakin, 'Curtain Call: "Eurydice" Was Well Worth While [*sic*]', an undated clipping from an unidentifiable Derbyshire newspaper (probably *The Advertiser*).

It was a terrifically good year: Zucker, p. 19.

Finney, O'Toole and Bates: Stephen Pile, 'The Rough and the Smooth', *Daily Telegraph*, 3 July 1993, p. 34.

Keith Baxter's recollections of life at Primrose Mansions were included in his tribute to AB at the Royal Court, 26 September 2004.

What a crew: Maureen A. Smith, 'He is an Englishman!', *Daily News Record*, 11 December 1964, p. 4.

I blew it: David Lewin, 'The ripening of Alan Bates', *Daily Mail*, 29 June 1987, p. 24; see also, 'Master of the Roles', *Time Out*, 11–18 October 1995, p. 18.

The RADA report by AB's teachers covered the summer 1955 term, for the Finals 2 Division. The assessments were written in long-hand on a single large, undated sheet.

I was terrific: Georgina Brown, art.cit.

It was a very: Zucker, p. 19.

I didn't really know: Ibid.

The Piper anecdote is included in an interview conducted by Kate Dorney on 12 March 2005 for the British Library Theatre Archive Project; see www.bl.uk/projects/theatrearchive/piper.html

I stage-managed: Osborne, p. 18.

In rehearsal: Morley, art.cit., p. 34.

rehearsals were: Richardson, cited in Mark Lawson, 'Fifty Years of Anger', *Guardian*, 31 March 2006.

I doubt if: Kenneth Tynan in the *Observer*, 13 May 1956.

cosy young: Philip Hope-Wallace in the *Guardian*, 9 May 1956.

made us the theatre: Richardson, p. 59.

It was the first time: Michael Owen, 'An Appetite for Big Things', *Sunday Telegraph*, 8 August 1999.

It was a real stroke of luck: From the unpublished Beasley interview.

I sometimes look back: In the *Birmingham Post*, 28 September 1996, p. 39.

Booing is: Osborne, p. 27.

I just felt lucky: Jasper Gerard, 'Chinks in a lonely knight's armour', *Sunday Times* (news review), 5 January 2003, p. 5.

Even though it offered: Lewin, art.cit., p. 24.

I didn't want to be: Gerard, art.cit., p. 5.

Bates went through: Telex from Jerene Jones to New York offices of *Time*, 24 October 1972. Her extensive, lengthy research became the basis for a brief, uncontroversial essay in the magazine's issue of 6 November 1972; the original draft of Jones's message was kept by AB among his private papers.

Chapter Three

Five British actors: Brooks Atkinson in the *New York Times*, 2 October 1957.

little more than: Osborne, p. 78.

He was sexually: Paul Taylor to DS, 24 May 2006.

We always had a good time: Arthur Laurents to DS, 5 October 2006.

I got stale: Ki Hackney, 'The State of Bates', *Women's Wear Daily*, 20 December 1968.

Long runs are very bad: Peter Buckley, 'Alan Bates: An Actor Who Prefers To Be Anonymous', *Show*, May 1972.

a valiant ambassador: John Bates to DS, November 2006.

It was a great mistake: O'Neill, p. 154.

Alan's awfully good: Recalled by Martin Bates to DS, July 2006.

At that time: Ian Auger and Stephen James Walker, '*Doctor Who* Magazine', issue no. 141 (October 1988), n.p.

The production: *The Times*, 16 February 1959.

the number one pin-up boy: 'Bates Beats the Jinx', *Picturegoer*, 19 March 1960.

I think he was seeking: From the transcript of a 1995 interview with AB, conducted by Brian McFarlane.

I watched Alan: Harold Pinter, in the memorial tribute to AB at the Royal Court, 26 September 2004.

Well, there isn't much: The dialogue here, and that which followed on opening night of *The Caretaker*, was recalled by AB in a BAFTA tribute that honoured Harold Pinter with a fellowship (1997). AB kept his written remarks among his papers.

I didn't immediately: Jane Edwardes, 'Master of the Roles', *Time Out*, 11–18 October 1995.

It is a study: AB, on his DVD commentary for *The Caretaker*, released by the British Film Institute (2002).

I don't find my own behaviour: Quoted in the *Sunday Times*, 16 June 1991.

a national masterpiece: Marowitz confirmed this description in a message to DS, 30 August 2006.

I went with fear: Coward, p. 436; entry for 2 May 1960.

Mr Pinter is neither pretentious: *Sunday Times*, 15 January 1961; the play was still in its successful first run.

playing the most straightforward: *Tatler & Bystander*, 15 June 1960.

Mick is a fantasist: Zucker, p. 23.

three rather isolated people: Ibid.

I think eight performances: Ibid., p. 21.

You can't really: Ibid., pp. 20–21.

the dark period: The phrase, quoting AB, was used by, among others, Nickolas Grace, Gerard Hastings and Michael Linnit.

Chapter Four

wholly convincing: *The Times*, 21 February 1961.

How very lucky I was: Bryan Forbes, at the memorial tribute to AB at the Royal Court Theatre, 26 September 2004.

He was wonderfully pleasant: Hayley Mills to DC, 2 August 2006.

It was my first: McFarlane, p. 58.

Do congratulate Alan: Claude W. Gibson to Mary Bates, letter dated 14 August 1961.

unerring tenderness: *Daily Mirror*, 19 June 1961.

Locked in a cycle: *Time*, 13 October 1961.

one of the most important properties: 'When Actor Is a Property', *Derby Evening Telegraph*, 4 September 1961.

It had a lot of human understanding: McFarlane, p. 59.

human difficulties: Mann, p. 7.

The secretary of the Board: Gareth Wigan to DS, 21 April 2006.

A Kind of Loving: Buckley, art.cit.

It was a wonderful experience: Mann, pp. 173–174.

such a good, intuitive actor: Ibid., p. 175.

Had Alan been willing: Ibid., p. 189.

wasn't really: From the draft of a 1982 interview with Sharon Feinstein for the magazine *Woman's Realm*.

I didn't think: 'Reflections: Alan Bates, interviewed by Gordon Gow', *Films and Filming*, June 1971.

I felt I was working: Ibid.

On the filming of *The Running Man*, see Harvey Matofsky, 'Reed's "Running Man" on a Spanish Course', *New York Times*, 12 August 1962.

It was done out of: Ibid.

The scenes between: Gow interview, *Films and Filming*.

I was called: Interviewed by Jerene Jones for *Time* in 1972; her research resulted in a brief, polite essay in the magazine: 'The Colors of

Bates', 6 November 1972. The lengthy transcript of her research notes was forwarded to the New York office of the magazine, where its receipt was dated 24 October 1972.

I don't want to be a star: From AB's tribute to Harry Andrews, who died on 6 March 1989. The eulogy was written for AB by Gerard Hastings.

a really ambitious little creep: Ibid.

Bates is attractive: Eugene Archer, 'The Best of "The Best"', *New York Times*, 16 August 1964.

Chapter Five

At his best: Gow interview, June 1971.

Alan was easy: Michael Cacoyannis, in his commentary provided for the Fox Studio Classics DVD release of *Zorba the Greek* (2004).

He's rather: McFarlane, p. 60.

It was something new for me: 'Bates – at the crossroads', *Showtime*, March 1967, p. 30.

an incredibly difficult thing: Gow interview, June 1971.

he was 'miscast': 'Bates – at the crossroads', *Showtime*, March 1967, p. 30.

It was a double agony: Margaret Hinxman, 'An Enigma Called Alan', *Woman*, 6 October 1967.

For most actors: 'The Colors of Bates', *Time*, 6 November 1972.

easily pushed around: Bosley Crowther in the *New York Times*, 18 December 1964.

Living on Crete: Anne Hooper, '15 Minutes with Alan Bates', *Photoplay*, April 1966.

Poor Richard was billed: Joanna Pettet to DS, 22 April 2006.

another winner: The New York *Journal American*, 3 December 1964.

Alan Bates is so poised: *New York Times*, 3 December 1964.

but as a charmer: *Time*, 11 December 1964.

Even when both our disappointments: Chris Chase, 'Alan Bates, or Who Says Nice Guys Finish Last?', *New York Times*, 29 October 1972, p. D-1.

I chose it myself: The incident with Coward was later recounted by AB to Gerard Hastings, thence to DS: 24 May 2006.

a great thinker: Letter of Valerie Ward to a friend – henceforth in this book, designated 'Victoria,' the name she had adopted and by which everyone knew her; and as VW in the notes. As often in her letters, there is no salutation or addressee: letter typed and dated Friday, 21 August 1964, from New York.

It was marvellous: Zucker, p. 20.

On Victoria's name: her birth, marriage and death certificates (among other papers such as her passport) are unambiguous: she was legally Valerie June Ward.

Alan Bates rang: VW in a letter to an unidentified recipient, 29 January 1965.

A small group of us: Yardena Harari to DS, 5 October 2006.

Why am I bitchy: VW, letter to Jane Gilchrist, dated from London, 17 September 1965.

What's it like: VW, to Jaffray Cuyler, 1 November 1965.

Trouble with a mammoth: VW, to 'Anna': 2 November 1965.

He's gentle and intelligent: VW, to Jaffray Cuyler, 7 October 1965.

As usual: Ibid.

in a pad with girls: VW, to Jane Gilchrist, 17 September 1965.

You must think: VW, to Jane Gilchrist, 25 October 1965.

I don't feel: VW, to 'Gérard', 17 October 1965.

Chapter Six

I've been miserable: VW, letter to 'Paul', 10 November 1965; also, frequently in conversations.

I have a great need: VW, to 'Gérard', 16 November 1965.

splendid: Bosley Crowther, '"Georgy Girl" Is Puddin' and Pie', *New York Times*, 6 November 1966.

I didn't think he: Rasky, art.cit.

He was really a bit past: Hinxman, art.cit.

He's having this great time: 'Bates – at the crossroads', *Showtime*, March 1967.

Oh, Mr Bates: Ibid.

What was your: Hooper, art.cit.

Peter Wyngarde gathered: Michael Linnit to DS, 19 May 2006.

Peter had apparently: Nickolas Grace to DS, 23 May 2006.

he talked about his time: Felicity Kendal to DS, 16 June 2006.

He finally looked up: 'Bates – at the crossroads', art.cit.

Nothing about this comedy: *Time*, 14 July 1967.

The film started off: Ibid.

The mad element: Gow, art.cit.

I have always resisted: McGill, art.cit.

I spent three quarters: VW, to 'Jane,' 7 February 1966.

She was without doubt: Marie Malavieille to DS, 21 October 2006.

Why is it: VW, to 'Anna', 17 May 1966.

My dreams: VW, to 'Anthony', 25 May 1966.

slightly stilted: VW, to 'Anthony', 21 May 1966.

Now there's richness: VW, to 'Anthony', 23 May 1966.

sure touch: *The Times*, 29 September 1966.

Alan was very reluctant: Gareth Wigan to DS, 22 April 2006.

I didn't want to play: Gow, art.cit.

On the filming of *Far From the Madding Crowd*, see the brief report in *Motion Picture Herald*, March 1967.

a jolly difficult: Ibid.

What's good about the film: Gow, art.cit.

a strong, direct man: 'Bates – at the crossroads'.

It's a rather difficult role: Sarah Meysey-Thompson, *Petticoat*, no. 40 (19 November 1966).

AB received the Langham telegram in Dorset on 24 January 1967.

The part is absurd: Cited in Frank Rasky, 'He's a real gasser', *Toronto Daily Star*, 3 June 1967, p. 18.

Chapter Seven

There was an immediate rapport: Paul Taylor to DS, 24 May 2006.

I'm going to do: William Rice, 'Bates Sharpens His Acting Skill in Rep,' *Los Angeles Times*, 14 August 1967.

clear, cool: Walter Kerr, 'When Is a Throne Truly Occupied?' *New York Times*, 25 June 1967.

singularly miscast: 'Outpost of Habitual Culture', *Time*, 30 June 1967.

fragmented: Barbara Frum, 'A Date with Alan Bates', *Chatelaine*, August 1967.

I hadn't actually lost: Romany Bain, 'Alan Bates', *She*, December 1968, p. 41.

When you go between: Zucker, p. 25.

I was on my knees: Bain, art.cit., p. 41.

It was totally different: Buckley, art.cit.

We did it all in real dungeons: Ki Hackney, 'The State of Bates', *Women's Wear Daily*, 20 December 1968.

I think it made me aware: Nicholas de Jongh, 'A kind of love', *Guardian*, 17 November 1969

He is the finest: From the Jones research notes for *Time*, 1972, as above.

Alan Bates was divine: See Champlin.

He doesn't understand: Fred Robbins, 'How Do You Look Jewish?', *New York Times*, 11 February 1968.

I think . . . that the movie: Unedited McFarlane interview (1995).

sexually ambivalent: Russell, p. 58.

Not only did he want: Jasper Gerard, 'Chinks in a lonely knight's armour', *Sunday Times*, 5 January 2003.

one of the most exposed: From the unpublished Beasley interview.

We didn't think too much: Buckley, art.cit.

very uncommunicative: From the transcript of an unpublished interview with AB conducted by Andy Warhol and Paul Morrissey in New York 1972. See also Michael Owen, 'An Appetite for Big Things', *Sunday Telegraph*, 'Arts', 8 August 1999, p. 1.

I had him earmarked: Russell, p. 59.

would be protected: Letter from Gareth Wigan, of Gregson & Wigan Ltd, to Martin Rosen of Brandywine Prods Ltd (co-producer, *Women in Love*), 10 January 1969.

When you were around Alan: Glenda Jackson to DS, 9 May 2006.

I gave him a certain: Gow, art.cit.

All I do is eat: Hackney, art.cit.

Oh, he's back: Quoted by Lauretta Feldman to DS: 24 April 2006.

Residential care emphasised: From Barnardo's history, outlined in their website:www.barnardos.org.uk/who_we _are/history/history2.htm; the citation refers to the institution circa 1900–1939, but little changed before 1950.

Chapter Eight

Lindsay sent me the play: AB's remarks on *In Celebration* were included in a March 2003 on-camera interview, accompanying the release of the DVD of the American Film Theatre production (completed in 1974, seen in limited theatrical release in 1975): Kino Video K290 (DVD release, 2003).

Americans have a neurosis: Sydney Edwards, 'The Sloane Square deserter', *Evening Standard*, 11 April 1969.

At one point: David Storey to DS, 23 November 2006.

made the play vibrate: Harold Hobson in the *Sunday Times*, 27 April 1969.

The play – it is like: Quoted by David Storey, on the Kino Video interview cited above (2003).

a somewhat highbrow: Quoted by AB; his comments on *Three Sisters* are part of the long 2003 interview detailed above, on the same disc as *In Celebration*.

spectacular in its: Jack Zink in the *Miami News*, 1 February 1974.

With that subject: Catherine Stott, 'Actor without an image', *Guardian*, 21 October 1971.

I felt more uncertain: Gow interview, 1971.

We took care: *Sunday People*, 14 May 1972.

I think they were afraid: Peter Buckley, 'Alan Bates: An Actor Who Prefers To Be Anonymous', *Show*, May 1972.

I had the impression: Elizabeth Grant to DS, 14 June 2006.

I gather: Benedick Bates to DS, 25 April 2006.

Victoria wanted Alan Bates: Nickolas Grace to DS, 23 May 2006.

When Alan brought me to his mother: Quoted by Niema Ash to DS, 28 November 2006; see also Ash, p. 75.

The reasons for Alan's marriage: Simon Gray to DS, 22 May 2006.

The script was marvellously: Stott, art.cit.

He's a deeply sensitive: Gow interview, 1971.

the best of his contemporaries: Wanda Hale in the New York *Daily News*, 25 July 1971.

I've done certain parts: Peter Ansorge and Peter Roberts, 'A Pride of Hamlets', *Plays and Players*, February 1971.

I think I am rather: Sydney Edwards, 'What Hamlet has done for Alan Bates', *Evening Standard*, 1 January 1971.

Nothing he does: John Barber in the *Daily Telegraph*, 13 January 1971.

Alan Bates, virile and handsome: Milton Schulman in the *Evening Standard*, 12 January 1971.

had little magnetism: Trewin.

masterly: Philip Hope-Wallace in the *Guardian*, 13 January 1971.

admirably dashing: Michael Billington in *The Times*, 12 January 1971.

I loved that part: AB's comments on *Butley* are part of the long 2003 interview detailed above, on the same disc as *In Celebration* and *Three Sisters*.

I recall very clearly: Ros Chatto to DS, 24 May 2006.

I spent the first three weeks: Judy Klemesrud, 'He's Charming, He's Sympatico – And a Reluctant Heart-throb', *New York Times*, 16 April 1978.

Have you told her: AB in a tribute to Harold Pinter at BAFTA (1997).

You can go to town: Zucker, pp. 22–23.

You could count on him: Gray, *The Year of the Jouncer*, p. 81ff.

a remarkable creation: Harold Pinter, 'Introduction', in Simon Gray, *Key Plays*, p. vii.

He took such relish: Harold Pinter at the memorial tribute to AB, 26 September 2004.

It was his merriness: Gray, *The Year of the Jouncer*, p. 83.

I find it much more: Buckley, art.cit. in *Show*, 1972.

haunting solitary beauty: Niema Ash to DS, 28 November 2006; see also Ash, p. 70.

But she didn't seem: Niema Ash to DS, 28 November 2006.

Victoria was for the most part: Rosemary Geddes to DS, 16 May 2006.

Chapter Nine

We were highly incompatible: Suzie MacKenzie, 'Alan Bates on life beyond 65', *Evening Standard*, 18 February 2000.

We women: Elizabeth Grant to DS, 14 June 2006.

inflexible, unreal: 'Bates Talks About Acting and the "Butley" Character', *New York Times*, 27 October 1972, p. 28.

In some ways, perhaps: Sheridan Morley, 'Messrs Bates, Gray & Co.', *Radio Times*, 11–17 October 1975, p. 70.

The leading character: *Time – Showbiz*, art.cit., 1972.

after months of driving: Lewis Funke, 'News of the Rialto', *New York Times*, 23 April 1972, p. D-1.

astonishing compassion: Clive Barnes in the *New York Times*, 1 November 1972, p. 54.

sticky . . . I can't have it: *New York Times*, 27 October 1972, p. 28.

I could never understand: Ronald Hayman, 'Gray, Pinter and Bates: a triangular alliance', *The Times*, 26 July 1975.

was cut from the production: Gray, *Key Plays*, p. 89n.

I don't like flying: Robert Taylor, 'Stage and Screen', *Oakland Tribune*, 9 March 1973.

It's nice: Barbara Frum, 'A Date with Alan Bates', *Chatelaine*, August 1967; AB was referring to success onstage and screen.

You could come: Sheila Ballantine at the memorial to AB at the Royal Court, 26 September 2004.

I'm ready to have it: Taylor, art.cit.

It comes closest: Andrew Clarke, 'Interview', *East Anglian Magazine*, 1–7 November 2003, p. 25.

I had met Alan: Nickolas Grace to DS, 23 May 2006.

I hated being in it: Sheridan Morley, 'Laughing with horror', *The Times*, 23 June 1987.

The account of the fracas with a spectator at *The Taming of the Shrew* was recounted by Nickolas Grace and by AB in a tribute to Grace.

Lindsay Anderson taught me: Morley, 'Messrs Bates, Gray & Co.', art.cit., p. 70.

I was knocked out . . . He works very fast: Sydney Edwards, 'The Arts', *Evening Standard*, 4 July 1975.

It makes me: Quoted by Malcolm McDowell at the memorial to AB at the Royal Court, 26 September 2004.

We were both always: Georgina Hale to DS, 25 May 2006.

He always took: Michael Lindsay-Hogg to DS, 27 April 2006.

because he's the most: Morley, 'Messrs Bates, Gray & Co.', art. cit.

Peter is very much: Ibid.

at his most magisterially comic: Clive Barnes, 'London Likely to Be "Otherwise Engaged"', special to the *New York Times* from London, 18 August 1975, p. 33.

who only gives permission: Gray, *Key Plays*, p. 164.

Chapter Ten

the quintessential Pinter menace: *Time*, 30 October 1978.

Affinities: Paul Vallely, 'Affinities that brought Alan Bates back home', *Yorkshire Post*, 13 July 1976.

Acting is too mysterious: Jonathan Miller, 'The Hot New Actor is Old Pro Alan Bates', *US* magazine, 3 October 1978.

Mr Bates's role: Vincent Canby in the *New York Times*, 5 March 1978.

I have been in rubbish: Jasper Gerard, 'Starry starry knight', *Sunday Times*, 5 January 2003.

such a full character: Minty Clinch, 'Tea and Sensuality', 7 *Days*, 10
September 1989, p. 14.

I don't know: Zucker, p. 29.

What was so impressive: John Schlesinger (from 10 Victoria Road,
London) to AB (122 Hamilton Terrace, London), 23 January
1978.

He was born: Gray, *The Year of the Jouncer*, p. 87.

She was very exciting: AB, interviewed by John Dunn on BBC Radio
2, 27 July 1983.

driving him mad: Lauretta Feldman to DS, 24 April 2006.

I've been lucky enough: 'Alan Bates Talking to Sheridan Morley',
Flair, January 1970.

I saw Alan: Michael Linnit to Midgley Snelling, 1 June 1978.

I made a conscious: Zucker, p. 25.

I don't think as an English: Georgina Brown, 'Master of disguise',
Evening Standard, 13 October 1995.

Chapter Eleven

He was the most: Michael Owen, 'The Filming of "Nijinsky",' *New
York Times*, 1 April 1979, pp. 19–20.

It was not, I think: Zucker, p. 24.

We got on: Gemma Jones to DS, 18 May 2006.

I was completely overwhelmed: John Osborne to AB, 3 February
1980.

pale, rather tired-looking: P. N. Gilchrist, 'Confidential Psychological
Assessment of Tristan Bates and Benedick Bates', dated 17 July
1980.

The picture of the elegant actress: Bennett, *Writing Home*, p. 330.

Burgess never tried: Michael Owen, 'Bates: a spy at the drag ball',
Evening Standard, 8 April 1983.

A beautifully controlled: Michael Church in *The Times*, 30 November
1983.

He was a brilliant: AB, interview on BBC Radio 2, 27 July 1983.

masterly: Richard Findlater in *Plays & Players*, July 1983.

All concerned: John J. O'Connor, 'Mason and Bates in "Fischer",' *New
York Times*, 11 October 1985.

It took me: McGill, art.cit., p. 8.

Chapter Twelve

He was enchanting: David Hughes in the obituary for Patrick Willis Woodcock, *Independent*, 19 June 2002.

sleek, calm and vicious: Rosalind Carne in the *New Statesman*, 23 April 1984.

the most restrained: Gray, *An Unnatural Pursuit & Other Pieces*.

The King Alfred School reports were handwritten evaluations from the summer term 1984, each teacher signing a summary of academic and personality impressions.

a buoyant, springy: Martin Hoyle in *Plays & Players*, July 1985.

to see themselves: Irving Wardle in *The Times*, 31 May 1985.

a very tender: Gerard Hastings to DS, 24 May 2006.

who dominates the evening: Benedict Nightingale in the *New Statesman*, 13 December 1985.

like all great actors: Peter Hall to DS, 24 May 2006.

Gerard Hastings was present at *Yonadab* to hear the exchange between AB and the audience.

I don't get them at first: AB to Gerard Hastings.

I'm dominated by work: From an interview with Ghislaine Edwards and R. T. Witcombe, April 1986.

Acting consumes me: Minty Clinch, 'Tea and Sensuality', *7 Days*, 10 September 1989.

was not the most: from the press kit for *Duet for One*, issued in 1986.

a lifeless artefact: Peter Heyworth, 'Purcell's Arthurian Incidental Music', *Observer*, 27 July 1986.

his vanity got in the way: Gray, *The Year of the Jouncer*, p. 84.

who advocates promiscuity: Ibid., p. 18.

It's crack-up time: Philip Oakes, 'Survival of the fittest', *Mail on Sunday* (*You* magazine), 21 June 1987. See also the important article on Gray, Bates and *Melon* in Frank Granville Barker, 'The method in his madness', *Plays International*, June 1987, pp. 12–13, 44.

I've always been able: Ibid.

masterly: Michael Billington, 'A case for treatment', *Guardian*, 25 June 1987.

easy, if querulous: Charles Osborne, 'A thin slice of "Melon"', *Daily Telegraph*, 25 June 1987.

half-manic: Peter Kemp, 'Gray's strange fruit', *Independent*, 25 June 1987.

hid behind the furniture: Gray, *The Year of the Jouncer*, pp. 84–85.
Ackerley sought: Clinch, art.cit.

Chapter Thirteen

Sometimes during rehearsals: Felicity Kendal to DS, 16 June 2006.
Specific details of the death of Tristan Bates are derived from the
    report of the coroner in Tokyo, 'on matters relative to a certain
    death occurring at 3.30 on the morning of 13 January 1990'.
    Tristan was identified as living in Room 401, Mansion Azabu
    Court, Tokyo. The autopsy report was kept by AB among his
    private papers.
It was horrendous: Sharon Feinstein, 'How Laughter Conquered My
    Grief', *Daily Express*, 8 July 1996.
Tristan's death: Quoted in the *Birmingham Post*, 28 September 1996.
It's a very shocking thing: From the unpublished Julia Beasley essay,
    art.cit.
It's tempting to go: Nicci Gerrard, 'At Home with Tragedy', *Observer*,
    23 January 2000.
I don't expect to get over it: Andrew Duncan, 'Farther from the
    Madding Crowd', *Radio Times*, 5–11 December 1992.
People ask: Suzie MacKenzie, 'Alan Bates on life beyond 65', *Evening
    Standard*, 18 February 2000.
Three handsome men: Duncan, art.cit.
Another nineteen-year-old: Gerrard, art.cit.
in highly unorganised chaos: Graham Leader, quoted in William
    Grimes, 'Filming Turns Out to Be Just the Beginning', *New York
    Times*, 13 February 1994.
I had read the script: Ibid.
It's difficult to follow: Ibid.
mired in complexity: Bruce Williamson in *Playboy*, April 1992.
tortuous and repetitive: *Daily Mail*, 25 September 1992.
Gray's most openly confessional: Michael Coveney in the *Observer*, 2
    May 1993.
Partt watches his life: Duncan, art.cit.
Alan Bates played me: Gray, *The Year of the Jouncer*, p. 155.
I am not at all sure: AB's speech was prepared by him and preserved
    among his private papers.

Chapter Fourteen

You either collapse: Jasper Gerard, 'Chinks in a lonely knight's armour',
    Sunday Times, 5 January 2003.

I wasn't mad with grief: Nicci Gerrard, 'At Home with Tragedy',
    Observer, 23 January 2000.

out of step with the world: Andro Linklater, *Sunday Telegraph Magazine*,
    15 November 1992.

one of the great performances: Jack Tinker in the *Daily Mail*, 19
    November 1992.

He effortlessly holds the stage: Benedict Nightingale in *The Times*, 19
    November 1992.

I did not know: Irving Wardle in the *Independent on Sunday*, 22
    November 1992.

with his powerful: Lambert, p. 276.

Mr Bates simply: John J. O'Connor, 'A Downsized Professor, a
    Missing Wordsmith and Murder', *New York Times*, 3 October
    1996.

I'm not really sure: Mel Gussow, 'What's a 6-Letter Word for Detective?',
    New York Times, 29 September 1996.

He embraced: Mark Stephens, in the commemorative programme for
    the AB memorial tribute, 26 September 2004.

I sometimes wonder: Jill Lawless, 'Alan Bates: British star smoulders
    in Nordic drama', *Now*, 11–17 January 1996.

I knew this was a hard: Jane Edwardes, 'Master of the Roles', *Time
    Out*, 11–18 October 1995.

Solness and I: H. J. Kirchhoff, 'Mastering the art of Ibsen', *Globe and
    Mail* (Toronto), 16 January 1996.

Alan Bates enters: John Peter in *The Times*, 23 October 1995.

I like doing things: Colin Donald, 'Fool's gold', *The Scotsman*, 24
    September 1996.

He is someone who: Anthony Hatter, 'Bates gets connected', *Hounslow
    Chronicle*, 6 June 1996.

beautifully executed: John Peter, 'All the wrong connections', *Sunday
    Times*, 12 May 1996.

harrowing anguish: Charles Spencer, 'A moving comedy of manners',
    Daily Telegraph, 15 May 1996.

We come to each other: Colin Donald, art.cit.

In Chichester: Gray, *The Year of the Jouncer*, p. 79.

He's given me: Michael Owen, 'Why the talking never stops', *Evening Standard*, 1 August 1997.

This play has been: Simon Fanshawe, 'But seriously?', *Sunday Times*, 3 August 1997.

I do know: Ibid.

magnificent: *Daily Telegraph*, 16 August 1997.

Chapter Fifteen

You don't want: *San Francisco Examiner*, 23 April 1998.

a catharsis: Ibid., 23 December 1997.

The memory of the loss: Reg Green's tribute is among those gathered by the BBC on their memorial website for AB: http://newsvote.bbc. co.uk/mpapps/pagetools/print/news/bbc.co.uk/1/hi/ entertainment/film/33528

It's a strange and exciting place: Michael Owen, art.cit.

It took me nine months: Ibid.

completely absurd: Laura Fries, '*St Patrick* stretches credibility', *Reuters/Variety*, 9 March 2000. In the original casting, AB was to have played a bishop, but he preferred a smaller and less time-consuming role.

I'm sure you will be relieved: Bennett, *Untold Stories*, p. 341.

Bates is gloriously reinstated: Michael Coveney in the *Daily Mail*, 24 June 1999.

Even his jealous rages: Benedict Nightingale, 'Noble obliges at the RSC', *The Times*, 21 January 2000.

We didn't really know: Angharad Rees to DS, 26 May 2006.

Has friendship touchingly turned: *Express*, 21 February 2000.

her new love: Maureen Paton, 'Angharad's second act', *You*, 13 May 2001.

You cannot help: This and AB's subsequent comments on *Love In A Cold Climate* are excerpted from an interview in a BBC press release in 2001, at the time of broadcast (and subsequently syndicated in many UK newspapers).

the support and encouragement he gave: Kate Harwood's tribute is among those gathered by the BBC on their memorial website for AB: http://newsvote.bbc.co.uk/mpapps/pagetools/print/news/bbc.co.uk/1/hi/entertainment/film/33528

delicious acidity: Elysa Gardner, '"Unexpected" delights fill minimalist drama', *USA Today*, 26 October 2000.

made the character's: Charles Isherwood, review in *Variety*, 19 October 2000.

Alan went over: Mike Palmer's tribute is among those gathered by the BBC on their memorial website for AB: http://newsvote.bbc.co.uk/mpapps/pagetools/print/news/bbc.co.uk/1/hi/entertainment/film/33528

It's a part like: Dave Kehr, 'For Alan Bates, a Role's a Role', *New York Times*, 31 May 2002.

The script: Andrew Clarke, art.cit., p. 24.

I liked playing: Bill Desowitz, 'Busy Bates does more than brood', *Los Angeles Times*, 10 December 2002.

Alan clung to him: Robert Altman in his commentary for the Universal Studios-released DVD of *Gosford Park* (2002).

He stood in the background: Desowitz, art.cit.

Benedick Bates is made: Clare Brotherwood, 'Theatrical feast', *Observer*, 20 July 2001.

an evil influence: Sandy Baker, 'No Nude Wrestling These Days for Alan Bates', *Farnham Herald* and other regional UK newspapers near Windsor, 27 July 2001.

the little details: Desowitz, art.cit.

Noël Coward's poem 'I am No Good at Love', originally published in *Not Yet the Dodo*, has been reprinted in Payn and Tickner, p. 5.

We are very good friends: Katie Nicholl, 'Romance is over for Bates and Angharad', the *Mail on Sunday*, 27 January 2002.

absolutely not: Ibid.

Chapter Sixteen

full examination: AB's medical report, based on the routine executive screening of 19 December 2001, was sent to him on 17 January 2002 by his primary care physician, Dr Paul Ettlinger.

It is: Clive Barnes, 'Fortune's Priceless', *New York Post*, 3 April 2002.

Mr Bates brings: Ben Brantley in the *New York Times*, 3 April 2002.

masterly: John Simon in *New York* magazine, 15 April 2002.

Bates is still: Charles Isherwood in *The Times*, 8 April 2002.

The things that: Gray, *The Year of the Jouncer*, p. 79.

a ridiculous car: Ibid., p. 80.

I've had a good life: Ibid., p. 86.

imperial in his dying: Ibid., p. 91.

Bibliography

Ash, Niema, *Travels with My Daughter* (Bridgnorth, Shropshire, UK: TravellersEye Ltd, 2001).

Bennett, Alan, *Untold Stories* (London: Faber and Faber/Profile, 2005).

——*Writing Home* (London: Faber and Faber, 2006).

Champlin, Charles, *John Frankenheimer: A Conversation* (Burbank, CA: Riverwood Press, 1995).

Coward, Noël, *Not Yet the Dodo* (London: Heinemann, 1967).

Gray, Simon, *Key Plays: Butley, Otherwise Engaged, Close of Play, Quartermaine's Terms, The Late Middle Classes* (London: Faber and Faber, 2002).

——*Life Support* (London: Faber and Faber, 1997).

——*Simply Disconnected* (London: Faber and Faber, 1996).

——*An Unnatural Pursuit & Other Pieces: A Playwright's Journal* (London: Faber and Faber, 1985).

——*The Year of the Jouncer* (London: Granta Books, 2006).

Hobson, Harold, *Theatre in Britain – A Personal View* (Oxford: Phaidon Press, 1984).

Kerr, Jean, *Poor Richard.* (Garden City, NY: Doubleday, 1965).

Lambert, Gavin, *Mainly About Lindsay Anderson: A Memoir* (London: Faber and Faber, 2000).

Loney, Glenn, *Twentieth Century Theatre*, vols I and II (New York: Facts on File, 1983).

Mann, William J., *The Edge of Midnight: The Life of John Schlesinger* (London: Hutchinson, 2004).

Manvell, Roger and John Huntley (rev. Richard Arnell and Peter

Day), *The Technique of Film Music* (London and New York: Focal Press, 1975).

McFarlane, Brian, *An Autobiography of British Cinema as told by the film-makers and actors who made it* (London: Methuen, 1997).

O'Neill, Eugene, *Long Day's Journey into Night* (New Haven: Yale University Press, 1955).

Osborne, John, *Almost a Gentleman: An Autobiography*, vol. II, 1955–1966 (London: Faber and Faber, 1991).

Payn, Graham and Sheridan Morley, eds, *The Noël Coward Diaries* (London: Papermac, 1982).

Payn, Graham and Martin Tickner, eds, *Noël Coward: Collected Verse* (London: Methuen, 1999).

Richardson, Tony, *The Long Distance Runner: An Autobiography* (New York: Morrow, 1993).

Russell, Ken, *Directing Film from Pitch to Premiere* (London: Batsford, 2000).

Scavullo, Francesco, *Scavullo on Men* (New York: Random House, 1977).

Shipley, Joseph T., *The Crown Guide to the World's Great Plays: From Ancient Greece to Modern Times*, rev. ed. (New York: Crown, 1956).

Spoto, Donald, *Laurence Olivier: A Biography* (New York and London: HarperCollins, 1992).

Storey, David, *Life Class* (London: Jonathan Cape, 1975).

—— *Plays: I – The Contractor, Home, Stages, Caring* (London: Methuen Drama, 1992).

Trewin, J. C., *Five and Eighty Hamlets* (London: Hutchinson, 1987).

Zucker, Carole, *In the Company of Actors: Reflections on the Craft of Acting* (London: A & C Black, 1999; New York: Theatre Arts Books/Routledge, 2001).

Index

Index